A Guide to Te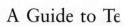

*Teaching Psychological Science*
Series editors: William Buskist and Douglas A. Bernstein

The *Teaching Psychological Science* series focuses on critical aspects of teaching core courses in psychology. The books share ideas, tips, and strategies for effective teaching and offer all the pedagogical tools an instructor needs to plan the course in one handy and concise volume. Written by outstanding teachers and edited by Bill Buskist and Doug Bernstein, who are themselves well-respected authors and teachers, each book provides a wealth of concrete suggestions not found in other volumes, a clear roadmap for teaching, and practical, concrete, hands-on tips for novice teachers and experienced instructors alike.

Each book includes

- Ideas for beginning the course
- Sample lecture outlines for the entire course
- Examples and applications that link the course content to everyday student experience
- Classroom demonstrations and activities with an emphasis on promoting active learning and critical thinking
- Discussion of sensitive and difficult-to-teach topics and ethical issues likely to be encountered throughout the semester
- Course-specific options for evaluating student performance
- A chapter on available resources for teaching the course

1.  *A Guide to Teaching Research Methods in Psychology*
    Bryan K. Saville

2.  *A Guide to Teaching Introductory Psychology*
    Sandra Goss Lucas

3.  *A Guide to Teaching Statistics*
    Michael R. Hulsizer and Linda M. Woolf

4.  *A Guide to Teaching Developmental Psychology*
    Elizabeth Brestan and Ember Lee

# A Guide to Teaching Statistics

## Innovations and Best Practices

Michael R. Hulsizer and
Linda M. Woolf

A John Wiley & Sons, Ltd., Publication

This edition first published 2009
© 2009 Michael R. Hulsizer and Linda M. Woolf

Blackwell Publishing was acquired by John Wiley & Sons in February 2007.
Blackwell's publishing program has been merged with Wiley's global Scientific,
Technical, and Medical business to form Wiley-Blackwell.

*Registered Office*
John Wiley & Sons Ltd, The Atrium, Southern Gate, Chichester, West Sussex,
PO19 8SQ, United Kingdom

*Editorial Offices*
350 Main Street, Malden, MA 02148 5020, USA
9600 Garsington Road, Oxford, OX4 2DQ, UK
The Atrium, Southern Gate, Chichester, West Sussex, PO19 8SQ, UK

For details of our global editorial offices, for customer services, and for information
about how to apply for permission to reuse the copyright material in this book please
see our website at www.wiley.com/wiley-blackwell.

The right of Michael R. Hulsizer and Linda M. Woolf to be identified as the authors
of this work has been asserted in accordance with the Copyright, Designs and
Patents Act 1988.

*Library of Congress Cataloging-in-Publication Data*

Hulsizer, Michael R.
   A guide to teaching statistics : innovations and best practices / Michael R. Hulsizer,
Linda M. Woolf.
      p. cm. — (Teaching psychological science ; 3)
   Includes bibliographical references and index.
   ISBN 978-1-4051-5573-1 (hardcover : alk. paper) — ISBN 978-1-4051-5574-8
(pbk. : alk. paper)   1. Statistics—Study and teaching.   I. Woolf, Linda M.   II. Title.

   QA276.18.H86 2009
   519.5071—dc22

                                                                    2008010968

A catalogue record for this book is available from the British Library.

Set in 10.5/12.5 point Sabon by Graphicraft Ltd, Hong Kong
Printed in Singapore by Utopia Press Pte Ltd

1   2009

This book is dedicated to
Michelle and Dylan Hulsizer,
Mark Muehlbach,

*and especially to the memory of*
*William HuddlestonBerry,*
*who taught us what it means to be a teacher*

# Contents

# Series Editors' Preface

As the best teachers among us can surely attest, teaching at the college and university level is no easy task. Even psychology, as inherently interesting as it may be, is a difficult subject to teach well. Indeed, being an effective teacher of any discipline requires a steadfast commitment to self-improvement as a scholar, thinker, and communicator over the long haul. No one becomes a master teacher overnight.

Compared to other disciplines, though, psychology has been way ahead of the curve when it comes to taking its teaching seriously. The Society for the Teaching of Psychology (www.teachpsych.org/) was founded in 1946 and continues to be a powerful force in supporting the teaching of psychology in high schools, community colleges, and four-year schools. The annual National Institute on the Teaching of Psychology, or as it more informally known, NITOP (www.nitop.org), has been featuring an impressive venue of pedagogical presentations for the past 30 years. In addition, several annual regional teaching of psychology conferences offer a variety of talks, workshops, and poster sessions on improving one's teaching.

Psychologists have also led the way in writing books on effective teaching. Perhaps the best-known among these texts is McKeachie's (2006) *Teaching Tips*, now it's in 12th edition (the first edition was published in 1951!). Although McKeachie wrote *Teaching Tips* for all teachers, regardless of discipline, other books focused specifically on teaching psychology have appeared in the past several years. (e.g., Buskist & Davis, 2006; Davis & Buskist, 2002; Forsyth, 2003; Lucas & Bernstein, 2005). The common theme across these books is that they offer general advice for teaching any psychology course, and in McKeachie's case, for teaching any college course.

Blackwell's *Teaching Psychological Science* series differs from existing books. In one handy and concise source, each book provides all an instructor needs to help her in her course. Each volume in this series targets a specific course: introductory psychology, developmental psychology, research methods, statistics, behavioral neuroscience, memory and cognition, learning, abnormal behavior, and personality and social psychology. Each book is authored by accomplished, well-respected teachers who share their best strategies for teaching these courses effectively.

Each book in the series also features advice on how to teach particularly difficult topics; how to link course content to everyday student experiences; how to develop and use class presentations, lectures, and active learning ideas; and how to increase student interest in course topics. Each volume ends with a chapter that describes resources for teaching the particular course focused on in that book, as well as an appendix on widely available resources for the teaching of psychology in general.

The *Teaching Psychological Science* series is geared to assist all teachers at all levels to master the teaching of particular courses. Each volume focuses on how to teach specific content as opposed to processes involved in teaching more generally. Thus, veteran teachers as well as graduate students and new faculty will likely find these books a useful source of new ideas for teaching their courses.

As editors of this series, we are excited about the prospects these books offer for enhancing the teaching of specific courses within our field. We are delighted that Wiley Blackwell shares our excitement for the series and we wish to thank our Editor Christine Cardone and our Development Project Manager Sarah Coleman for their devoted work behind the scenes to help us bring the series to fruition. We hope that you find this book, and all the books in the series, a helpful and welcome addition to your collection of teaching resources.

Douglas J. Bernstein
William Buskist
April 2007

# References

Buskist, W., & Davis, S. F. (Eds.). (2006). *Handbook of the teaching of psychology*. Malden, MA: Blackwell.

Davis, S. F., & Buskist, W. (Eds.). (2002). *The teaching of psychology: Essays in honor of Wilbert J. McKeachie and Charles L. Brewer*. Mahwah, NJ: Erlbaum.

Forsyth, D. R. (2003). *The professor's guide to teaching: Psychological principles and practices*. Washington, DC: American Psychological Association.

Lucas, S., & Bernstein, D. A. (2005). *Teaching psychology: A step by step guide*. Mahwah, NJ: Erlbaum.

McKeachie, W. J. (2006). *McKeachie's teaching tips: Strategies, research, and theory for college and university teachers* (12th ed.). Boston: Houghton Mifflin.

Perlman, B., McCann, L. I., & Buskist, W. (Eds.). (2005). *Voices of NITOP: Memorable talks from the National Institute on the Teaching of Psychology*. Washington, DC: American Psychological Society.

Perlman, B., McCann, L. I., & McFadden, S. H. (2004). *Lessons learned: Practical advice for the teaching of psychology* (Volume 2). Washington, DC: American Psychological Society.

# Preface

Early in our psychology graduate careers, we each learned an indispensable lesson about success in academia—become a statistics teacher! Regardless of whether you are a social, developmental, or clinical psychologist, a biologist or sociologist, knowing how to teach statistics makes you a valuable and marketable commodity. Moreover, it is one of the most rewarding teaching opportunities across the curriculum. Few books devoted to teaching highlight the inherent satisfactions associated with teaching statistics. In addition, those of us that teach the course often do little to advertise our successes. Our hope is that this book will lift the veil of silence that shrouds the teaching of statistics and sparks in others the joy of both teaching and learning statistics.

Certainly, myths abound concerning the odious nature of teaching statistics. Many teachers firmly believe that most students hate statistics, perceive it to be a necessary but painful class to teach, and imagine that it will naturally result in poor course evaluations. Unfortunately, these myths can become self-fulfilling prophecies, particularly if one is unfamiliar with the literature concerning the scholarship of teaching statistics. We are very fortunate to have taught over 100 sections of statistics. The course continues to be as much fun and as fresh as the first time we each taught the course. For both of us over the years, our teaching methods have evolved in response to changes in technology and statistics education reform. What has remained consistent is that our statistics classes normally fill within a day or two of open registration, we have waiting lists for our classes, and our statistics course evaluations are among our best ratings. Of course, the best part of teaching statistics every semester is being a witness to student transformation as they come to enjoy, value, and understand that statistics is a fundamental tool for critical thinking, a necessary component of the research process, and an integral part of psychological knowledge.

Although this book is part of the *Teaching Psychological Science* series, we researched and wrote this book for anyone, regardless of discipline, who desires to learn more about the teaching of statistics. We conducted exhaustive reviews across disciplines such as education, mathematics, biology, statistics, health, psychology, and social sciences and included both specific and cross-disciplinary discussions and methods throughout the text. Ideally, readers will find the book serves to confirm and provide evidence for their current approaches but more importantly, will also serve as a transformative tool to upgrade course content based on the most recent literature concerning the scholarship of teaching statistics.

## Organization of the book

We have divided the book into four parts. Part I, which contains Chapters 1 and 2, is devoted to course preparation. Topics range from historical and current controversies in the field to the basics of statistics course preparation (e.g., textbook selection, creation of an effective syllabus, and the use of multimedia). Part II, consisting of Chapters 3 and 4, details both theoretical and practical pedagogical concerns related to issues of statistical literacy, thinking, reasoning, and most importantly, assessment. Included are a host of teaching techniques designed to enhance student comprehension and active learning as well as strategies aimed at reducing fear and anxiety.

Part III contains a rich deposit of course suggestions related to the teaching of specific concepts present in most undergraduate statistics courses, particularly in the behavioral and social sciences. Specifically, Chapter 5 focuses on descriptive and bivariate distributions. Chapter 6 is devoted to teaching hypothesis testing and includes topics such as inferential statistics, the analysis of variance, and non-parametrics. Included are helpful examples, techniques, computer applications, and suggestions for encouraging student comprehension of these key areas of statistical knowledge. The final part, consisting of Chapters 7 and 8, introduces transformative issues, topics, and pedagogical approaches appropriate for a typical undergraduate statistics course. Topics include the importance of using real data, incorporating data analysis software tools (e.g., SPSS), the role of ethics and diversity in statistical education, introducing advanced statistical techniques, and the effectiveness of online statistical education. In addition, we have included a wealth of additional materials on the book Web site at www.teachstats.org.

Writing this book, much like the teaching of statistics, has been a labor of love for both of us. If you have never taught statistics before, we hope that this book will spark your interest to explore this wonderful teaching opportunity. If you currently teach statistics, we believe this text will either serve as a catalyst to rejuvenate and transform your existing statistics course or serve to confirm what you already know—that the rewards of teaching statistics are among the best kept secrets in academia.

## Acknowledgments

We would like to thank our friends and family for their invaluable support during the writing of this book. They sacrificed much to insure that this book came to fruition and we are very appreciative. In addition, we owe a debt of gratitude to our statistics students who have provided us with invaluable insights through student evaluations, class comments, and informal discussion. The creation of this book has been an ongoing collaborative process. Numerous colleagues, through conversation, offhand remarks, statistical mentoring, and research findings, have had a profound impact on the shaping of the book's content. Specifically, we would like to thank Casey Cole, Mary Harmon-Vukić, Maureen McCarthy, Geoff Munro, Brad Shepherd, and Kevin Waghorn. We are also enormously indebted to our past mentors, William HuddlestonBerry and Stuart Taylor, for instilling in us a passion for teaching. We are also very appreciative of the skillful editorial assistance and patience provided by William Buskist and members of the Blackwell team: Christine Cardone and Kelly Basner. Finally, the book would not have been possible without the ever-present support, assistance, and encouragement of Debi Aholt, we give her our deepest thanks.

# I

# Course Preparation

# Chapter 1

## Teaching Statistics
### A beginning

*For some students, it is the course about which their peers have warned them. They have heard the horror stories and believed them. – Schutz, Drogosz, White, & DiStefano, 1998, p. 292*

Statistics as both a course to take and one to teach has a dreaded reputation. If they are able, students invariably put off the course to the very last moment and appear visibly anxious on the first day of class. They seem to believe the scuttlebutt that any statistics course really deserves the title, "Stadistics." Of course, faculty are not much better. Our departmental chairperson joked that he does not like the three of us who teach statistics traveling together to a conference. "What if something happened! Who would teach statistics?" If truth be told, most of our colleagues, with a bit of time to prepare, could teach introductory statistics. However, they also seem to believe the mythology that the course is a drudge and more importantly, the notion that the course is ripe for less than stellar course evaluations.

However, nothing could be farther from the truth. Statistics can be one of the most fun and gratifying courses to teach. When we talk to fellow statistics teachers at various conferences, it is not unusual for one of us to comment on how much we enjoy teaching statistics. Oddly, what we have noticed is that individuals will often lower their voices a tad and look around before expressing similar thoughts.

It is as if some teachers do not want others to know about one of the best-kept secrets in academia. Teaching statistics can be eminently rewarding and, more importantly, meets a fundamental need in helping students develop a solid knowledge foundation in psychology.

Nonetheless, as Mulhern and Wylie (2004) commented, "Teaching statistics and research methods to psychology undergraduates is a major pedagogic challenge" (p. 355). The challenge, however, lies not with the complexity of the material, which ranges in difficulty from easy to conceptually complex, but rather with the type of information communicated. Evans (1976) provided an interesting perspective on the differences between teaching most content-oriented courses in psychology and quantitative methods courses. In most content courses, we teach students to "know that," whereas in statistics we teach students to "know how." Evans draws the following apropos analogy: Teaching statistics via lecture and handouts, with a clear explication of concepts, is as useful as providing someone with a lecture and handout on how to ride a bicycle. The pedagogical challenge for statistics teachers is to move beyond the lectern, put away the static PowerPoint (the current equivalent of yellowing notes), and to try out some alternate teaching strategies.

Students also face new challenges when taking statistics or research methods courses for the first time. Unfortunately, students may perceive these challenges principally as threats versus opportunities. This point is particularly true for those students who may not utilize sophisticated learning techniques. If students have succeeded primarily by studying in spurts, memorizing materials, or relying heavily on recall for exams, they may find statistics to be difficult terrain to navigate. Hence, the familiar lament from struggling students that they feel "lost" in the course. If students cling to their traditional study methods and learning strategies, they may experience a drop in their usual performance level and hence, a subsequent drop in their self-efficacy in relation to the course, which can then spiral into a well of deepening frustration and potential failure. Therefore, statistics teachers might consider structuring their courses in ways that facilitate new and more adaptive learning strategies.

The aim of this book is to provide statistics teachers with the best information available to assist in the development or restructuring of their statistics course. We designed this book to meet the needs of both novice and seasoned teachers of statistics. In addition, we have created a companion Web site (www.teachstats.org) that contains additional instructional techniques, activities, topics, and resources.

Throughout the book, we provide information concerning a range of topics from pedagogical methods and activities designed for teaching specific concepts to broader issues related to the unique learning needs of statistics students. We draw heavily on the small but growing empirical and scholarly literature related to the teaching of statistics in each chapter (Becker, 1996). As a result, this book extends beyond the content you might typically find in an instructor's manual. Our goal is to introduce you to the best practices in teaching statistics so that you can turn a potential course prison—the incoming perception of many students—into a pedagogical haven for learning.

## So Why Teach Statistics?

Although statistics may be tangential to your primary area of research, it is beneficial to examine why the course is an important one to teach. After all, if you do not find meaning in the material, neither will your students. On the most transparent level, it simply is a good idea for everyone to have a basic understanding of statistics. In other words, knowledge of elementary statistics is an end goal in itself. In today's world, statistical literacy is fundamental given the tendency for the media, politicians, and corporate America to deluge us daily with quantitative information (Ben-Zvi & Garfield, 2004; Gal, 2004; Rumsey, 2002; Utts, 2003). Individuals need to be able to make sense of numerical information to avoid falling prey to the influence of data that looks incontrovertible simply because it is quantitative in nature. Over a half century ago, Wishart (1939), an early statistician, commented that the teaching of statistics is important because it protects individuals from the misleading practices of "the propagandists" (p. 549). It is just as important an issue today.

Two similes often describe the teaching of statistics. Hotelling (1940), perhaps best known for the multivariate technique called Hotelling's T, remarked that teaching students statistics is like teaching them to use a tool. More commonly, instructors comment that teaching of statistics is like teaching a foreign language (Hastings, 1982; Lalonde & Gardner, 1993; Walker, 1936). Both comparisons are insufficient, as they emphasize discrete skills that, once learned, students may fail to apply to other domains of knowledge or to the broader research process. Hence, one can learn to use a power sander and circular saw but not necessarily see any connection from those skills to building a doghouse. Students need to be able to apply their underlying knowledge to other contexts. We also do not want students to perceive statistics as a foreign language requirement only to be left unvisited once completed. It is imperative that students come to see statistics as a set of critical thinking skills and knowledge structures designed to enhance their ability to explore, understand, reason, and evaluate psychological science. In teaching the course, instructors need to make connections to material from other courses to emphasize the role that research methods and statistics plays in creating a foundation for the study of psychology as well as other disciplines.

We all cringe when we see a paper handed in that has as its most scholarly reference, *Rolling Stone* or *Newsweek*. Students need to be able to read and evaluate the empirical literature. This ability is particularly important given the dangers associated with blindly trusting the translations presented in the popular press. Consequently, we often ask our students how many of them actually read the results section of an empirical paper and how many simply skip over that section hoping that the author will eventually put it into English for them. Sheepishly, a large percentage of our students confess to such practices. As demonstrated by Rossi (1987), the statistical computations themselves in journal articles may even be incorrect. Therefore, our students need basic statistical literacy, thinking, and reasoning skills with which to begin their evaluation of empirical results. Buche and Glover (1988) demonstrated that students who are provided with training in the fundamental skills necessary to review and study research articles, particularly in relation to methods and an understanding of statistical techniques, are better able to read, evaluate, and appreciate research in their field. Thus, such training is not only essential in their other coursework, but also beneficial for their future careers regardless of whether they choose a path as a researcher, clinician, lawyer, manager, or medical practitioner.

Hotelling (1940) commented that "a good deal of [statistics] has been conducted by persons engaged in research, not of a kind contributing to statistical theory, but consisting of the application of statistical methods and theory to something else" (p. 465). The vast majority of our students will not develop careers specializing in quantitative methods or theory. However, we may hope, and in some instances require, that our students engage in research as part of a class project or independent study. Unfortunately, not all students immediately see the connection between research methods and statistics. They may hold the false belief that one can simply design a study, collect data, and then hire a statistician to analyze those data. Of course, the concepts of research methods and statistics are inextricably interwoven and students must recognize the interrelationships to conduct research effectively. Indeed, students must begin their statistical planning while designing their study.

Finally, and perhaps it should go without saying, psychology is a science. Thus, research methods and statistics are foundation courses necessary for understanding and critically evaluating all of the research presented, studied, and evaluated in the remainder of our students' coursework. Psychology instructors can enhance students' appreciation of statistics by drawing connections to other content-focused domains of psychology. Although taking statistics alone does not decrease students' beliefs in pseudoscientific claims (Mill, Gray, & Mandel, 1994), statistical literacy combined with other content-focused coursework stressing research evaluation, may better prepare our students to be critical consumers of information both within and outside of psychology.

## Historical Pedagogical Controversies

Occasionally, one may hear statistics teachers state that they love teaching the course because the material never changes. This point is simply not true. Although there is much that has remained the same, the field of statistics and its application to psychological research is constantly developing. Three main pedagogical controversies have been associated with the teaching of statistics since the field was in its infancy: (a) who should teach statistics; (b) the use of statistics labs and technology; and (c) the content of statistics courses.

### Who should teach statistics?

One source of discussion among statisticians, decades ago, was the question of who should teach statistics. Should statisticians and mathematicians be the only individuals allowed to teach statistics or is it more appropriately taught within the departments, such as psychology, conducting research? Wishart (1939) argued that non-statisticians should not teach statistics. He believed that such practices were fraught with danger, as non-statisticians were unprepared to handle the difficulties of teaching and supervising statistical research. However, Fisher (1937) felt that the goal of teaching statistics should be toward the application of these concepts to research in one's field and he argued for offering statistics coursework in research departments such as psychology or biology. Hotelling (1940) commented that professors usually do not want to teach a class outside their main area of interest. He noted further that anyone attempting to digest mathematical statistics outside of one's discipline faces a largely unreadable task. Therefore, he made a case for individuals within particular disciplines keeping current with the quantitative methods literature in their field and teaching the statistics course within respective academic departments. Although some individuals may feel unprepared to teach statistics due to a lack of extensive training in quantitative methods, Hotelling argued that being an excellent mathematician is, in and of itself, a poor predictor for becoming a good statistics instructor. Rather, Hotelling stated that in addition to knowledge of the fundamentals, statistics instructors need to have "a really intimate acquaintance with the problems of one or more empirical subjects in which statistical methods are taught" (p. 463). Accordingly, psychologists today are in a good position to make the world of statistics contextually meaningful for students by relating statistical concepts to applied problems in psychology.

By 1950, it was evident that psychology had adopted Hotelling's (1940) approach to teaching statistics and the majority of psychology departments included coursework in statistics, research methods, experimental, and tests and measurements (Sanford & Fleishman, 1950). More recently, approximately 77% of universities and colleges required statistics courses within departments of psychology (Bartz, 1981). According to Garfield (2000), today's students receive the vast majority of statistical training from instructors outside the field of mathematics (e.g., education, psychology). Many individuals who teach statistics within psychology departments do not have quantitative methods as their primary focus of scholarship (Hayden, 2000). The departmental location of a statistics class may reflect philosophical differences and pragmatic concerns due to limited numbers of faculty within any one department (Fraser, 1962; Friedrich, Buday, & Kerr, 2000; Perlman & McCann, 1999).

## Statistics labs and related technology

Many early statisticians cared deeply about the pedagogy of statistics and endeavored to sort out best practices in relation to their craft. For example, there was uniform agreement that teaching statistics primarily through lecture was a death knoll for learning. Indeed, Cohen and Firestone (1939) commented that "a lecture is a process whereby the notes of the professor become the notes of the student without passing through the minds of either" (p. 714). Although there was agreement on some issues related to teaching methods, there were still significant areas of disagreement among statistics instructors. For example, Walker (1936) and Olds (1954) argued for the importance of laboratory work. On the other hand, Cohen and Firestone stated that a lecture–laboratory combination was not enough to facilitate learning and only assisted the best students. They suggested that students take smaller, informal statistical workshops designed to provide them with the opportunity to learn a range of concepts and apply these techniques to real-world problems.

Few teachers today would argue that lecture alone is ideal for any course. However, Perlman and McCann (1999) found that only 12% of statistics courses included an identified laboratory component. Although one can argue that Perlman and McCann's methods may have undercounted the number of available statistics courses including a laboratory experience, the reported limited availability of laboratory experiences for students studying statistics is still a potential concern.

The Guidelines for Assessment and Instruction in Statistics Education (GAISE) Project (American Statistical Association: ASA, 2005) noted that the biggest change in the teaching of statistics over the past decade was the increased use of technology. Interestingly, the use of technology as a means to assist faculty and students with the computation of data was also an issue for the early statisticians. For example, Wishart (1939) argued that teachers should only introduce students to "calculating machines" after they had enough practice computing data by hand (p. 547). He also stressed that everyone in the class should have access to their own machine. Clearly, the argument for a well-stocked lab predates the use of computers. Although we occasionally witness the media lament that students just are not as mathematically literate as they were years ago, early statisticians also remarked that not all of their students appeared to be mathematically prepared. Walker (1936) expressed concern that some students appeared to spend hours working formulas and checking for errors at the expense of genuinely understanding the concepts behind formulas. She further mused that some students appeared to spend an inordinate amount of time fruitlessly attempting to read the textbook.

## Content of statistics courses

There is relatively little debate as to the importance of including statistics as a core area in psychology. The St. Mary's Conference included statistics and methodology as a core content area within psychology (Brewer, 1997). Understanding research methods, including knowledge of data analytic techniques, is one of the learning goals listed in the APA *Guidelines for the Undergraduate Psychology Major* (American Psychological Association: APA, 2006). Basic statistical concepts, from descriptive through inferential statistics, are also included in the *National Standards for High School Psychology Curricula* (APA, 2005).

Psychology departments have largely complied with the recommendations put forth by the APA regarding the infusion of statistics into the curriculum. For example, Bartz (1981) found that the majority of psychology programs required coursework in statistics either through their own department or through another department on campus. More recently, Friedrich et al. (2000) sampled top ranking national and regional universities/colleges (defined according to *U.S. News & World Report*) as well as an unranked sample of colleges on a range of variables related to the teaching of statistics. Based on the 255 returned surveys, Friedrich et al. found that 93% of departments included one or more courses devoted entirely to statistics. Moreover, Perlman and McCann (1999) found in a survey of 500 college catalogs that introductory psychology, a capstone course, and statistics composed the core course requirements at the majority of institutions they surveyed.

Although departments have been quick to adopt statistics as a core course in their curriculum, they have been reticent to adopt many of the concepts recommended by the APA Task Force on Statistical Inference (Wilkinson & the Task Force on Statistical Inference, 1999). For example, this task force argued for greater inclusion, both in data analysis and reporting, of effect sizes, confidence interval estimation, and statistical power. Unfortunately, Friedrich et al. (2000) found most teachers included one hour or less on these topics. Instead, they found that most introductory statistics courses covered traditional topics such as correlation, independent t-tests, and one-way ANOVA. Byrne (1996) argued that psychology was lagging behind other disciplines in clinging to teaching traditional quantitative methods. She stated that instructors ignored topics such as path analysis, multivariate techniques, time series analysis, and analysis of covariance methods in introductory statistic courses. She further commented that the course excluded field research in favor of basic laboratory methods and statistical analysis.

One might argue that these newer themes are unnecessary in an introductory statistics course. However, as Friedrich et al. (2000) highlighted, the introductory course serves as a "conceptual framework" for future courses given students are encouraged to think about statistics within a research context. Giesbrecht, Sell, Scialfa, Sandals, and Ehlers (1997) noted that many students would only take one statistics course in their entire academic career. If instructors do not introduce these concepts to students in the first course, they may never see them during their undergraduate training. Byrne (1996) argued that several problems arise from not teaching current techniques in the course. First, students and future researchers may design studies that are less than optimal to address the research question being asked, potentially leading to false conclusions. Second, the information presented in journals may fail to include much needed analyses such as effect sizes and instead demonstrate an "over-reliance on evidence of statistical significance, with little or no attention paid to practical significance" (p. 78). Finally, students may be unprepared for future positions in psychology, higher education, business, or other fields due to lack of familiarity with the newer techniques expected by future employers.

## Statistics in Relation to the Discipline

Many students put off taking a course in statistics until the very end of their undergraduate studies because they fear the difficulty of the course (Barnette, 1978). Of course, this educational strategy makes little sense on either a pragmatic or a logical level. Therefore, most departments recommend that students take statistics and research methodology coursework early in their academic careers, given that these courses provide the necessary foundation upon which to take more advanced coursework in psychology (Friedrich et al., 2000; Lauer, Rajecki, & Minke, 2006).

Although psychology departments as a whole seem to prefer that students undertake quantitative methods courses early, students seem to be of a different opinion. Lauer et al. (2006) examined the transcripts of psychology major alumni from four different universities. For all universities, a significant difference was found between when students completed non-methodological psychology courses (e.g., abnormal or cognitive) and methodological coursework. Students consistently completed quantitative methods courses later in the academic careers. This finding is not surprising, given researchers have revealed that psychology majors tend to prefer "human interest" courses such as developmental or personality as opposed to methodological courses (Rajecki, Appleby, Williams, Johnson, & Jeschke, 2005).

Lauer et al. (2006) suggested that departments consider the following recommendations to counter student bias against quantitative methods courses and to ensure that such courses are taken early in a student's academic career. First, offer a lower-level methods course with no prerequisites. Second, require students to take more than one methods-related course. Third, develop a hierarchically structured curriculum organized such that the quantitative methods course is a requirement for future coursework. Finally, and perhaps most importantly, articulate the link between developing statistical, research, and technical skills and future success in more applied psychology courses and in the job market.

Currently, there appears to be little consistency across departments in relation to statistics serving as a prerequisite for other courses. In their survey of psychology departments, Friedrich et al. (2000) found that only 15% of departments required introductory statistics as a prerequisite for "most" of their intermediate or advanced courses. In fact, many of the respondents revealed that statistics either was not required (22%) or was a prerequisite for "only a very few" intermediate or upper division courses (45%).

Although making statistics a prerequisite for additional content courses might be pedagogically sound, doing so has at least one important pragmatic implication. Individuals who are fearful of statistics might avoid psychology classes altogether if a statistics course was a prerequisite. Thus, potential majors might be lost. Additionally, students from other disciplines might also not register for more advanced psychology coursework if statistics was a prerequisite. Consequently, prerequisites might have the unintended consequence of reducing class registrations—an issue at many institutions, particularly smaller schools.

## Sequence of the Class and Topics

Teachers must decide what material is optional or imperative to teach and in what order. Most individuals who teach statistics find themselves faced with too much information to teach in too short a time. They must strive to balance the needs of heterogeneous students of variable abilities. You do not want to sacrifice rigor leaving the best students in a state of perpetual boredom, but you also do not want to present the information in such depth that you leave other students behind. This challenge is not a new one. Walker (1936) compared the teaching of statistics to "walking a tightrope" (p. 610). In terms of sequencing, teachers face a challenge to integrate fundamental statistical concepts and ideas. As we tell our students, learning certain concepts will be like constructing a picture puzzle. The entire picture may not be clear until we have put all of the pieces in place.

An introduction to statistics covering a range of essential topics is often useful to students later as they take coursework in other departments or pursue career opportunities that require a broader range of quantitative knowledge (Giesbrecht et al., 1997). For those students seeking a more in-depth study of methods and statistics, departments can always offer advanced coursework. Walker (1936) suggested that departments offer three different introductory statistics courses: (a) statistics for students who plan to become statisticians; (b) statistics for students who plan on research careers; and (c) a statistical appreciation course for students who want to develop a general statistical literacy. However, then as now, most universities do not have the staffing required to offer such a range of introductory courses.

Bossley, O'Neill, Parsons, and Lockwood (1980) recommended that teachers begin the course with a general overview of both descriptive and inferential statistics, thereby providing a conceptual framework for use throughout the course. Such a cognitive map would enable students to conceptualize the overall schema of the course and the material to be covered. They also noted that teachers might introduce nonparametric statistics early in the semester, as this material tends to be less challenging mathematically. Therefore, teachers can place a greater emphasis on introducing ideas such as significance levels and statistical power as opposed to teaching complex mathematical formulae. Finally, they suggested that an introductory statistics course should focus on a broader understanding of the material to build general statistical literacy as opposed to developing specific skills.

Two studies have identified the most important topics to teach in the introductory statistics course. Giesbrecht et al. (1997) compiled a list of statistical topics based on an evaluation of research articles and statistics textbooks. Forty-four professors who taught at least one statistics course at the introductory level ranked the importance of each topic. The results revealed 49 topics that fell into the following nine categories: (a) summarizing data and graphs (e.g., frequency histograms, regression lines); (b) summarizing data using descriptive data (e.g., measures of central tendency and variability); (c) probability and probability distributions (e.g., normal distribution, central limit theorem); (d) estimation (e.g., sampling distributions, least squares estimation); (e) hypothesis testing (e.g., t-tests, Type I and Type II errors); (f) categorical data analysis (e.g., chi-squared test for independence); (g) correlation and regression; (h) ANOVA; and (i) nonparametric tests. Readers may also be interested in a similar analysis conducted on core topics in teaching research methods (see Giesbrecht et al., 1997).

Because Giesbrecht et al. (1997) used professors representing four different disciplines, it is possible that their results do not accurately reflect of the perspectives of psychologists who teach statistics. Landrum (2005) conducted a study to identify the primary topics of importance in an introductory statistics course for psychology students. Using a similar procedure, he compiled a list of statistical terms appearing in statistics textbooks and mailed a survey to psychology departments. Faculty who taught statistics and participated in the survey rated the importance of each concept on a four-point scale ranging from "not at all important" to "extremely important." Based on the return of 190 surveys, Landrum developed his Top 100 list (see Table 1.1). This study, together with Giesbrecht et al.'s findings, provided teachers with the most important concepts to cover in an introductory statistics course.

Finally, instructors rarely address tests and measurement within the introductory statistics course. This point most likely reflects pragmatic concerns such as time limitations and staffing issues. Nonetheless, to augment the introductory course, Friedrich et al. (2000) recommended the addition of an advanced hybrid course that combines research, statistics, and measurement into the curriculum.

Regardless of topics covered or course sequencing, the GAISE Project (ASA, 2005) recommended six strategies for teaching statistics:

1. Emphasize statistical literacy and develop statistical thinking.
2. Use real data.
3. Stress conceptual understanding rather than mere knowledge of procedures.

*Table 1.1*   Landrum's (2005) Top 100 List[1]

| | |
|---|---|
| 1. Normal curve | 52. Distribution of sample means |
| 2. Statistically significant | 53. Student's *t* test |
| 3. Bell-shaped curve | 54. Linear relationship |
| 4. Significance level | 55. Independent-samples design |
| 5. Hypothesis testing | 56. *z* score transformation |
| 6. Normal distribution | 57. Random |
| 7. Standard deviation | 58. Random assignment |
| 8. Sample | 59. Sampling error |
| 9. Alpha level | 60. Correlational method |
| 10. Mean | 61. *z* score |
| 11. Null hypothesis | 62. Null-hypothesis population |
| 12. Central tendency | 63. Frequency |
| 13. Inferential statistics | 64. Independent groups design |
| 14. Variability | 65. Frequency distribution |
| 15. Arithmetic mean | 66. Independent variable |
| 16. Correlation | 67. Type II error |
| 17. Pearson correlation | 68. One-tailed probability |
| 18. Dependent variable | 69. Random selection |
| 19. Two-tailed probability | 70. Nondirectional hypothesis |
| 20. Positive correlation | 71. Sampling distribution |
| 21. Data | 72. Estimated population standard deviation |
| 22. Hypothesis | |
| 23. *t* test | 73. Overall mean |
| 24. Descriptive statistics | 74. Correct decision |
| 25. Variance | 75. Sampling distribution of the mean |
| 26. Negative correlation | |
| 27. Not significant | 76. Sampling distributions of a statistic |
| 28. Variable | |
| 29. Population | 77. Regression |
| 30. Statistic | 78. Causation |
| 31. Level of significance | 79. Scatterplot |
| 32. Critical values | 80. Sum of squares |
| 33. Type I error | 81. Positive relationship |
| 34. Degrees of freedom | 82. Sampling distribution of *t* |
| 35. Median | 83. Sum of squared deviations |
| 36. Significant effect | 84. Test statistic |
| 37. Rejection region | 85. Chi-square distribution |
| 38. *t*-test for independent-samples design | 86. Between-groups sum of squares |
| | 87. Simple random sample |
| 39. One-way ANOVA | 88. Population variance |
| 40. Statistical inference | 89. Random sampling |
| 41. Two-tailed test of significance | 90. *t*-distribution |
| 42. *t*-test for independent groups | 91. Chi-square statistic |
| 43. *t*-statistic | 92. One-tailed test of significance |
| 44. Standard error of the mean | 93. Probability |
| 45. Critical region | 94. Standard score |
| 46. Standard error | 95. *F* distribution |
| 47. ANOVA | 96. Distribution of scores |
| 48. Inferential process | 97. ANOVA summary table |
| 49. Alternative hypothesis | 98. Treatment |
| 50. *F* ratio | 99. Levels/treatments |
| 51. Deviation | 100. Subjects/participants |

4. Foster active learning in the classroom.
5. Use technology for developing conceptual understanding and analyzing data.
6. Use assessments to improve and evaluate student learning. (p. 1)

Throughout this text, we will discuss research supporting the above recommendations and describe the best teaching practices to translate these recommendations into statistics learning outcomes.

## Introducing Research Methods within the Context of Statistics

The story of research methods and statistics is the story of the chicken and the egg. Can one conduct research without some knowledge of statistics and can one truly understand the fundamentals of statistics without some knowledge of research methods? Certainly, in departments of psychology around the country, prerequisites for both statistics and methods courses vary. In addition, many departments have opted for a combined research methods and statistics course or a sequence of integrated courses (Friedrich et al., 2000).

Byrne (1996) argued that students do not develop an appreciation, let alone an excitement, about studying statistics until they see real-world applications of statistical concepts and methods. She argued that all statistics courses should include an applied research component. In other words, students should be able to work with and make practical sense of data sets provided for the course.

The value of student involvement in research includes not only the development of a greater appreciation for statistics but extends to an increased understanding of them as well (Pfannkuch & Wild, 2004; Starke, 1985). One key component of statistical literacy is the ability to apply statistical thinking correctly to different situations. In their own lives, in evaluating media information, or in reading research, students do not regularly arrive at accurate conclusions when the situation involves issues of statistics or probability (Schwartz & Goldman, 1996). Instead, students tend to rely on "statistical heuristics to reason and make judgments about the world" (Nisbett, Krantz, & Jepson, 1983, p. 339). Unfortunately, these statistical cognitive shortcuts are not always useful and may lead to faulty conclusions. Friedrich et al. (2000) concluded that greater learning in statistics courses results when methods used to teach statistics highlight reasoning, understanding, and interpretation of data rather than merely the computation of statistical formulas. As research opportunities facilitate both critical and independent thinking (Starke, 1985), instructors can accomplish the goals outlined by Friedrich et al. by incorporating research methods into their statistics courses. Conversely, statistics education increases reasoning skills across a variety of domains and thus, may facilitate the study of research methods (Kosonen & Winne, 1995).

In addition, Thompson (1994) recommended that teachers include research as a fundamental component of any statistics course. However, he stressed that students generate their own data for analysis as opposed to being passive recipients of pre-existing data sets. He also emphasized that involvement in the collection of data and the development of specific research questions for testing generates greater excitement for learning statistics (see also ASA, 2005; Bradstreet, 1996; Cobb & McClain, 2004; Jowett & Davies, 1960; Rumsey, 2002; Singer & Willett, 1990; Stallings, 1993; Tanner, 1985; Thompson, 1994). We will discuss this topic more in subsequent chapters.

## Student Populations

The far-ranging heterogeneity of undergraduate statistics students provides a wonderful backdrop for discussion, exploration, and learning of new course content. However, such diversity also creates challenges. The most commonly noted concerns for teachers include variability in mathematical ability, cognitive abilities and learning styles, and attitudes and motivation toward learning statistics (Schutz et al., 1998; Tremblay, Gardner, & Heipel, 2000).

### Mathematical ability

Quantitative literacy and statistical literacy are distinct but interrelated concepts (delMas, 2004; Moore, 1998). Research examining the development of students' statistical knowledge base in middle and high school demonstrates that general math courses often ignore concepts related to statistics and probability (Wilkins & Ma, 2002). Using data drawn from the national *Longitudinal Study of American Youth* study (LSAY: Miller, Kimmel, Hoffer, & Nelson, 2000), Wilkins and Ma documented the progressive rate of student learning related to algebra, geometry, and statistics during middle and high school. The LSAY followed a cohort of 3,116 middle to high school students over a period of 6 years from 12 different geographic areas. Each year, students completed measures of mathematics achievement, mathematics attitude and self-concept scales, and other background information. Using hierarchical linear modeling, Wilkins and Ma measured patterns of growth for each student related to mathematical learning. They found that learning rates related to statistics literacy lag far behind the other two content areas. For example, the growth rate of algebra learning is three times that of statistics at the high school level. Wilkins and Ma (2002) hypothesized that, at the secondary school level, concepts related to statistics and probability topics are often in the "back of the book" (p. 296) and thus rarely covered.

As a result, many undergraduate students arrive on college campuses unprepared to study advanced mathematics or statistics (Brown, Askew, Baker, Denvir, & Millett, 1998; Mulhern & Wylie, 2004; Phoenix, 1999; Tariq, 2002). Additionally, high school seniors in the United States lag behind students in other countries on measures of mathematical literacy (Mullis, Martin, Beaton, Gonzalez, Kelly, & Smith, 1998). The lack of mathematical ability among many incoming students may haunt them in future statistics courses given the reported positive correlations between highest mathematical grade level completed, mathematical achievement, and performance in an introductory statistics course (Lalonde & Gardner, 1993).

Unfortunately, the situation may be worsening. Mulhern and Wylie (2004) argued that mathematical competencies are uniformly decreasing at the college level. In a comparison of two psychology undergraduate cohorts, 1992 and 2002, they found significant reductions in mathematical competencies for all six of the components that they measured (calculation, graphical interpretation, algebraic reasoning, probability and sampling, proportionality and ratio, and estimation). This finding is important because research consistently underscores the relationship between mathematical skills and performance in statistics courses (e.g., Elmore & Vasu, 1980; Elmore & Vasu, 1986; Feinberg & Halperin, 1978; Schutz et al., 1998; Woehlke & Leitner, 1980).

Although some researchers paint a less than stellar picture of mathematics, and in particular, statistical literacy and learning at the post-secondary level, the GAISE project (ASA, 2005) is much more optimistic. It noted that the number of students taking advanced placement (AP) statistics has grown from 7,500 in 1997 to over 65,000 in 2004. They also report that enrollments in introductory statistics courses on the community college level have increased substantially. Mills (2004a) examined student attitudes towards statistics with the *Survey of Attitudes Toward Statistics* (SATS: Schau, Stevens, Dauphinee, & Del Vecchio, 1995). She administered the survey to 203 undergraduate psychology students and found that their attitudes tended to be more positive than negative in relation to statistics. Students agreed with items such as, "I like statistics" and "Statistics should be a part of my professional training" and disagreed with items such as "I feel insecure when I have to do statistics problems" (2004a, p. 361). She credited the statistics education reform movement for improved student attitudes towards statistics.

   Although there is some positive news at the college level regarding statistics education, the GAISE (ASA, 2005) project introduced an important caveat. Current statistics students exhibited great variability in quantitative abilities and motivational levels. Consequently, statistics instructors need to begin developing strategies to address the increasing diversity among statistics students. Schutz et al. (1998) recommended the use of pre-tests to identify potential at-risk students. With proper identification, students may receive remedial assistance related to math competencies and assistance in developing highly effective, alternative learning strategies aimed at increased understanding of statistics as well as other content in other courses. This early work can help establish and build feelings of confidence and self-efficacy leading to greater motivation in the course. Schutz et al. also found that individuals of different ability levels working together during the course helps all achieve a higher level of performance.

## Cognitive ability and learning styles

Researchers have also studied levels of cognitive ability and learning styles in relation to learning statistics. For example, Hudak and Anderson (1990) examined the hypothesis that students operating below Piaget's level of formal operations would have more difficulty learning and conceptualizing statistical methods. At the beginning of the semester, they tested students in both statistics and computer science classes for level of cognitive ability using the Formal Operational Reasoning Test (FORT: Roberge & Flexer, 1982) by comparing final course grades to performance on the FORT. They discovered a positive correlation between formal operational reasoning ability and successful course performance for both statistics and computer science students.

Hudak and Anderson (1990) also tested learning styles, specifically concrete experience and abstract conceptualization using Kolb's (as cited in Hudak & Anderson) Learning Style Inventory. They found that both sets of students exhibiting a high level of abstract conceptualization skills performed better than did students reliant on a high level of concrete experience. Forsyth (1977) also found students differed on measures of cognitive ability, most notably the factors related to Guilford's (1959) defined categories of memory, intellectual ability, divergent thinking, and convergent thinking. Forsyth found lower performance on each measure was associated directly with poorer performance in a statistics and research methods course.

Teachers may need to provide some students with concrete learning experiences to facilitate understanding of statistical concepts particularly as those concepts increase in difficulty. Involving students in direct experimentation and data collection is one potentially effective method for providing students such concrete experience.

## Self-efficacy and motivation

Levels of self-efficacy and motivation also differ among students, potentially having a significant impact on their course performance. For example, Lane, Hall, and Lane (2004) studied the relationship between performance in a statistics class and self-efficacy. They measured self-efficacy using the Self-efficacy Towards Statistics Questionnaire (STSQ; Lane, Hall, & Lane, 2002) at the beginning and the middle of the course. The researchers found a positive correlation between self-efficacy and final performance in the class, particularly the mid-course measure. They recommended that teachers use the STSQ to identify students at the beginning of the course who may be at risk of poor performance due to low self-efficacy.

Mills (2004a) found a relationship between high statistical self-efficacy and positive attitudes about learning statistics. Of course, students may have a low level of self-efficacy based on their realistic self-assessment of their mathematical skills. As such, a math pre-test in addition to the STSQ may be beneficial in isolating the source of low self-efficacy. Lane et al. (2004) also recommended that instructors gradually provide the means for students to establish an adequate level of statistical competency early the course. Such shaping of statistical competency would simultaneously enhance student's confidence in their abilities. As part of this process, Lane et al. encouraged instructors to design the course to first increase student interest in statistics before attempting to teach highly complex tasks that might threaten students' self-efficacy.

Student motivation is also an important factor to consider in teaching the course. For example, Harris (1974) met individually with students who performed poorly (received a grade of D or F) in a statistics course. Harris found that students' low performance resulted from several factors ranging from failing to understand a major concept to lack of studying and missed classes. He continued to work with students the following semester and concluded that motivational factors played a significant role in the majority of the students' poor experiences. Harris used group review sessions to address these motivational issues rather than individual tutoring sessions. At retesting, the majority of the students passed the class.

Schutz et al. (1998) systematically studied the role of motivation in relation to performance in a statistic course. They broadly defined motivation using the learning beliefs, elaboration, and test anxiety scales of the Motivated Strategies for Learning Questionnaire (MSLQ: Pintrich, Smith, Garcia, & McKeachie, 1991) and included whether students spent additional time using alternative learning strategies such as relating the material studied to other coursework, visualization, and the development of analogies. The results confirmed earlier findings (e.g., Elmore & Vasu, 1986; Feinberg & Halperin, 1978; Presley & Huberty 1988; Woehlke & Leitner, 1980) demonstrating that students with higher pre-statistics mathematical abilities performed better than did students with lower math and statistics pre-scores. However, Schulz et al. found some students with low pre-test scores who were successful in learning statistics. The major difference between the two groups of students with low pre-test scores was motivation and effort. Students who performed well in statistics regardless of whether they had prior knowledge of math and statistics used very different learning strategies than those students who did not do well in the course. Those who performed well used the traditional methods of reading, highlighting, memorization, and working sample problems. However, they also sought out tutoring, read other textbooks related to statistics, completed programmed instructional texts, used visualization, rewrote notes into their own words, and engaged in regular daily studying. Students who preformed poorly in the class used the traditional studying methods but did nothing more. They reported feeling more overwhelmed and lost in the course. These students relied heavily, if not solely, on rehearsal and repetition strategies, highly unproductive strategies when aimed at learning to "know how" (Evans, 1976).

Tremblay et al. (2000), extended the socio-educational model of Lalonde and Gardner (1993), and examined the role of motivation in statistics learning. Tremblay et al. defined motivational intensity as "the amount of effort students expend in learning statistics" (2000, p. 43). They found a positive correlation among motivational intensity, final exam performance, and students' positive attitudes towards the teacher. Although a correlational design, these results highlight the potential role that teachers may play in students' motivation and the importance of factors such as listening, humor, and student–teacher rapport.

## Gender

Some researchers have pondered whether there is a gender difference related to learning statistics. Although Mulhern and Wylie (2004) found that men performed significantly better on a series of tests of mathematical abilities, Brooks (1987) found women had higher overall grades than did male students over the previous decade of his course. Similarly, Elmore and Vasu (1986), in a study of 188 students enrolled in a statistics class, found that women performed at a significantly higher level than did their male counterparts. However, Buck (1985) in an analysis of 13 semesters of both introductory and advanced undergraduate statistics course grades, found no gender differences related to performance in a statistics course.

In a meta-analysis of 13 articles, Schram (1996) examined the relationship of gender to performance in a statistics class, and determined that when the evaluation criterion was an exam, men performed better than did women. However, when the evaluation criterion was the total overall performance in the course, women outperformed men. In relation to attitudes, Mills (2004a), in her study of 203 undergraduate statistics students, found that women had more negative attitudes towards statistics than did men.

The question of whether gender differences exist in mathematical ability is a hotly contested issue. For example, Dr. Lawrence H. Summers, President of Harvard University from 2001–2006, initiated a maelstrom of controversy when he suggested at the National Bureau of Economic Research Conference on Diversifying the Science and Engineering Workforce that gender differences in math and science were primarily due to genetics (Summers, 2005). On the other hand, Spencer, Steele, and Quinn (1999) asserted that math differences between men and women largely result from stereotype threat versus genetically rooted sex differences. Subsequent studies have confirmed the role of stereotype threat as one explanation for gender differences in mathematics (e.g., Martens, Johns, Greenberg, & Schimel, 2006; Marx & Roman, 2002; McIntyre, Paulson, & Lord, 2003; O'Brien & Crandall, 2003). Although the question of gender differences in mathematics is still unresolved, it is likely that the issue is much more complex than simply who gets the highest grade at the end of the term.

## Helping Your Students Survive Statistics

There are many ways that teachers can help their students survive and even thrive as they make their way through a semester of introductory statistics. Given the tendency for math anxiety to drive students' perceptions of statistics, instructors should assure students that statistics is not primarily a math class. Indeed, as noted by the GAISE Project (ASA, 2005), it is important to foster conceptual understanding as opposed to simply procedural understanding of the material. Nonetheless, a look of panic on students' faces at the first glimpse of a formula or a table practically assures that conceptual learning will be lost given the negative correlation between learning and statistics anxiety (Lalonde & Gardner, 1993; Onwuegbuzie & Seaman, 1995; Onwuegbuzie & Wilson, 2003; Tremblay et al., 2000; Zanakis & Valenza, 1997; Zeidner, 1991). Consequently, teachers must incorporate strategies aimed at reducing math anxiety and enhancing self-efficacy in the course structure from the first day of class. We will discuss strategies aimed at reducing statistics anxiety and increasing self-efficacy in greater depth in Chapter 4.

Instructors can also teach students to self-monitor their learning process during the course. For example, Lan (1996) tested the effects of self-monitoring on class performance. Lan assigned students to one of three groups: self-monitoring, instructor-monitoring, and control. Students in the self-monitoring group kept a daily log documenting the time they spent using various learning strategies (e.g., group discussion, tutoring, problem solving), the amount of time they spent studying a particular statistical concept, and they recorded their confidence level in understanding the material. Students in the instructor monitoring condition had the same list of statistical concepts but evaluated the instructor's teaching. Lan found that students in the self-monitoring group performed at a significantly higher level than the other two groups and demonstrated a better ability to organize and understand course content. Relative to the other two groups, the self-monitoring group also engaged in a higher number of self-regulatory learning strategies such as environmental structuring, review of previous work, and self-evaluation. However, Lan noted that students' self-regulatory behavior declined when they faced complex learning tasks, particularly when those tasks required an increased focus on the processing of the new information. Lan found no difference in motivation levels among the groups, suggesting that the self-monitoring was equally beneficial for all students.

In some small measure, encouraging self-monitoring behavior facilitates students' use of good study habits. Hastings (1982) and Schutz et al. (1998) stressed the importance of good study habits and keeping up with the material. Students who self-monitor may be quicker to realize that they are in need of tutoring, including peer tutoring, both of which can be beneficial for students in statistics courses (Conners, Mccown, & Roskos-Ewoldsen, 1998; Ward, 1984). In addition, students and instructors can use self-monitoring to recognize the warning signs of future trouble and as a guide to adopt new learning strategies or seek assistance.

Finally, students' motivation increases when they recognize the practical benefits of a course. Students entering graduate school with weak statistical and methodological training are at greater risk for dropping out than well-prepared students (Jannarone, 1986). Clough (1993) argued that employers expect that potential employees with undergraduate psychology training have skills in both statistics and methodology. Unfortunately, alumni do not appear to recognize the benefit of these skills, or perhaps, that they even have these skills (Grocer & Kohout, 1997).

If students avoid quantitative methods coursework and view it as having little relevance, then such biases will most likely shape and limit their future career choices as well. Exposing students to exciting careers possibilities that require knowledge of methodology and statistics can help reverse this trend. For example, Beins (1985) described a statistics class project whereby students contacted companies and requested data related to studies mentioned in advertising claims. Through such creative projects, students can discover that statistics have real world usefulness and context. With greater emphasis on the opportunities available to students with a background in quantitative methods, students will begin to incorporate such ideas into their own thinking, studying, and potential career opportunities.

## Conclusion

Statistics can be a challenging, engaging, and positive educational experience for students. However, to realize this potential, instructors need to pay particular attention to the design of the course to maximize the learning experience. Specifically, instructors need to attend to a host of details from selection of teaching strategies aimed at anxiety reduction to the selection of activities designed to maximize the development and assessment of students' statistical literacy, thinking, and reasoning skills. To make informed choices about the best methods to teaching statistics, instructors need to be familiar with the growing literature on statistics education. Ideally, the journey through statistics is much like a well-planned, but oft repeated, road trip. The route remains relatively the same but the company and process of exploration are dynamic and interactive with each journey. Thus, the trip is never dull.

### Note

1   From "Core terms in undergraduate statistics," by R. E. Landrum, 2005, *Teaching of Psychology, 32*, p. 250. Copyright 2005 by Taylor & Francis Ltd. Adapted with permission.

# Chapter 2

# Nuts and Bolts of Teaching Statistics

*The mediocre teacher tells. The good teacher explains. The superior teacher demonstrates. The great teacher inspires. – William Arthur Ward*

Texts devoted to assisting novice and seasoned educators improve their teaching skills highlight a similar theme—it is never too early to begin planning and preparing your course (Buskist & Davis, 2006; Dunn & Chew, 2006; Forsyth, 2003; Lucas & Bernstein, 2005). According to McKeachie (2002), "for teachers, courses do not start on the first day of classes. Rather a course begins well before you meet your students" (p. 9). In this chapter, we will discuss course development including topics such as syllabus creation, textbook or study guide selection, and the possible use of an electronic bulletin board, Java applets, and/or Flash exercises during lecture. To maximize the success of your course, and consequently your students' success, you need to tackle each topic well before the first day of class.

The goal of this chapter is not to tell you which textbook, study guide, calculator, online tutorial or Web animation to use for your course. Rather, we aim to provide you the necessary tools to make an informed choice. To that end, we have created several online appendices for use with this chapter. Appendix A contains a listing of nontraditional and electronic undergraduate statistics textbooks.

Appendix B is an analysis of traditional psychologically oriented undergraduate introductory statistics textbooks. A listing of Web sites hosting useful interactive applications such as Java applets, Flash animations, tutorials, and simulations is in Appendix C. All online materials are available at our Web site at www.teachstats.org.

## Syllabus Construction

The syllabus is often a student's first introduction to any course and the statistics course is no exception. In fact, some students download available syllabi prior to or immediately following registration. For courses where syllabi are not available prior to the course, Pan and Tang (2005) recommended that instructors send students an orientation letter a week before the beginning of a term. Such a letter may include information about the textbook, the level of math knowledge required for the class, and available student resources (e.g., tutoring services). In addition to ameliorating student fears, the instructor can utilize an orientation letter to convey warmth and genuine interest in student success. In turn, students' positive attitudes toward statistics teachers positively correlated with lower class anxiety and higher performance (Tremblay et al., 2000).

In their analysis of over 200 course syllabi, from a variety of disciplines, Parkes and Harris (2002) posited three basic functions of a course syllabus. The first purpose is to provide a contract between the instructor and student. The contract should clearly delineate course goals, outcomes, methods, and expectations for the students. As part of that process, instructors need to construct syllabi that unambiguously outline the course requirements with applicable dates for the entire semester. In addition, teachers should detail policies regarding attendance, late assignments, make-up exams, incompletes, plagiarism, and special accommodations. A well-constructed statistics syllabus provides a clear roadmap of course expectations and requirements, which can be instrumental in reducing first day jitters among anxious students.

The second function of a syllabus is as a permanent record of the course goals, outcomes, and assessment techniques (Parkes & Harris, 2002). The recent focus on assessment in academia has resulted in institutional pressure for instructors to communicate clear goals on their syllabi and detail how various assignments and exams allow students to reach these goals. Indeed, accrediting agencies, such as the North Central Association Commission on Accreditation and School Improvement may request syllabi, complete with goals and measured outcomes, for each course offered in a particular discipline. Parkes and Harris also pointed out that tenure and promotion committees may request course syllabi to assess course content, the degree to which the assignments, exams, etc. are appropriate for the course level, and as a measure of the instructor's attitudes towards students. In addition, students often need to provide undergraduate syllabi, particularly for statistics and research methods courses, to graduate institutions to demonstrate educational exposure to a particular subject matter.

According to Parkes and Harris (2002), the final function of a syllabus is to serve as a learning tool. They asserted that a learning-centered syllabus provides students with information on how to develop self-management skills, expresses clear expectations regarding the amount of effort students need to expend mastering the subject matter, and details whether students have the skills necessary for success. For example, statistics teachers may find it useful to address math concerns in the syllabus. Our introductory statistics syllabi often include the phrase "No prior statistical knowledge is required for this class" to reassure students. In addition, we also include information as to where students can find assistance outside of class. Parkes and Harris suggested instructors include information about the availability of tutors, useful Web sites, and contact information for student services on the course syllabus. A learning-centered syllabus can also provide students with a sense of context as to where the course fits within their discipline (Parkes & Harris, 2002). Such contextual information is particularly important in an undergraduate statistics course in psychology given the tendency for students to view the discipline as primarily human interest in focus (Rajecki et al., 2005).

Regardless of how well you craft your syllabus, you should recognize that not all students will attend to every aspect of the syllabus. Becker and Calhoon (2000) had students rate the degree to which they attended to 29 syllabus items. They found that students paid the most attention to exam and assignment due dates and the least amount of attention to general course information, withdrawal dates, and details about assigned readings. First-year students were more apt to pay attention to prerequisites, late assignment and dishonesty policies, and support services as compared to continuing students. Nontraditional students rated course goals, type of assignments, and details about assigned readings higher than did traditional students. All students tended to focus less attention on syllabus items as the semester ended, suggesting that instructors may need to reiterate aspects of the syllabus pertinent to the last portion of the class.

Teachers should strive to create a syllabus that conveys a positive attitude towards statistics. A reduction in anxiety and the presence of positive instructor attitude are both associated with increased student performance in a statistics course (Onwuegbuzie & Wilson, 2003; Pan & Tang, 2005; Tremblay et al., 2000). To reduce anxiety, teachers may insert some humor into their syllabi and lectures. Lomax and Moosavi (2002) stated that inserting humor into a statistics course reduced statistics anxiety, motivated students, facilitated a deeper understanding of the material, and made for a more engaging classroom (see our Web site at www.teachstats.org for suggestions on incorporating humor in your courses).

Creating an effective statistics syllabus takes considerable time and effort. Indeed, you will likely be tweaking the syllabus each time you teach the course. However, there are several recent resources devoted to teaching psychology that include a section on the creation of course syllabi to help reduce future edits and rewrites (e.g., Buskist & Davis, 2006; Forsyth, 2003). Additionally, Lucas and Bernstein's (2005) guide to teaching psychology has an excellent chapter entitled "Preparing Your Course" that includes advice on syllabus creation, setting up a grading system, and communicating with students in person and via email.

## Textbook Selection

A textbook is your students' at-home window into the world of statistics. As such, its selection is an important consideration when preparing to teach any quantitative methods course. Although there are several notable publications devoted to aid instructors in selecting an introductory psychology textbook (e.g., Koenig, 2006; Woolf, Hulsizer, & McCarthy, 2002a, 2002b), there are no such resources available for statistics instructors in psychology. The lack of resources is surprising given the fact that three major publishers alone currently market almost two dozen introductory statistics texts for use in psychology departments.

The lack of statistics textbook evaluation aids is not unique to psychology. Although several journals in education and mathematics routinely publish reviews of recently published statistics textbooks, these evaluations are typically very subjective, lack any theory-based rationale, and fail to compare and contrast among existing texts (Harwell, Herrick, Curtis, Mundfrom, & Gold, 1996). Cobb (1987) was one of the first authors to compare and contrast statistics texts used in the fields of education and mathematics. In his evaluation of 16 statistics texts, Cobb rated each book on: (a) technical level and quality of exposition; (b) topics covered; and (c) the type of data sets and quality of the exercises present in the text. Although Cobb's analysis was subjective, the criteria he developed became the basis of several more advanced analyses of statistics textbooks in these fields (e.g., Halvorsen, 2000; Harwell et al., 1996; Huberty & Barton, 1990). We based the following statistics textbook evaluation criteria on the guidelines used by Griggs (2006) in his analysis of introductory psychology textbooks and the approaches advocated by Cobb (1987) and Hayden (2000) in their analyses of education and mathematics statistics texts.

## Conceptual orientation

When selecting a statistics textbook, instructors need to be cognizant as to whether the text is primarily conceptual or computational in nature. Research suggests that the conceptual approach to teaching undergraduate statistics is more pedagogically sound than focusing solely on calculation. Guttmannova, Shields, and Caruso (2005) suggested that teachers refrain from focusing on computational formulas in a statistics course. They noted that most computational formulas bear little resemblance to the theory at the core of each statistical technique. Consequently, students may become good at computing a particular statistic but have little understanding as to its meaning. Instead, Guttmannova et al. argued that coursework should focus on definitional or theoretical formulas. Not only can students use theoretical formulas to compute a statistic, but more importantly, these formulas reinforce the underlying theory behind the statistic. Unfortunately, Guttmannova and colleagues found that only a few of the textbooks reviewed highlighted definitional as opposed to computational formulas.

Layne and Huck (1981) examined whether computational procedures facilitated student's ability to read and understand empirical literature using two sections of a research methods class. The researchers provided the experimental group with information concerning the computation of traditional introductory statistical techniques (e.g., Pearson's product moment correlation coefficient, independent t-tests). The control class was identical in content with the exception that the researchers did not provide computational procedure information. Students in both classes completed exams at the end of the term evaluating their ability to read and comprehend statistical information including tables photocopied from professional journals. The researchers used pre-course math tests as a covariate. They found no significant differences between the two groups' ability to read and interpret journal information. It appeared, at least in relation to journal interpretation, that students experienced no benefit from learning to compute statistical techniques by hand.

Paradoxically, textbooks that focus exclusively on theory are sometimes the perfect choice for students with math phobias. A conceptual approach allows the instructor to focus less on math and more on logical reasoning, thus reducing anxiety and better enabling students to learn the material. This approach can be particularly successful when coupled with statistical software packages (e.g., SPSS) which further remove students from working with raw data (and therein may lie the root of their anxiety troubles). It was not until relatively recently that instructors had the tools available (e.g., computer SPSS labs) to shift from time-consuming hand calculations to computer programs. In fact, psychology departments now routinely use computers in about 70% of their introductory statistics classes (Bartz & Sabolik, 2001). Moreover, it is unlikely that students will ever compute the vast majority of statistics by hand when conducting research. Consequently, researchers have argued that it is pedagogically unsound for teachers to continue to focus largely on hand computations in light of current computer methodologies (Bear, 1995; Guttmannova et al., 2005).

Despite the growing body of literature supporting the conceptual approach to teaching statistics, there still appears to be a market for textbooks that emphasize computation. One potential explanation for this incongruity is the fact that many of those teaching undergraduate statistics have very little training in statistics (Hayden, 2000). As a result, instructors may avoid entering into a lengthy discussion of statistical theory because they are less sure of their ability to convey such information to their students in an understandable fashion. In addition, instructors may encounter a classroom composed of students with a low need for cognition (Cacioppo, Petty, Feinstein, & Jarvis, 1996) when it comes to statistical reasoning. In this situation, students may only be interested in getting the final answer and extremely resistant to any discussion of why a particular theory or approach works. The existence of these factors may predispose instructors to believe that they have no choice but to devote the majority of class time to computation.

## Level of difficulty

As the march to the end of the semester quickens, statistics instructors only have a finite amount of time to devote to any one topic in their courses. Unfortunately, some students will need to spend additional time digesting the material. In these situations, students will need to rely on the text to provide supplementary instruction. Consequently, it is crucial for instructors to choose a textbook that best matches the mathematical background of their students. "No one enjoys being ambushed by a textbook whose technical arsenal turns out to be more powerful than expected" (Cobb, 1987, p. 322).

To determine the true difficulty level of a statistics textbook, Cobb (1987) suggested that researchers avoid relying solely on the author's own assessment (often provided in the Preface). Instead, Cobb recommended that researchers also assess the degree to which the author's use of formulas obscures (or focuses attention) on the relevant basic concepts. In addition, researchers need to judge the extent to which the author relies on algebra to make connections among concepts.

Initially, there were relatively few texts designed for students that traditionally struggle with mathematics. Historically, small publishing companies such as Pyrczak Publishing produced texts appropriate for this population. However, recently larger psychology publishers have been more active producing textbooks in this area (see online Appendix A at www.teachstats.org for a listing of nontraditional statistics texts). These texts use a variety of techniques, most often humor, to take the focus off math and instead emphasize the ideas behind the numbers. It is important to note that some of these texts may not be appropriate as preparation for a graduate or postgraduate career in psychology given they may not cover more advanced topics. However, they can be very good at preparing students to become good consumers of scientific information.

The diverse mathematical abilities of psychology majors have resulted in authors creating statistics textbooks appropriate at the intermediate level. As a result, these textbooks are a nice fit for most introductory statistics courses at community and four year colleges and universities. Unfortunately, a high proportion of intermediate level texts focus on computation versus the theoretical underpinnings of statistical reasoning. According to Griggs (2006), the decision to adopt an intermediate versus a more advanced text hinges on the extent to which you wish to challenge students. In addition, instructors who add supplemental readings may wish to use an intermediate text given the fact that the text will not be the sole focus of the course. Finally, instructors need to consider the extent to which they want to add material during lecture versus asking students to skip material in their book.

There are only a handful of textbooks appropriate for advanced undergraduate students. Advanced level texts cover the basics as well as more advanced topics such as logistic regression and repeated measures analyses of variance. The focus is often more theoretical than computational. Some psychology departments offer an introductory statistics course as well as an upper level statistics course for students who wish to pursue graduate coursework. Advanced texts can be a very good preparation for graduate school, particularly if coupled with a data analysis program (see Chapter 7). Although having students take an introductory statistics course followed by an advanced course results in some significant content overlap, most students can use this refresher to sharpen their statistical skills for graduate work.

## Chapter topics and organization

We reviewed the contents of 30 statistics textbooks published since 2000 (see online Appendix B at www.teachstats.org). All the texts included several sections devoted to descriptive statistics including chapters on central tendency, variability, and the normal curve. In addition, all texts had at least one chapter devoted to correlation and regression. Furthermore, all the textbooks included a chapter introducing inferential statistics (central limit theorem, sampling distributions, confidence intervals etc.) as well as chapters devoted to the one sample t-test, two sample t-test (independent and pairwise), and the analysis of variance (ANOVA). All textbooks discussed nonparametric tests; many had a separate chapter devoted to the chi-square statistic.

Although most authors included some discussion of advanced statistics, the extent to which these analyses were included as separate chapters varied. For example, although 87% of textbooks included a discussion of power analyses, only 38% of those textbooks included the material as a separate chapter. Similarly, although 70% of the textbooks included a chapter on factorial ANOVA, only 43% included a chapter on repeated measures analysis of variance (several of these chapters were in the appendices or online). A small handful of authors elected to go beyond simple regression and include a chapter on multiple regression (13%). Finally, only a few authors included a substantive discussion of analysis of covariance (ANCOVA), multivariate analysis of variance (MANOVA), logistic regression, factor analysis, and structural equation modeling. Despite the popularity of meta-analysis in psychological research, not one book covered the topic in any detail. Note, though, that several resources exist to assist instructors who want to infuse specific advanced statistical methods into their courses (e.g., Grimm & Yarnold, 1995, 2000; Tabachnick & Fidell, 2007). Consequently, instructors that wish to discuss, for example, analyses of covariance in their courses, should not feel obliged to select a text that covers this topic in detail.

## Core formulas and vocabulary

Another issue instructors need to consider when selecting a statistics text involves the extent to which they are comfortable with the formulas and symbols used in the text. The symbols authors use to represent statistical concepts (e.g., standard deviation) vary from text to text. Likewise, computational and conceptual formulas differ among the various statistics texts. Consequently, it is important for instructors to review the formulas highlighted by the author prior to using the text in the classroom. We have found that the use of alternative formulas in the classroom can result in particularly painful results for the students as well as instructor. A strong student might rise to the challenge of learning alternative approaches to answering a question. On the other hand, a student struggling with the material may be further confused (to the point of helplessness) when exposed to yet another formula.

Paradoxically, a university tutoring center can sometimes create confusion by assigning tutors from business or mathematics to work with psychology students seeking help in their statistics course. Although the tutors may be very competent, we have found that they sometimes insist on using personally familiar methods versus the formulas the student has encountered in lecture and their text.

A similar issue often arises when students borrow a friend's book to use while taking your class.

Texts also differ in their presentation of key terms and concepts. Landrum (2005) conducted an analysis to determine the top 100 statistics terms and concepts (see Table 1.1 for the complete list). He used a convenience sample of three statistics textbooks to create a list of 374 terms. Landrum reported that only 44 terms appeared in all three books. Although statistics texts may share similar chapter titles, the results of Landrum's analysis suggested that the content within each chapter is markedly heterogeneous.

## Type of data sets/quality of the exercises

Cobb (1987) recommended that when evaluating a statistics text, instructors should examine whether the text (a) contains real data (versus contrived data); and (b) contains exercises in which the solutions answer realistic questions. In other words, the data sets and accompanying problems need to involve more thinking than number crunching. A growing body of research supports Cobb's suggestions. For example, Lutsky (1986) required students in his introductory psychology class to develop research questions, navigate, and analyze a previously collected data set using SPSS. The experience resulted in students reporting less anxiety about using and interpreting statistics. Students also reported a deeper understanding of the complexities associated with conducting scientific research in psychology. Similarly, Thompson (1994) produced a realistic data set in his introductory statistics class using the Student Information Questionnaire (SIQ). When given a choice between an artificial data set and the SIQ data, most students found the data set created in class to be more interesting. In addition, students revealed that the SIQ data set made it easier to learn statistics.

Given the focus on data calculation, instructors might expect that textbooks with a computation orientation would be more apt to use real data sets and exercises than books with a more conceptual approach. However, in her analysis of 15 mathematics statistics texts, Halvorsen (2000) examined the nature of the exercises and examples and found the opposite pattern. She found that theoretical texts were more likely to use real data or provide exercises that had a realistic setting than texts that were more computational in orientation. Theoretical statistics books were also more likely to cite from newspaper, magazine, or journal articles than computational textbooks. Cobb's (1987) statement that instructors should "judge a book by its exercises, and you cannot go far wrong" is particularly relevant in light of the current research (p. 339). See Chapter 7 for additional information on the use of data sets in statistics education.

## Traditional Versus Electronic Textbooks

College textbook prices have increased twice the general rate of inflation since the academic year 1987–1988 (US Government Accountability Office, 2005). Predictably, students and parents have become increasingly more vocal in their protests over the high costs of college texts. Consequently, in April 2006, Virginia Governor Timothy M. Kaine (D) signed legislation that required public colleges in his state to develop policies aimed at minimizing the cost of texts (Walters, 2006). Lawmakers have championed similar measures in other communities and states around the country. One possible solution to rising textbook costs involves the use of electronic texts (see online Appendix A at www.teachstats.org). Many of these texts are either free or charge a nominal access fee. Unfortunately, only a few studies have examined whether electronic statistics texts are effective pedagogical tools.

Utts, Sommer, Acredolo, Maher, and Matthews (2003) compared a traditional statistics course to a hybrid course on such measures as student performance, satisfaction, and the amount of time the instructor put into the course. Students in the traditional course met regularly with the instructor three times a week and during an hour-long discussion session. The instructor required a standard statistics text for all students taking the traditional course. In contrast, the hybrid course required that students meet in person with the instructor once a week for 80 minutes to take a quiz. The instructor used the remaining time to provide an overview of the upcoming material and provide some demonstrations of relevant material. Students in the hybrid course used a traditional statistics text, as well as CyberStats, an online statistics text from Thomson Learning. The groups did not differ on test performance. In addition, there was no difference between the traditional and hybrid course in the total amount of time spent by the instructor on each course. However, students in the traditional class were more satisfied with the course organization, pace, and expectancies as compared to students in the hybrid course.

Symanzik and Vukasinovic (2003) compared three popular electronic textbooks—ActivStats (www.datadescription.com), CyberStats (www.thomsonlearning.com), and MM*Stat (www.quantlet.com/mdstat). All three of these books contain features typically found in an introductory statistics textbook (e.g., theoretical concepts, computational formulas, exercises). ActivStats and CyberStats target undergraduate students whereas MM*Stat is aimed at advanced statistics courses. In addition, the statistics authors have integrated a data analysis application into each textbook. Symanzik and Vukasinovic (2006) discussed some of the issues they encountered when teaching a "Web-enhanced" version of an introductory statistics course. Unlike the Utts et al. (2003) study, students in the Web-enhanced course described by Symanzik and Vukasinovic only used one text, CyberStats, but did so during three face-to-face 50-minute lectures each week throughout the semester. The course took place in a computer lab to allow each student access to their online text during the lecture period. According to the authors, teaching with an online text like CyberStats sometimes created unique challenges, most of them related to technology glitches. Other issues revolved around the electronic text medium—not having a printed copy of the text was at times an issue for the instructor and students. For example, Symanzik and Vukasinovic reported that it took several steps through online links to find definitions. In addition, some students did not have Internet access at home, which impaired their ability to study and complete homework assignments. Consequently, many students eventually printed out the online material.

In spite of these issues, electronic texts do offer some distinct advantages. The primary advantage is cost. Many electronic textbooks are available at no cost or a fraction of the cost of traditional texts. In addition, electronic texts can incorporate multimedia features such as animation, Java applets, and interactive applications that are not possible via print media. Finally, electronic texts may be ideal for distance education and individualized instruction.

## Supplemental Materials

When selecting a text it is important to examine what supplemental resources are available for students. In fact, we often use the availability of supplemental materials as the "tie-breaker" when trying to decide which text to adopt. However, it is important to recognize that not every student will need or want to take advantage of these tools. Consequently, we tend to shy away from bundling these resources with the text (unless it does not increase the cost of the text), choosing instead to have them available as optional purchases. Additionally, instructors should assign study guides and other ancillary materials judiciously. If students use these aids as a means to assess their learning and strengthen specific skills and knowledge, they may benefit from their use (Dickson, Miller, & Devoley, 2004). However, if misused largely as a means to memorize information, study guides result in little benefit and may detract, in fact, from time spent studying more wisely (Gurung, 2003). As noted by Dickson et al. (2004), "not all study time is equal; time spent learning must be actively used and students need to engage in productive activities that correspond to the testing method" (p. 38). Therefore, students may need instruction as to how best to use various ancillary course materials.

## Study guides

Study guides, paper-bound and electronic versions, are available for the majority (67%) of the traditional statistics texts reviewed in online Appendix B. The typical study guide consists of a combination of chapter outlines, learning objectives, glossary of statistics terms, flash cards, and most importantly, additional multiple-choice, essay, and problem solving questions. Although the pedagogical tools provided in most study guides are limited, some students benefit from the additional problems and seem to find comfort in the flash cards. However, instructors may need to warn students that the test questions in the study guide may bear little resemblance to the exam questions used in the course (Christopher, 2006) and this disparity may impact test performance (Dickson et al., 2004). Regardless, these guides are likely to remain popular because they are relatively cheap to produce and they are tremendously appealing to anxious statistics students.

## Companion Web sites

Increasingly, text authors and publishing companies are creating companion Web sites for students. Indeed, 63% of the texts we examined provided online resources. Although the vast majority of companion Web sites are just simple versions of study guides, a small percentage contain multimedia exercises, multimedia demonstrations, additional Web chapters, and links to additional Web resources. For example, Portier, Hermans, Valcke, and van den Bosch (1997) created an "electronic workbook" for students to use as a supplement to their course. Others have created class Web pages with interactive exercises, PowerPoint lecture notes, and other resources for students to use as a supplement to class lecture and the text (e.g., Couch, 1997). Given the fact that Web sites are relatively inexpensive to create and maintain, the number of text authors providing Web materials will likely continue to increase. However, the challenge facing publishers and authors is to make these supplemental Web sites pedagogically sound.

## Computer tutorials

There has always been an interest in facilitating the ability of students to learn the material after they leave the classroom, particularly using computer-based applications. For example, Dixon and Judd (1977) described the advantages associated with requiring students to use a computer-managed instruction (CMI) system. The primary advantage was the fact that instructors could now require that students learn specific areas of inquiry outside the classroom using the CMI system versus relying on a traditional lecture in class. Consequently, instructors would have more time to discuss additional topics.

Previously, researchers advocated the use of audio-tutorials as an adjunct to an introductory statistics course (Carter & Cooney, 1983). Students equipped with audiotapes and a corresponding workbook performed significantly better in statistics courses than those students studying notes and the textbook. Today, statistics instructors have implemented a variety of innovative strategies aimed at utilizing electronic media outside of the classroom (see online Appendix C at www.teachstats.org for a representative list). For example, Hurlburt (2001) created a series of what he termed "lectlets" (p. 15), mini-lectures delivered via the Internet with audio and graphic components, for use with statistics courses. Each lectlet is relatively short with the maximum length being approximately 9 minutes. Students can listen, forward, reverse, and pause the audio-lecture with an accompanying graphic-text display or download a transcript of the audio portion of the lectlet.

Aberson, Berger, Emerson, and Romero (1997) described the Web Interface for Statistics Education support site (WISE; www.wise. cgu.edu). The WISE site has several online statistics tutorials each designed using cognitive learning-based teaching techniques (Romero, Berger, Healy, & Aberson, 2000). Although the exact content varies from tutorial to tutorial, students can expect to encounter an overview of the topic, sample questions that force the student to elaborate on what they have learned and monitor their progress, interactive Java-based exercises, downloadable follow-up questions, and lecture suggestions for instructors. Britt, Sellinger, and Stillerman (2002) introduced the Estimating Statistics (ESTAT) tutorial as a means of introducing students to statistics using a variety of activities such as graphics, eyeball estimating procedures, and data analysis techniques. Following the use of the program, most students responded that ESTAT was interesting, engaging, and helped their understanding of statistics. Students also encouraged instructors to continue to offer this program in future classes.

Ben-Zvi (2000) described several online simulation or "microworlds" that were useful for high school and undergraduates in introductory statistics courses. For example, Ben-Zvi introduced *Prob Sim*, a Macintosh program designed to teach probability via simulations to grades 6–13 (www.umass.edu/srri/serg/software/probsim. html). *Sampling Distributions* is another Macintosh-based microworld intended to assist high school and undergraduates develop an understanding of sampling distributions via graphics and visual feedback (www.tc.umn.edu/~delma001/stat_tools/). Ben-Zvi also introduced several tutorials designed to improve students' knowledge of a wide variety of statistical concepts. Examples included ActivStats (www.datadesk.com/products/mediadx/activstats/), ConStats (www.constats.atech.tufts.edu/), and The Authentic Statistics Project (ASP; Lajoie, 1997).

There are several advantages associated with the development of computer-based tutorials for students' use outside of the classroom. First, tutorials may improve student understanding of the material. Marcoulides (1990) found that students given the opportunity to use computer-assisted instructional (CAI) programs outside the classroom scored significantly higher on a statistics achievement test than did students who only received lecture. Second, many of the materials are self-paced, enabling students to spend as little or as much time needed to develop mastery of a specific information module. Third, additional materials that utilize a variety of learning modalities may be useful to students with special needs. For example, transcripts can be helpful for English as a Second Language (ESL) students and the pairing of visual-auditory information may benefit those with various learning disabilities. Fourth, students can focus their study on shorter chunks of information during a single study session to maximize learning. Finally, adjunct materials can help foster in students independent study skills and an increased sense of responsibility for learning of statistics. Indeed, Stockburger (1982) found that introductory statistics students who participated in the computer simulations (e.g., means, normal curve, correlation coefficient) attempted significantly more exercises with greater success than students that did not make use of the simulations. For additional information on supplemental materials such as CD-ROMs and calculator selection, see our Web site at www.teachstats.org.

## Electronic Discussion Boards

We all have that rare lecture that seems to fall flat. While discussing a topic, you look out into a sea of faces and see utter confusion among many of the students. Asking if anyone has any questions will sometimes coax some students to voice their concerns. However, more often than not, we find that confused students will often leave lecture hoping to achieve clarity by rereading their class notes or text. Although these techniques can be useful, sometimes it is more beneficial to have someone re-explain the difficult concept. Electronic discussion boards can provide students with the opportunity to interact with the instructor and their peers in a safe and non-threatening atmosphere. However, the research surrounding the use of electronic bulletin boards is decidedly mixed.

Several researchers have reported benefits associated with computer-mediated discussion. For example, Harasim (1990) suggested that online discussions differ from face-to-face sessions in that computer-mediated discussions allow students to join in on a discussion anywhere they have access to a computer and the Internet. Therefore, class discussion can continue outside of the formally scheduled class time. In addition, computer-mediated discussion can be asynchronous. Consequently, students can compose a thoughtful response without feeling pressured to produce a quick glib response in real time. Another important aspect associated with electronic discussion boards is the fact that students can talk among themselves without feeling pressured to interact with the instructor. Indeed, well-crafted questions can provoke lively discussions rivaling those experienced in the face-to-face medium (Duell, 2006).

Electronic discussion boards have added benefits beyond simply the extension of classroom discussion. For example, Althaus (1997) found that students who took part in face-to-face discussions in class as well as the computer-mediated discussion groups were more likely to earn higher grades than those students who only participated in the classroom discussions. Wang, Newlin, and Tucker (2001) found that the total number of student comments in an electronic chat room correlated with the final grade students' achieved in an Internet-based introductory statistics course. Kahn and Brookshire's (1991) results revealed that students who participated in a computer bulletin board consequently rated themselves as more computer literate. Of course, these results are correlational and thus, one cannot assume that the use of the electronic discussion board caused these benefits. However, Kahn and Brookshire found that electronic discussion boards freed up more time for in-class discussion, enabled the instructor to post announcements and examples for student use, and resulted in the instructor spending less time answering the same repeated questions. Finally, Newlin and Wang (2002) suggested that Web-based computer-mediated communication encouraged contact between faculty and students, facilitated cooperation among students, allowed instructors to provide prompt feedback, gave students a sense of how far along they should be on a particular assignment, and allowed faculty to establish their course expectations.

Unfortunately, Kahn and Brookshire (1991) found that despite the advantages, many students did not utilize electronic bulletin boards. The researchers speculated that the lack of student involvement was due to many factors including a lack of computer availability, a preference for oral communications versus written prose, and the perception that instructors were not rewarding student participation on the board with sufficient academic credit. In addition, the authors posited that instructors sometimes responded too quickly, not allowing students sufficient opportunity to respond, ultimately inhibiting student responses. Pena-Shaff, Altman, and Stephenson (2005) found that students sometimes refrained from participation due to fear that other students would view their posts as ignorant or unintelligent. In addition, the researchers reported that some students felt that the instructor forcing them to participate made the process a chore and many resented the fact that the discussions were graded. Other students reacted negatively when they received insufficient feedback and viewed the other postings as personal communication without any merit.

Sain and Brigham (2003) reported that students required to use an electronic bulletin board reported levels of satisfaction less than those taking a traditional class section of introductory psychology. The researchers concluded that "adding an interactive Web component is not sufficient to increase satisfaction and academic performance in a college course" (p. 428). In addition, a poorly run discussion board can cause many headaches for the instructor. One of the most significant problems that can develop is the emergence of discussion that gets off topic and fosters a dysfunctional environment. Finley (2006) suggested that there is also the potential for the misinterpretation of simple comments due to the lack of nonverbal behavior and/or proper "netiquette" (e.g., avoid writing in capital letters, as this is equivalent to shouting in the online environment). Consequently, the instructor should routinely monitor all material and keep the discussion centered on statistics. Instructors can also be proactive and routinely introduce applied statistical topics for discussion.

There are several tools available to set up a discussion board. However, it is important to maintain the privacy of the participants such that names and e-mail addresses are private (consequently listservs are not appropriate). In addition, instructors should construct the forum so that students have the choice of opting into the board versus initially enrolling all students in the group (and then having to opt out if desired). There are several easy to use free tools available to create electronic discussion boards including Google Groups and Yahoo! Groups. In addition, discussion boards are also a part of popular online teaching applications such as Blackboard and WebCT. Finally, your school or college may have their own software portal that allows for the creation of discussion groups.

## Multimedia Tools

Technological advances since the mid-1990s have allowed for the introduction of interactive technologies into statistics classrooms. Applications such as PowerPoint, Java applets, Macromedia Shockwave and Flash, and HTML have greatly enhanced the ability of instructors to make statistics come alive in the classroom. In their review of the research literature, Ludwig and Perdue (2005) reported that multimedia tools in the classroom raised interest levels, enhanced understanding, and increased encoding and retrieval. A growing body of research suggests that employing multimedia instructional methods, if done well, facilitates student performance (e.g., Eskicioglu & Kopec, 2003; Forsyth, 2003; Mayer, 2001; Velleman & Moore, 1996). For example, Erwin and Rieppi (1999) compared traditional and multimedia classes on a range of psychology topics (e.g., human development, abnormal, and statistics). Students in the multimedia classrooms, regardless of the topic, obtained significantly higher exam scores than those students in traditional courses.

Although there are many benefits associated with multimedia tools, there are some notable disadvantages associated with their use in educational settings. For example, Briggs and Sheu (1998) cautioned that Java applets available on the Internet are not always available for use due to Internet congestion, Web site reorganization, faculty migration, and lack of funds or continued interest. In addition, there is no way to get the coding for Java applets, Flash, and Shockwave without contacting the author (HTML sources can be viewed in your browser). Another issue that instructors need to address is the amount of time they wish to devote to developing multimedia tools for lecture. Some programs, like HTML and Java, are relatively easy to learn but instructors should keep online tutorials and reference texts handy. Others programs, like Shockwave, take considerable time and effort to master. Consequently, Huelsman (2006) suggested that instructors find someone with a strong computer application background to assist in the creative process.

Educators need to avoid becoming infatuated with the use of multimedia to teach statistical concepts. Despite grand expectations over the years, technology-centered approaches to multimedia learning have not lived up to the hype (Mayer, 2005). The failure of this approach was the result of forcing people to "adapt to the demands of cutting-edge technologies" rather than taking the more learning-centered approach of "adapting technology to fit the needs of human learners" (Mayer, p. 9). Before considering whether to incorporate multimedia tools into lecture, instructors need to make sure that multimedia content is essential to the understanding of the topic at hand and does not serve as a distraction (Lucas & Bernstein, 2005).

## Presentation technology

Microsoft PowerPoint and other presentation software (e.g., Corel's Presentations) have permeated all aspects of college teaching. Increasingly, it seems as though students are more likely to attend classes taught entirely via PowerPoint than traditional lectures involving a lectern and an overhead projector. So, does it make sense to teach statistics using presentation software such as Microsoft PowerPoint?

According to Mayer (2001), the extent to which students retained new information, integrated it into an existing knowledgebase, and were able to use this information to solve novel problems depended to a large degree on the how text, pictures, and animation were used in conjunction with spoken word. Specifically, retention increased when instructors presented text accompanied by images, graphics, or animation—as one would do in a typical PowerPoint lecture. However, Mayer noted that is important to avoid burdening slides with extraneous sounds, animation, and words. In addition, trying to make the material fit into an electronic medium such as PowerPoint may lead instructors to dumb down the material to ensure the slide is visually appealing.

Mayer (2001) also noted that not all material is suitable for visual representation. For example, although it might be very useful to demonstrate the theory behind linear regression using multimedia tools such as Java applets, it would be inappropriate to walk students through, slide after slide, the process of solving a regression formula. Simply showing students a completed regression problem is much less effective than having students interact with each other and the professor as the problem unfolds in real time. Accordingly, Mayer stated that students benefit greatly from hearing a professor discuss a topic. The worst retention occurs when an educator merely reads the bullet points or a formula presented in PowerPoint.

When presenting your slides, Zhu and Kaplan (2002) recommend that instructors face the class, use the slides as guides for discussion, do not turn out the lights, and avoid putting the students in a passive mode by combining the presentation with other activities such as writing on the board. Lucas and Bernstein (2005) recommended that instructors pass out handouts of slides prior to lecture to encourage active learning. Finally, Huelsman (2006) suggested that instructors using PowerPoint have a hard copy backup handy in the event technology fails (which inevitably will happen).

## Interactive applications: Java applets, Flash, Shockwave, and HTML

A Java applet is a software application that provides interactive features within an existing program such as a Web browser. Java applets offer several distinct advantages for instruction in education. According to Saucier (2000), Java applets can incorporate sound, text, animation, and graphics into the final product. In addition, although Java applets load slower than other Web applications (e.g., Macromedia Flash), they will cache in most browsers resulting in quick load times when an individual returns to that particular Web site. Finally, but most importantly, Java applets can be used on virtually any platform including Windows, Unix, Mac OS, and Linux. In addition, viewers do not need any special plug-in software. Briggs and Sheu (1998) suggested that Java is also very useful for educators because the program comes equipped with toolkits and built-in support to aid instructors who are not experienced in Web animation.

Several Web sites offer Java applets covering a wide variety of statistical topics (see online Appendix C at www.teachstats.org for a representative list). For example, Romero and colleagues (2000) described the Java applets provided on the Web Interface for Statistics Education site (WISE; www.wise.cgu.edu). Included on the site are applications that address concepts such as the sampling distribution of the mean, correlation and regression, and statistical power. Malloy and Jensen (2001) developed the Utah Virtual Lab using Java applets (www.psych.utah.edu/learn/statsampler.html). The lab, which is one tool in the University of Utah Department of Psychology's *StatCenter*, allows instructors to: (a) create a statistical virtual reality environment; (b) link theory and data; and (c) define independent, dependent, and predictor variables for a particular area of interest. Instructors can then have their students research the topic, develop hypotheses, design a study, collect and analyze data, and interpret their results. In addition, the *StatCenter* contains additional Java applets covering topics such as effect size and the normal probability curve. It contains a tool that allows instructors to create homework, quizzes, and exams. The site also contains Macromedia Flash interactive tools addressing ANOVA and the relations among alpha, beta, and power.

Macromedia Shockwave and Flash (recently acquired by Adobe) have great potential use in a statistics class. Shockwave, originally designed to provide multimedia content for CD-ROMs, can add movies, sound, and animation to a presentation. Flash, a newer application created for use on the Web, is a very popular tool for adding mouse-overs, animation, and special effects to presentations. Wender and Muehlboeck (2003) created five Macromedia Flash animations for use in a statistics course. These included the multiplication of two matrices, covariance, least squares in linear regression, the interconnectedness of Type I and II errors, and effect strength. When the researchers compared students exposed to a static versus an animated presentation, they found that the animation of the aforementioned statistical concepts was beneficial to student retention and performance.

Although both programs provide an excellent means to add multimedia content to a statistics presentation, they do differ from each other in several important ways. For example, Saucier (2000) reported that Flash animation is much quicker to load than Shockwave, is easier to learn for the novice, and produces smaller files. Shockwave, on the other hand, is more versatile and better suited for complex tasks. Macromedia applications require a free plug-in to view content. Nonetheless, over 54% of U.S. computers have the Shockwave player and almost 99% have the Flash player on their computer (Macromedia, 2007). Indeed, the ubiquitous presence of Flash makes it a powerful tool for the traditional multimedia-equipped classroom as well as online statistics courses.

HyperText Markup Language (HTML) aids in the creation of Web pages by defining the content of a Web page and establishing how to display the page in a Web browser such as Internet Explorer or Firefox. Although HTML is not difficult to learn, there are hosts of programs available that allow the user to create Web pages with little or no knowledge of HTML. Koch and Gobell (1999) used HTML to create a dynamic set of decision charts for use in an introductory statistics or methodology course illustrating the interconnectedness among scales of measurement, methodology, and statistical analyses. They found that students using the charts were more accurate, confident, and found the problems easier when using the HTML tutorial. In addition, practice on these tutorials improved the ability of these students to solve future problems. These results parallel the work of Schau and Mattern (1997) who demonstrated the learning benefits associated with the use of concept maps in a statistics course.

## Multimedia simulation programs

There is considerable promise associated with the use of multimedia in the teaching of undergraduate statistics. The use of multimedia simulation packages enables students to become active learners, provides a visual medium to assist student comprehension, and encourages students to apply statistical concepts to real-world problems (Velleman & Moore, 1996). For example, Hatchette, Zivian, Zivian, and Okada (1999) created an interactive computer program (STAZ) that enabled instructors to illustrate statistical concepts that were difficult to express verbally (e.g., central limit theorem). Similarly, the Friendly Introductory Statistics Help (FISH) program provides the scaffolding necessary for students to conceptualize statistical concepts (Brooks & Raffle, 2005). Fathom (Key Curriculum Press, 2007a) is a dynamic classroom statistics package that students can use to explore simulations, create sampling distributions, and conduct data analyses. For additional examples of simulation programs, see our Web site at www.teachstats.org.

Researchers have found that the classroom use of multimedia simulation programs can enhance student learning. For example, Meletiou-Mavrotheris (2003) concluded that the use of Fathom in the classroom promoted greater student understanding of key concepts related to statistical inference. Mills (2004b) determined that computer simulation methods (CSMs) improved student understanding of abstract statistical concepts. Although these are promising results regarding the use of simulations in the classroom, computers are unlikely to replace human instructors anytime in the near future. Rather, instructors should use multimedia simulations to free themselves from tasks better suited for a machine to focus instead on interaction, motivation, and assessment (Velleman & Moore, 1996).

## Conclusion

Garfield (1995) examined research in the areas of psychology, statistics, and mathematics education to formulate general principles by which students learn statistics. She asserted that students learn statistics by constructing relevant knowledge via active involvement in learning activities. As instructors, we need to facilitate student learning by providing an environment that allows students to reach their potential. The syllabus and textbook establish the personality of class. Consequently, instructors need to create a syllabus that strikes the right tone and select a text that best matches student abilities. There are a number of technological tools at the statistics instructor's disposal to create an active learning environment. Choices range from CD-ROMS, electronic discussion boards, and PowerPoint lectures to Java applets and Flash animation. However, too much multimedia can overwhelm content. Instructors need to be judicious when infusing multimedia content into a statistics course. There is "no substitute for the *motivation and encouragement* that a teacher can provide . . . technology should serve content and pedagogy" (Moore, 1997, p. 134).

# II

# Theoretical and Pedagogical Concerns

# Chapter 3

## Educational Reform
## in Statistics

*Lottery: A tax on people who are bad at math. – Author
unknown*

Science fiction author H. G. Wells in 1903 stated, "Statistical thinking will one day be as necessary for efficient citizenship as the ability
to read and write" (Mallows, 1998, p. 2). Wells was quite prophetic
as the ability to think and reason about statistical information is not
a luxury in today's information and technological age. Students who
lack fundamental statistical literacy, reasoning, and thinking skills
may find themselves unprepared to meet the needs of future employers or to navigate information presented in the news and media
(Bryce, 2002; Ritter, Starbuck, & Hogg, 2001).

The National Assessment of Adult Literacy (NAAL) Report defined quantitative literacy as:

> the knowledge and skills required to perform quantitative tasks—to
> identify and perform computations, either alone or sequentially, using
> numbers embedded in printed materials. Examples include balancing
> a checkbook, computing a tip, completing an order form, or deter-
> mining the amount of interest on a loan from an advertisement.
> (National Center for Education Statistics, 2003, p. 14)

At the highest level, the report cited the ability to compare, by
ounce, the cost of grocery items as an example of the proficient level.

Unfortunately, despite a general increase in quantitative literacy over the past 10 years, the report painted a bleak portrait of literacy in the United States. Specifically, the NAAL Report documented that quantitative literacy skills of the U.S. population were at approximately the following levels: 22% below basic, 33% basic, 33% intermediate, and 13% proficient. Although the NAAL Report was specific to quantitative literacy, it is reasonable to assume that statistical literacy, reasoning, and thinking may be lacking within the United States given the fact that these concepts involve knowledge and abilities that extend far beyond the skills required to balance one's checkbook (delMas, 2002; Garfield, 2002; Rumsey, 2002).

Fortunately, students are taking more statistics classes than ever at the high school and undergraduate level. In 1997, the College Board offered the first Advanced Placement (AP) test in statistics. At that time, 7,667 students registered for the exam. Since 1997, an additional 364,703 students have taken the test with 75,668 students completing the exam in 2005 (AP College Board, 2006). On the college level, Loftsgaarden and Watkins (1998) estimated that over 236,000 students register for statistics courses each semester in departments of mathematics and statistics. Garfield, Hogg, Schau, and Whittinghill (2002) argued that this number underestimates current enrollments for two reasons. First, they noted that the number of students taking statistics course continues to rise each year and second, the figure excludes students taking statistics courses in departments such as psychology, business, and economics.

# Educational Reform

Although students are taking more statistics classes than ever before, there remain two questions. First, do students take more than one course in statistics? Second, are students benefiting from the courses they are taking? In 1999, the American Statistical Association (ASA) launched the Undergraduate Statistics Education Initiative (USEI; *Amstat News*, 1999). The USEI focused on several aspects of statistics education including curriculum guidelines for an undergraduate major and minor in statistics, employer needs related to statistical literacy in future employees, and educational reform within introductory statistics courses.

One major concern raised by the USEI concerned the possibility that many students had a negative experience when taking introductory statistics such that "few desire a second course or make subsequent use of what they have been exposed to" (Bryce, 2002, p. 7). Scholars in the field of statistics education also questioned what students were learning in many statistical methods courses (Butler, 1998; Garfield, et al., 2002). They argued that heavily lecture-based courses, with a focus on computations and discrete methods, fail to teach adequately statistical literacy, thinking, and reasoning and leave students unprepared in today's data-driven world. Butler (1998), one of the most vocal critics of traditional methods of teaching statistics, argued that students are frequently unable to take what they have learned in statistics courses and apply that knowledge in the workplace. According to Butler, when former students attempt to use statistical methods in their jobs, often "the results are a shambles" (p. 84).

Both the American Statistical Association (ASA) and the Mathematical Association of America (MAA) issued a call for educational reform in statistics (ASA, 2005; Cobb, 1992). In 1991, the MAA convened the Curriculum Action Project including the Focus Group on Statistics Education headed by George Cobb. The Focus Group's final report, *Heeding the Call for Change*, included three primary recommendations for educational reform in statistics—an emphasis on statistical thinking, a greater use of real data, and active learning (Cobb, 1992). The report argued against lecture as the primary method of statistics education stating that students must experience statistics in a research context as opposed to passively receiving statistics education. Following this report, statistics scholars and educators endorsed the call for reform arguing for change throughout the undergraduate curriculum (e.g., Bryce, Gould, Notz, & Peck, 2001; Cannon, Harlaub, Lock, Notz, & Parker, 2002; Higgins, 1999; Hogg, 1999; Moore, 1997; Moore, 2001a; Roiter & Petocz, 1996; Snee, 1993; Tarpey, Acuna, Cobb, & De Veaux, 2002).

In an effort to evaluate progress within statistics education reform, Garfield (2000) surveyed over 300 statistics instructors to assess their current methods of teaching. This research, funded by the National Science Foundation, sampled not only teachers of statistics within mathematics and statistics departments but included instructors from other disciplines such as psychology, sociology, and business. Survey results highlighted improvement in statistics education particularly related to the use of technology and the analysis of real data. Indeed, two-thirds of all instructors surveyed reported that over the past few years, they had made significant changes to their courses. In addition, approximately half of the respondents reported specific substantive changes to teaching methods and course content.

Although the report documented positive efforts towards reform in overall instructional strategies, Garfield noted that instructors still were reporting lecture and traditional assessment measures such as quizzes, homework, and in-class exams as the most frequently used teaching and assessment methods.

As part of the ongoing reform effort, the ASA funded the Guidelines for Assessment and Instruction in Statistics Education (GAISE) Project in 2005. This project focused on two separate domains of statistics education: K-12 and introductory statistics courses at the undergraduate level. The GAISE College Report (ASA, 2005) contained six recommendations related to the teaching of an introductory statistics course on the undergraduate level (see Chapter 1). Unlike other studies highlighting a topical approach to what teachers should include in a statistics course (e.g., Giesbrecht et al., 1997; Landrum, 2005), the GAISE Report focused on broader methods of instructional practice.

The GAISE College Report represented "ASA-endorsed guidelines for assessment and instruction in statistics" (ASA, 2005, p. 1). In relation to proposed reforms, Garfield et al. (2002) commented,

> While many statistics instructors have readily adopted some of these reform suggestions, there are others teaching statistics, particularly in the biological and social sciences, business, and engineering as well as mathematics, who are harder to reach. We must find ways to inform and support these other teachers of statistics, so that they may learn about and implement ways to improve their courses. (p. 13)

In this and subsequent chapters, we will discuss the research related to these recommendations and provide information to enable instructors to integrate these reforms into the classroom. Although we will discuss each of the recommendations separately, be aware that a great deal of overlap exists between each of the recommendations.

## Statistically Educated Students

In a discussion of learning goals and outcomes, the GAISE report (ASA, 2005) argued that the primary goal of statistics education is to "produce statistically educated students" (p. 5). The report defines statistically educated students as those who are both statistically literate and who can think statistically. Although not specifically discussed in the GAISE Report, scholars in the field of statistics educational reform also have highlighted the importance of statistical reasoning as a fundamental goal within a statistics education (Ben-Zvi & Garfield, 2004; Cobb & McClain, 2004; delMas, 2004; Garfield, 2003; Jones, Langrall, Mooney, & Thornton, 2004; Tempelaar, Gijselaers, & Schim van der Loeff, 2006). To engage in the development of instructional practices and assessment measures, scholars must more fully explore and define these terms.

Numerous statistics education researchers such as Ben-Zvi and Garfield (2004), Chance (1997), Cobb and McClain (2004), delMas (2004), Hogg (1992), Jones, Langrall, Mooney, and Thornton (2004), Pfannkuch and Wild (2004), Rumsey (2002), Schield (2005a), and Utts (2003) have discussed concepts related to statistical literacy, thinking, and reasoning. Although all agree that these abilities are important, there is less consensus about the use or operationalization of each term (Ben-Zvi & Garfield, 2004; delMas, 2004). Indeed there appears to be much overlap among the terms and some researchers use the terms interchangeably (e.g., thinking and reasoning are not differentiated). Nonetheless, there is a consensus that students must become effective consumers of statistics and learn how to reason, think about, and critically question statistical information. Moreover, the next generation, particularly students involved in the sciences, need to be able to appreciate the role of statistics in the scientific process.

Effective instructional practices and assessment rest on the bedrock of clearly articulated goals and learning outcomes for each statistics course (Gal & Garfield, 1997). Given statistical literacy, thinking, and reasoning are fundamental learning goals in an introductory statistics course, it is imperative that we define and work to conceptualize these abilities and processes. delMas (2002) provided a good introductory schemata highlighting the three primary instructional domains of interest to statistics educators (see Table 3.1).

Table 3.1   delMas' (2002) model of statistical literacy, reasoning, and thinking[1]

| Basic Literacy | Reasoning | Thinking |
| --- | --- | --- |
| Identify | Why? | Apply |
| Describe | How? | Critique |
| Rephrase | Explain | Evaluate |
| Translate | (The Process) | Generalize |
| Interpret | | |
| Read | | |

Although researchers often approach literacy, reasoning, and thinking as separate but overlapping domains, delMas (2002) argued that basic literacy is the overarching ability with reasoning and thinking as overlapping abilities subsumed within literacy. Therefore, students cannot be considered statistically literate if they have not also developed statistical reasoning and thinking skills. This schematic provides a useful framework as we discuss further the concepts of statistical literacy, thinking, and reasoning. Table 3.2 contains a partial list of sample learning goals and outcome from the GAISE Report (ASA, 2005).

*Table 3.2*   Sample learning goals from the GAISE College Report

Goals for Students in an Introductory Course: What it Means to be Statistically Educated

Students should believe and understand why:

- Data beat anecdotes.
- Association is not causation.
- Statistical significance does not necessarily imply practical importance, especially for studies with large sample sizes.

Students should recognize:

- Common sources of bias in surveys and experiments
- How to determine when a cause and effect inference can be drawn from an association, based on how the data were collected (e.g., the design of the study).

Students should understand the parts of the process through which statistics works to answer questions, namely:

- How to obtain or generate data.
- How to graph the data as a first step in analyzing data, and how to know when that's enough to answer the question of interest.

Students should understand the basic ideas of statistical inference:

- The concept of statistical significance including significance levels and p-values.
- The concept of confidence interval, including the interpretation of confidence level and margin of error.

Source: ASA (2005, pp. 6–7).

## Statistical Literacy

Statistical literacy represents the minimum ability and knowledge needed by individuals traveling today's information superhighway. Whether one is reading a crime report in a newspaper or a research journal, the ability to use any of delMas' (2002) basic literacy skills is fundamental. However, it is important to differentiate between the basic literacy skills needed by the public and those abilities expected of undergraduate students, particularly those students completing advanced statistics courses. Teachers need to be cognizant of the exact literacy skill sets and domains of knowledge required for their specific statistics courses. Ultimately, teachers should link objectives, instruction, and assessment. Therefore, although delMas' goals may underlie all of statistical literacy, the specific degree of knowledge may vary depending on the level of statistics education. At the more advanced level, teachers need more specific and broader definitions of statistical literacy to complement the definition provided by delMas. The literature on statistics education contains several definitions and approaches to the study of statistical literacy. For example, Ben-Zvi and Garfield (2004) highlighted "basic and important skills that may be used in understanding statistical information or research results" (p. 7). Wallman (1993) included "the ability to appreciate the contributions that statistical thinking can make in public and private, professional and personal decisions" (p. 1). Utts (2003) identified a list of skills and ideas associated with statistical literacy such as knowledge of variability, the difference between "no statistically significant effect" and "no effect," and issues of causality (p. 75).

Regardless of the list or definition used, there is consensus about two overall abilities that underlie statistical literacy (Gal, 2004; Rumsey, 2002). First, students should be active consumers and evaluators of the broad range of statistical information they encounter on a daily basis. They should be able to interpret and critically evaluate statistical information. Second, students should possess and be able to communicate a basic understanding of the statistical terms, concepts, and approaches needed to make sense of data. It is not enough that students can read and interpret statistical information; they also should be able to discuss, relate, and articulate informed positions regarding data.

Gal (2004) presented a more detailed model of statistical literacy (see Table 3.3). This model is useful in further defining goals and

*Table 3.3*    Gal's (2004) model of statistical literacy[2]

| Knowledge elements | Dispositional elements |
| --- | --- |
| Literacy skills | |
| Statistical knowledge | Beliefs and attitudes |
| Mathematical knowledge | Critical stance |
| Context knowledge | |
| Critical questions | |

outcomes within a statistics course. He conceptualized the model into two broad categories of elements necessary for the development of statistical literacy. One particularly useful element of Gal's model is that it breaks down statistical literacy not only into those knowledge elements necessary within a literate individual but also those dispositions that facilitate the individual's use of those skills and knowledge.

## Knowledge elements

The first knowledge element inherent within Gal's (2004) formulation of statistical literacy is general literacy. Frequently, we watch students struggle with statistics and the cause may not be the result of specific deficits related to the learning of statistics but rather more general literacy deficits. Gal argued that for statistical literacy, individuals must be literate in a variety of abilities. According to Kirsch, Jungeblut, and Mosenthal (1998), literacy is composed of three abilities—prose literacy, quantitative literacy, and document literacy. Prose literacy is the ability to understand the written and spoken word. Quantitative literacy involves basic numeracy skills and the ability to perform computations. Document literacy is the ability to read and make sense of charts, graphs, and tables that may accompany text sources such as newspapers or journal articles as well as primarily non-text sources such as advertisements. Students lacking in any of these general literacy skills will have trouble developing statistical literacy and may need remedial coursework before taking a statistics course.

The second knowledge element required for statistical literacy is statistical knowledge. Students are most likely to achieve this knowledge base from careful attention to the material presented in statistics courses and textbooks. However, statistical knowledge should extend beyond the basic terms and ideas of probability or descriptive and inferential statistics. According to Gal (2004) and others involved in the reform movement of statistics education, statistical knowledge must extend to an understanding of the broader research context—why and how data are produced.

The third knowledge element required for statistical literacy is mathematical knowledge. However, leaders in the field of statistics education and reform have argued about the degree of mathematical knowledge required for an introductory statistics course (Cobb, 1992; Cobb & Moore, 2000; Gal, 2004; Moore 1998). On the one hand, Friel, Russell, and Mokros, (1990) argued that students learn many ideas such as averages, margin of error, and significant difference intuitively. According to this argument, it may be more important for students to focus on an understanding of basic statistical ideas such as those related to the concepts of variability and the process of data production than mathematical processes such as the derivation of formulas. This point is particularly true, given most individuals around the globe will never take a college-level statistics course (UNESCO, 2000). Consequently, basic numeracy skills taught to children and young adolescents may be fundamentally a more important element of statistical literacy than knowledge of more advanced quantitative procedures. On the other hand, according to Gal (2004), if students are to use statistical concepts with precision and demonstrate an ability to evaluate research data, they need a broader level of quantitative skills and abilities. For more information concerning the relationship between quantitative literacy and statistical literacy, visit our Web site at www.teachstats.org.

The fourth knowledge element required for statistical literacy is context knowledge. According to Gal, "Proper interpretation of statistical messages by adults depends on their ability to place messages in a context, and to access their world knowledge" (2004, p. 64). The GAISE Report (ASA, 2005) argued that teachers and students should use real data within the context of statistics instruction. Artificially produced numbers presented without a context do not facilitate the development of statistical literacy. Gal (2004) asserted that such examples do not enhance the development of statistical literacy and may instead serve to confuse and misinform students. After all, researchers produce data in real-world contexts and statistical literacy includes an ability to evaluate the context and methods of data collection as a fundamental component of data interpretation.

The final knowledge element required for statistical literacy is what Gal (2004) referred to as critical questions. We need to teach our students to arm themselves with common questions that they ask themselves when evaluating any statistical conclusion. The extent of critical evaluation can range from basic questions to comprehensive critiques. At a basic level, statistically literate individuals should ask questions when presented with statistical information numerically or in graph form (Gal, 2004). For example:

1.  Who are the researchers and is there any potential for conflict of interest or bias?
2.  How did the researchers collect their data?
3.  How did the researchers design their study (e.g., experimental, quasi-experimental, correlational, survey)?
4.  Who were the participants and how did the researchers find their sample? Was the sample representative of the population?
5.  Did the researchers use instruments and procedures that are reliable and valid?
6.  Did the researchers use appropriate statistical procedures to analyze these data?
7.  Do the results make sense? Are there alternative explanations for the research findings?

These sorts of questions should be in the forefront of anyone's mind when evaluating data. Of course, students can learn more comprehensive methods of critiquing studies based on threats to internal validity, external validity, statistical conclusion validity, and construct validity (e.g., Shadish, Cook, & Campbell, 2001).

## Dispositional elements

The first dispositional element discussed by Gal (2004) involves individuals' beliefs and attitudes about the value of statistics and their ability to use statistics. Gal stressed that individuals need to appreciate the "power of statistical processes" (p. 70). Individuals need to believe that statistical information is a powerful decision-making tool. Additionally, individuals need to view themselves as efficient and effective consumers of statistics. Such an appreciative stance may make them more likely to engage in problem solving and critical evaluation of statistical information.

The second dispositional element discussed by Gal (2004) involves the development of a critical stance. The phrase "lies, damned lies, and statistics" is attributed to a variety of authors including Mark Twain, Benjamin Disraeli, Henry Du Pré Labouchère, Leonard H. Courtney, and Cornelia Augusta Hewitt Crosse. The longevity and popularity of the phrase reflects the need for a critical stance when evaluating statistical data. Gal (2004) noted that it is not only important that individuals ask critical questions, but they must possess a dispositional stance that predisposes them to ask the tough questions when evaluating information. Gal (2004) further argued that individuals often fail to take a critical stance due to their lack of perceived familiarity with statistical issues and fear of embarrassment when discussing statistical matter that they perceive to be over their heads.

Milo Schield (2005a), Director of the W. M. Keck Statistical Literacy Project, argued that instructors have the responsibility to not only teach basic statistical competence but to become "evangelists" (p. 1) for statistical literacy. He argued that we should develop introductory statistics courses that attract students because students find the material enjoyable and beneficial. To foster statistical literacy, teachers and students must discuss and argue everyday, real-world examples of statistics from the media, news, and journal studies. As a result, the ultimate course evaluation should consist of measuring students' "appreciation for the value of statistics in everyday life" (p. 4).

Unfortunately, within the field of psychology, very few researchers have examined the concepts of statistical and quantitative literacy. For example, a search of PsycInfo of both terms yielded only 12 total citations. Moreover, only one citation, Walker (1951), discussed teaching statistical literacy within the social sciences.

## Statistical Thinking

In delMas' (2002) original schemata, statistical thinking involved the processes of application, critique, evaluation, and generalization. In general, statistical thinking involves the understanding of the big picture from research conceptualization to completion. However, the literature on statistics education contains several definitions and approaches to the study of statistical thinking. For example, Ben-Zvi and Garfield (2004) included "an understanding of why and how statistical investigations are conducted and the 'big ideas' that underlie statistical investigation" (p. 7). Melton (2004) highlighted "a philosophy of learning and action based on the following fundamental principles: 1) all work occurs in a system of interconnected processes, 2) variation exists in all processes, and 3) understanding and reducing variation are keys to success" (p. 1).

Pfannkuch and Wild (2004) presented a detailed model of statistical thinking that encompasses four dimensions. These dimensions may be useful when developing instructional practices and assessment measures relevant to statistical thinking and learning outcomes. According to Pfannkuch and Wild, it is necessary to address all four dimensions when teaching and modeling statistical thinking. Any instructional approach that fails to include all four dimensions may lead students to inaccurate or incomplete conclusions. Ultimately, they argued that individuals taught to think in a more comprehensive statistical fashion would make better decisions in both everyday life and research.

The first dimension discussed by Pfannkuch and Wild (2004) was investigative cycle. Students must learn that the research process, as a fundamental component of statistical thinking, involves the following steps: problem, plan, data, analysis, and conclusions. Students who do not see the connection between data and the research process may develop faulty or incomplete statistical thinking.

The second dimension involves thinking strategies. Pfannkuch and Wild (2004) subdivided these strategies into two categories: general strategies and strategies fundamental to statistical thinking. General strategies included strategic thinking and modeling. They considered five strategies fundamental to statistical thinking. First, students must recognize the need for data as well as an appreciation for data. Too often, individuals make decisions based on a "feeling" when data and an evaluation of these data would lead to more informed decisions. Second, students should be able to engage in "transnumeration" (p. 18). This term refers to the process of transforming real world situations into statistical/design questions and then applying that information back to the real world. Students who have learned the strategy of transnumeration can: (a) convert a real-world problem into something measurable; (b) collect, analyze, and represent data via graphs, tables, or statistical summaries; and (c) present statistical information in a manner that is understandable by others. Third, students must develop an appreciation and understanding of variation as it affects measures and the research process. Fourth, students should be able to think about and apply statistical models to research. Finally, students should be able to integrate the conceptual and the contextual. They should be able to take statistical information and evaluate that information from within a research or real-world context.

Pfannkuch and Wilds' (2004) third dimension was the interrogative cycle. Students should be able to ask questions and offer critiques throughout the process. The goals are to generate, seek, integrate, critique, and judge. In part, the interrogative cycle involves students: (a) anticipating questions, problems, and alternative explanations; (b) integrating new data and information collected throughout the research process; (c) incorporating new ideas into existing schemas; and (d) engaging in ongoing critique and evaluation.

Dispositions make up Pfannkuch and Wilds' (2004) fourth dimension. They identified eight dispositions that make up this dimension: "skepticism, imagination, curiosity and awareness, openness, a propensity to seek deeper meaning, being logical, engagement, perseverance" (p. 19). Similar to Gal's (2004) dispositional elements, these attitudes and cognitive predispositions propel much of their outline of statistical thinking.

Instructors may also place statistical thinking in the broader context of critical thinking across disciplines. For example, Halpern (2002) discussed the issue of critical thinking in relation to psychology instruction. She asserted that instructors should:

1. Explicitly teach the skills of critical thinking.
2. Develop the disposition for effortful thinking and learning.
3. Direct learning activities in ways that increase the probability of transcontextual transfer (structure training).
4. Make metacognitive monitoring explicit and overt (p. 95).

Teaching the skills associated with critical thinking, questioning, and skepticism for data are at the core of quality statistical instruction (Chance, 2002; Melton, 2004; Wild, 1994; Wild & Pfannkuch, 1999). Additionally, teachers must develop in students an appreciation for the value and effectiveness of statistics as a tool for decision making, (Gal, 2004; Pfannkuch & Wild, 2004) and they must stress the importance of deep or structural learning as opposed to surface learning (Broers & Imbos, 2005; delMas, Garfield, & Chance, 1999; Pfannkuch & Wild, 2004; Quilici & Mayer, 2002). Finally, students must develop self-monitoring and self-regulatory abilities as a corollary to their statistical thinking skills (Begg, 1997; Chance, 1997; Onwuegbuzie & Leech, 2003).

*Table 3.4*    McGovern's (2002) learning outcomes

| Thinking level | Verbs used to communicate assignment |
| --- | --- |
| Knowledge | State, list, name, define |
| Comprehension | Explain, identify, discuss, describe |
| Application | Apply, demonstrate, illustrate |
| Analysis | Analyze, compare and contrast, distinguish |
| Synthesis | Create, hypothesize, design, compose |
| Evaluation | Evaluate, criticize, judge, value |

In relation to broader cognitive objectives, McGovern's (2002) general course outcomes based on Bloom's taxonomy (Bloom, Englehart, Furst, Hill, & Krathwohl, 1956) may also be used when developing learning goals and outcomes relevant to instructional practices and assessment of statistical thinking within psychology courses (see Table 3.4). Ideally, students should come to realize that statistics involves a broad scope of skills, abilities, and dispositions that move beyond "number crunching" and that such skills can lead to more informed decision making in their research as well as every-day lives.

## Statistical Reasoning

"Statistics is an interpretive science" (Kelly, Sloane, & Whittaker, 1997, p. 90). delMas (2002) described statistical reasoning as the examination of the underlying process of statistical procedures and research—the why, how, and explanation of the process. It is not enough for someone to be able to compute a probability but they should be able to apply that reasoning to everyday life and situations involving probabilistic thinking in the real world. Garfield and Chance (2000) defined statistical reasoning as:

> The way people reason with statistical ideas and make sense of statistical information. This involves making interpretations based on sets of data, representations of data, or statistical summaries of data. Students need to be able to combine ideas about data and chance, which leads to making inferences and interpreting statistical results (p. 101).

Although the terms "thinking" and "reasoning" are often confused or used interchangeably in everyday discourse (Galotti, 1989), the literature on statistics education tends to draw heavily on Garfield and Chances' definition.

Statistical reasoning is a primary learning outcome for any introductory statistics course (Gal & Garfield, 1997). Students need to develop an understanding of the underlying processes involved in research methods and statistics and learn to ask questions that challenge their reasoning about these processes. One of the goals of the GAISE Report (ASA, 2005) was that teachers should "stress conceptual understanding rather than mere knowledge of procedures" (p. 1). We will discuss this issue more directly in Chapter 4 but the message is relevant to the discussion of statistical reasoning. Without an understanding of the underlying concepts related to statistical procedures, students will not be able to apply reason effectively or engage efficiently in statistical problems and solutions (Schau & Mattern, 1997).

It is important to recognize that statistical reasoning is not only a learning outcome but also a necessary process used by students to learn statistics (Tempelaar et al., 2006). As such, teachers should model and apply statistical reasoning in the classroom. Additionally, assignments and assessment practices should have a reasoning component.

delMas (2004) provided an extensive list of human reasoning errors and noted that individuals tend to reason better in situations in which they have a high degree of familiarity. Unfortunately, for most students, the world of statistics is not a highly familiar domain. As such, students often will attempt to make up rules rather than rely on underlying statistical reasoning. They may reason less about the underlying methods and assumptions of a problem and instead try to match up surface similarities as a cue to what procedure they should use (Quilici & Mayer, 2002). If instructors test students using problems similar to their homework exercises, they will do fine. However, any deviation from the practice problems will result in incorrect answers as the student may use rule-based as opposed to reasoning-based learning (Hubbard, 1997). Indeed, students may often ask for additional practice problems in an attempt to learn by rote and utilize memorized responses. Unfortunately, researchers have correlated such strategies with lower levels of performance (Onwuegbuzie & Leech, 2003; Tempelaar et al., 2006). If students ask for additional study problems, it is beneficial to provide dissimilar problems, which challenge students underlying reasoning and thinking. Moreover, teachers need to stress the importance of reasoning about data as opposed to the process of simply plugging numbers into formulas to get specific results (Chance, 1997; Cobb & McClain, 2004).

Often students who complete an introductory course in statistics can describe, but not justify, their answers, do not understand the concepts underlying their statistical solutions, and cannot recognize their own errors or understand why they have come up with an ineffective statistical solution (Kelly, Sloane, & Whittaker, 1997). This problem is often due to rote learning, the creation of faulty statistical rules, and surface recognition as opposed to a deeper understanding. According to Kelly et al., teachers need to recognize that students construct meaning relative to the statistical concepts they are learning. Therefore, it is important for teachers to listen carefully to what students are saying. Are they just using words mindlessly based on memorized phrases in an attempt to create an impressive answer or do their comments demonstrate learning? Kelly et al. cautioned that teachers should be alert to answers that sound perfect. They also asserted that teachers should make sure that students discuss their answers and apply similar reasoning to other problems. "It is not enough to be able to 'do' the routine (either by hand or on the computer); one must know why one has chosen it, what its applications tells one, and what limitations one must place upon its conclusions" (p. 90).

Jones, Langrall, Mooney, and Thornton (2004) argued that statistical reasoning is not an either-or skill but rather undergoes levels of development. They stated that we could apply several models of cognitive development to an understanding of statistical reasoning. Consequently, researchers have grounded their models on the results of clinical studies, structured interviews, and classroom studies involving primarily elementary and middle schoolchildren (e.g., Jones et al., 2000; Jones et al., 2001).

Jones et al. (2000) and Mooney (2002) presented similar models of statistical reasoning and placed students' abilities at one of four levels: Idiosyncratic, Transitional, Quantitative, and Analytical. At the Idiosyncratic level, predictions and reasoning are disorganized, inaccurate, or irrelevant. Students cannot explain the reasoning behind their answers and appear to be randomly guessing at solutions to problems. At the Transitional level, students will often draw on their own personal anecdotal experiences, use a variety of heuristics and evidence all sorts of biases in their responses. Additionally, they are unable to draw connections between inferences and data. At the Quantitative level, students can make predictions and inferences based on specific data sets but do not have an understanding of broader comparisons. Their answers may appear to be rule-based, thus demonstrating lower levels of statistical reasoning. Unfortunately, students are unlikely to make accurate inferences in comparable but somewhat dissimilar situations. At the Analytical level, students engage in deeper levels of statistical reasoning, make good inferences, and are able to see comparisons to other situations.

If teachers plan to facilitate the development of statistical reasoning skills, they need to be aware of each student's developmental reasoning level. Teaching the more advanced levels of statistical reasoning is unreasonable for students operating at the lower levels of reasoning abilities. Jones et al. (2004) recommended the use of a constructivist approach aimed at teaching reasoning. In part, students must learn to recognize the structural similarities between problems as opposed to surface similarities (Quilici & Mayer, 2002). Simulations and concept maps can help students form the cognitive schemata necessary for conceptual understanding of statistics (Broers & Imbos, 2005; delMas, Garfield, & Chance, 1999; Quilici & Mayer, 2002). Even the simple use of handouts emphasizing the role of selection skills related to the use of appropriate statistical procedures may improve performance (Ware & Chastain, 1991).

Teachers need to be aware of students' level of statistical reasoning as it influences not only the student but also the classroom as a learning community (Cobb, 1999). It is particularly important that teachers do not exclude or marginalize students at the lower levels of statistical reasoning. Additionally, teachers should coordinate group or dyadic exercises to facilitate movement towards more developed levels of statistical reasoning. Matching students of different levels of ability has been found to be beneficial to both the student at the lower level of ability as well as the higher performing student assigned as tutor (Ward, 1984).

Derry, Levin, and Schauble (1995) developed a course that focused specifically on the development of statistical reasoning as distinct from a traditional introductory statistics course. The focus of the course was on increased statistical authenticity as a means to help students develop the necessary abilities and tools needed in today's information-driven age. Derry et al. conceived of their course on two orthogonal dimensions: cultural relevance and social activity. Cultural relevance referred to the degree of meaningfulness in relation to real world problems and situations. Data collected on issues of relevance to students would have a high degree of cultural relevance whereas numbers simply provided or contrived to perform a specific statistical analysis with no grounding in research would be of low cultural relevance. Social activity described the degree of active participation or learning required on the part of the student. The design, collection, analysis, and interpretation of data related to a specific student generated research question would involve a high level of social activity whereas lecture with no student interaction would be low social activity. Ideally, a course high in statistical authenticity would be high on both social activity and cultural relevance. Such a course enhances students' statistical reasoning abilities (Derry et al., 1995).

One does not need to design an entire course focused on the goal of statistical reasoning development. Lawson, Schwiers, Doellman, Grady, and Kelnhofer (2003) provided students with information (a handout) concerning statistical reasoning and engaged students in practice related to problems involving statistical reasoning. A statistical reasoning quiz demonstrated improved reasoning skills in students who had received the reasoning information compared to the control group. Gains in statistical reasoning appear to be long-term and levels of reasoning remain high upon retesting (Cobb, McClain, & Gravemeijer, 2003).

## Misconceptions Impacting the Development of Literacy, Thinking, and Reasoning

Researchers agree that statistical literacy, thinking, and reasoning move well beyond the ability to crunch numbers and complete homework problems. Indeed, there is general agreement that traditional learning approaches associated with practice and conventional instruction are not particularly effective when teaching courses associated with statistics or mathematics (Cooper & Sweller; 1987; Paas, 1992; Quilici & Mayer, 2002; Sweller, 1988; Sweller, Chandler, Tierney, & Cooper, 1990).

The statistical reform movement argued that it is imperative that teachers of statistics focus on teaching underlying process or reasoning skills (ASA, 2005). Unfortunately, if courses are technique driven, students may not see the big picture or develop basic literacy, thinking, or reasoning skills. Rumsey (2002) identified three common misconceptions related to the teaching of statistics: (a) "Calculations demonstrate understanding of statistical ideas;" (b) "Formulas help students understand the statistical idea;" and (c) "Students who can explain things in statistical language demonstrate their understanding of a statistical idea" (pp. 5–6). Thus, students completing statistics courses founded on such misconceptions may be able to demonstrate some statistical knowledge, but not statistical understanding or literacy. Indeed, such rote, formula-based approaches to the learning of statistics results in limited transfer of learning (Onwuegbuzie & Leech, 2003).

Garfield (2002) studied the relationship between grades in statistics and statistical reasoning and found that students who do well on homework, exams, projects, etc. do not always score high on statistical reasoning measures. She argued that traditional homework problems may only lead to improved surface understanding of statistics but do not facilitate the development of deeper levels of learning that involve reasoning skills. Tempelaar et al. (2006) examined the relationship between course grades, amount of work on homework assignments, and statistical reasoning. They found a slight positive correlation between overall course grades and reasoning, but a weak negative correlation between effort on homework assignments and statistical reasoning. Thus, simply working harder or effort alone does not guarantee improvements in statistical reasoning.

Nicholson, Ridgeway, and McCusker (2006) argued that one of the reasons why we fail to teach statistical reasoning is the focus on univariate and bivariate data and techniques. Such representations do not represent the complexity of interactions as they occur in the real world and fail to take into account the messiness of most data (Moore, 1998). Fortunately, today's computer applications do not limit statistics instructors to such simple representations of data (Nicholson et al., 2006).

A cookbook approach to the teaching of statistics may make the material more assessable to students. Edirisooriya (2003) nicely diagramed this process. Students need to decide what to bake (what to study), collect the ingredients (data collection), prepare the ingredients (data preparation), prepare the dish (data analyses), finish preparing the dish (interpretation of the results), and present the food to one's guests (publication/presentation). Although such an approach may connect students with the research process, others argue that this metaphor is too linear (Singer & Willett, 1990). Cobb and McClain (2004) argued that a cookbook approach to statistics assumes that statistical reasoning is fundamentally the same as mathematical reasoning. Problems of type X, Y, or Z require an X, Y, or Z procedure to achieve the appropriate answer. However, this strategy belies that fact that in statistics, data are not always neat or precise and researchers can use more than one procedure to explore a problem.

Cobb and McClain (2004) highlighted that a detective metaphor may be more appropriate when teaching statistics. They argued that researchers act as detectives working to provide juries with evidence that will meet particular levels of certainty. Regular viewers of various court television programs such as *Law & Order* or *Judge Judy* are likely familiar with levels of certainty in the courtroom such as preponderance of the evidence, beyond a reasonable doubt, or even greater levels of surety as translated from the realm of probability. Therefore, as students work to understand research, they can learn to view data collection as part of a process of evidence collection subject to all of the messiness, variability, and potential sources of bias that exist in the real world. They may learn to view statistics as grounded in a real-world process as opposed to a definitive result encapsulated by a belief that "numbers do not lie." For more discussion on the distinction between statistics and mathematics, see our Web site at www.teachstat.org.

## Final Thoughts on Statistical Literacy, Thinking, and Reasoning

We have discussed a number of ideas regarding statistical literacy, thinking, and reasoning and argued for careful consideration of these issues when developing instructional practices. The GAISE Report (ASA, 2005) provided the following general suggestions for teachers when considering these issues:

1.  Model statistical thinking for students, working examples and explaining the questions and processes involved in solving statistical problems from conception to conclusion.
2.  Use technology and show students how to use technology effectively to manage data, explore data, perform inference, and check conditions that underlie inference procedures.
3.  Give students practice developing and using statistical thinking. This should include open-ended problems and projects.

4.  Give students plenty of practice with choosing appropriate questions and techniques, rather than telling them which technique to use and merely having them implement it.
5.  Assess and give feedback on students' statistical thinking. (p. 8)

In Chapter 4, we will discuss a range of instructional and assessment strategies aimed at the development of statistical literacy, thinking, and reasoning skills. Methods commonly used to develop and assess these skills include case studies, authentic tasks, concept maps, critiques of journal articles or news reports, minute papers, writing assignments, and specific reasoning assessment measures (ASA, 2005; Garfield, 2002).

## Assessment

"Will this be on the test?" How many instructors have heard this mantra and inwardly sighed? Students often appear to be studying for the test as opposed to studying for learning. However, teachers also must work to insure that they are not fostering such an attitude—they should teach for understanding and not simply to prepare students for testing (Begg, 1997). Requests for study guides and queries such as the above may mean that instructors are not effectively creating clear linkages for students between learning outcomes, instructional practices, and methods of assessment. Additionally, students may view assessment solely as summative (e.g., grades) and therefore, not see the beneficial role that formative assessment plays in their learning. In this section, we will discuss the role of assessment in statistics education.

### What is the role of assessment?

Before 1990, few researchers studied or examined the role of assessment in statistics education (Gal & Garfield, 1997). However, education shifted after 1990 from a teaching-centered model to a learning-centered model of statistics education (Barr & Tagg, 1995). When classes operate from a teacher-centered testing model, students may perceive grades as rewards or punishments given out by instructors. However, when student learning drives assessment, it not only guides *what* students learn, but if developed properly, also drives *how* they learn. In addition, a major component of student learning is self-assessment. Students need to ask themselves what they have learned and find ways with which to demonstrate their learning (Dunn, McEntarffer, & Halonen, 2004). This paradigmatic shift from a teacher-focused to a learner-focused model emphasizes the interactive and collaborative nature of education and the interrelationship among course outcomes, student learning, course instruction, content, context, and assessment (Hubbard, 1997; Onwuegbuzie & Leech, 2003).

One thing is clear from a review of the statistics assessment literature—teachers need to assess everything that they want students to know (Chance, 1997; ASA, 2005). Ideally, assessment should focus on the development of statistical literacy, thinking, and reasoning skills (Chance, 1997) and be both summative and formative (Chance, 1997; Garfield & Ben-Zvi, 2004). Summative assessment, epitomized by final course grades, involves the evaluation of prior learning. Formative assessment is an interactive process whereby teachers and students assess what they have learned but also use that information to facilitate future teaching and learning (Osborne & Wagor, 2004). Students should receive feedback that informs them of their weaknesses and strengths, motivates and challenges them to think and reason in new ways, and assists them in developing tools for enhanced learning and new schemas (Chance, 1997; Onwuegbuzie, 2000; Osborne & Wagor, 2004). Ideally, students should be actively engaged in assessment, and hence, motivated to learn (Colvin & Vos, 1997).

As teachers develop learning outcomes and goals, they should view formative assessment as an integral part of the process. Teachers need to develop focused course learning outcomes and goals, develop instructional and assessment measures that will lead to those outcomes and goals, and use assessment as a means to revise teaching strategies continuously to achieve those goals (Garfield & Ben-Zvi, 2004). Ideally, formative assessment can serve as a diagnostic tool informing teachers about concepts and skills that students have not yet learned or perhaps, have misunderstood. Teachers can then use this knowledge to make informed decisions about what material to reintroduce and the selection of appropriate methods of instruction (Onwuegbuzie, 2000; Osborne & Wagor, 2004).

## What is the role of authentic assessment?

Authentic assessment "emphasizes that the assessment task should be as true to life as possible" (Bosack, McCarthy, Halonen, & Clay,

2004, p. 141). Onwuegbuzie and Leech (2003) argued that courses that focus on authentic statistics must of necessity also use authentic assessment—evaluation methods that would most closely mirror the real-world application of concepts learned in a classroom. An example of authentic assessment in a statistics course might include students' involvement in and evaluation of the design and implementation of a research study. Another example would be students' evaluation and critique of research articles. The key to authentic assessments is that they are highly applied in nature. Can students demonstrate that they can apply what they have learned in a real-world context? Authentic assessments have the benefits of active learning, student ownership of the material, increased independent learning, increased student sense of responsibility, and the development of higher-order thinking skills (Baron & Boschee, 1995; Derry, Levin, Osana, Jones, & Peterson, 2000; Onwuegbuzie & Leech, 2003). Authentic assessments also have the added benefit of increasing student motivation levels, particularly if students see the connection to real-world usefulness (Chance, 1997).

Colvin & Vos (1997) outlined the difficulties that teachers must address when moving from a traditional performance-based method of assessment to authentic assessment. First, it is challenging to develop appropriate assessment measures and methods of scoring such measures. Additionally, teachers must address issues of reliability and validity when developing new measures. Finally, students and colleagues may be resistant to new methods of assessment. According to Onwuegbuzie (2000), students rate performance assessment higher than other forms of assessments. With traditional methods of testing and grading, students can perform well in their statistics course, but unfortunately still demonstrate low levels of statistical reasoning (Garfield & Chance, 2000). On the other hand, authentic assessment results in higher levels of statistical reasoning and thinking (Onwuegbuzie, 2000) and promotes active learning (Cobb, 1993). Therefore, although a change to authentic assessment may be challenging, it has long-term benefits for student learning.

## Assessment and learning outcomes or goals

Assessment is not possible with ill-defined or ambiguous learning outcomes or goals (Colvin & Vos, 1997). As such, it is imperative that statistics teachers have clear learning goals and outcomes articulated to enable linkages between instructional techniques, assessment, and learning (Gal & Garfield, 1997). According to the *APA Guidelines for the Undergraduate Psychology Major* (American Psychological Association, 2006), "current best practices in higher education rely on setting clear expectations for student learning, aligning curricula with these expectations, assessing student attainment, and using assessment results to effect changes to promote better student learning" (p. 3). In their discussion of introductory statistics courses, Roiter and Petocz (1996) stated, "Having clearly defined goals that the students see as relevant and attainable is the most important aspect of course design. If relevance or attainability of goals is missing, the course will not be effective" (p. 2).

Scholars within the field of statistics have recommended different learning outcomes and goals, many of which focus directly on the development of statistical literacy, thinking, and reasoning skills. For example, Begg (1997) argued an approach to assessment based not on statistical topics but broader learning outcomes such as problem solving, reasoning, communicating, making connections, and using tools. Hogg (1992) recommended that students should be able to ask appropriate research questions, know the fundamentals of data collection, have the ability to summarize and interpret data collected, and know how to evaluate their methods and statistical inferences. Garfield and Chance (2000) proposed seven learning goals for students of statistics. Students should be able to "understand the purpose and logic of statistical investigations; understand the process of statistical investigations; learn statistical skills; understand probability and chance; develop statistical literacy; develop useful statistical dispositions; and develop statistical reasoning" (pp. 100–101). As previously discussed, the GAISE Report (ASA, 2005) included a broader set of learning goals. Ultimately, however, each teacher must select the learning goals and outcomes best suited for their student population and educational program. These goals and outcomes will affect the instructional and assessment strategies selected.

Teachers should also assess students' attitudes and beliefs due to the impact they have on statistics learning and education (Gal, Ginsburg, & Schau, 1997). Attitudes and beliefs affect the process (the actual learning of statistics), the outcome (what students think about the course and the material once the course is complete and whether they will use the material in their everyday lives), and access (whether students pursue further coursework in statistics and research methods).

# Conclusion

Educational reform is a driving force in the field of statistics today. Scholars in statistics education have made substantial progress towards elucidating the needed reforms and designing strategies aimed at implementing and studying these reforms (ASA, 2005; Garfield, 2000). Researchers have focused many of their efforts on the study of statistical literacy, thinking, and reasoning (e.g., Cobb & McClain, 2004; delMas, 2004; Jones et al., 2004; Pfannkuch & Wild, 2004; Rumsey, 2002) as well as assessment (e.g., Garfield & Ben-Zvi, 2004; Onwuegbuzie, 2000; Osborne & Wagor, 2004).

Unfortunately, two issues remain. First, much of the work related to educational reform has been largely theoretical in nature. Researchers are working to define and operationalize terms with an eye towards empirical testing but this research is still in its infancy. Early research related to educational reform in statistics is promising and thus far supportive of the underlying hypotheses associated with educational reform. Nonetheless, researchers need to engage in more testing within the classroom. This is particularly true in relation to the teaching of statistics at the college level, as researchers have conducted much of the work examining the development of statistical literacy, thinking, and reasoning at the pre-college levels (i.e., elementary, middle, and high school levels).

Second, most of the work related to educational reform has come from the field of statistics. Few scholars within disciplines outside of statistics have been involved in studying and researching issues related educational reform or to teaching and statistical literacy, thinking, and reasoning. As such, we must engage in greater efforts to incorporate this research into the teaching literature beyond the discipline of statistics. On the bright side, these domains of study fall squarely within the purview and intersection of cognitive psychology and the scholarship of teaching. Therefore, a world of opportunities exists for researchers and teachers who want to study teaching and statistical processes such as thinking or reasoning.

## Notes

1 From "Statistical literacy, reasoning, and learning: A commentary," by R. C. delMas, 2002, *Journal of Statistics Education, 10*(3). Copyright 2002 by the American Statistical Association. Reprinted with permission.

2   From "Statistical literacy," by I. Gal, 2004, in D. Ben-Zvi & J. Garfield
    (Eds.), "The challenge of developing statistical literacy, reasoning, and
    thinking" (p. 51), Dordrecht, The Netherlands: Kluwer Academics. Copy-
    right 2002 by Wiley-Blackwell Publishing. Adapted with permission.

# Chapter 4

# In the Classroom

*Of course, I'm communicating; I lecture every day. – Wulff &*
*Wulff, 2004, p. 92*

Lecture remains the most frequent instructional method used by
undergraduate statistics teachers on the undergraduate level (Garfield,
2000). Yet both the American Statistical Association (ASA) and
the Mathematical Association of America (MAA) have argued against
a traditional lecture approach (ASA, 2005; Cobb, 1992). Traditional methods, such as lecture, tend to facilitate rote learning, poor
transfer of learning, and inadequate statistical literacy, thinking, or
reasoning skills except with the brightest students (Butler, 1998;
Cooper & Sweller, 1987; Garfield et al., 2002; Paas, 1992; Sweller,
1988). As such, the ASA-funded Guidelines for Assessment and
Instruction in Statistics Education (GAISE) Project (2005) proposed
educational reforms directly applicable to the classroom. The recommendations outlined in the report included the promotion of conceptual learning, the use of active learning strategies, and a focus on
real data.

# Conceptual Learning, Active Learning, and Real Data

Moore (1998) argued that anyone with a laptop could do statistics. Unfortunately, students may become quite competent at computing statistics but remain clueless as to understanding the when, how, and why of statistics. Layne and Huck (1981) compared students trained in computational methods and a control sample; they found no difference between the two groups in relation to their ability to read and interpret research articles. The computation of examples did not enhance students' understanding of statistics nor the role of statistics in the research process. Conversely, Lesh, Amit, and Schorr (1997) presented students with real-world information and found that they could extrapolate to the types of needed analyses based on the presentation of conceptual models. They also found no correlation between an understanding of conceptual models and mathematical ability. Schwartz and Martin (2004) presented students with novel problems related to descriptive statistics and had them work toward inventing solutions. They found that students given the novel task paired with lecture demonstrated significant gains in learning. Thus, instructors may best serve students by focusing on developing statistical thinking and reasoning skills as opposed simply to teaching computational techniques. Additionally, if instructors approach the course conceptually, the material may be more relevant to students (Dillbeck, 1983).

## Conceptual learning versus rote memorization

Rote memorization is a particularly ineffective and inefficient means of learning statistics. Students lacking confidence in their ability to understand the abstract nature of statistics often attempt to learn through rote memorization (Broers & Imbos, 2005). As long as the surface elements of a problem remain the same, these students can successfully complete the course. However, if the surface elements are changed, they will typically fail due to limited transfer of learning (Onwuegbuzie & Leech, 2003). Students who memorize material may perform well on formula questions but may do poorly on word problems that require deeper levels of learning (Hansen, McCann, & Myers, 1985; Myers, Hansen, Robson, & McCann, 1983). Surface similarities between problems also may mislead students towards false conclusions and analyses. As such, instructors need to facilitate students' recognition of and focus on the structural conceptual similarities between problems and teach students to ignore the surface similarities (Quilici & Mayer, 2002).

Rote learning does not help students developmentally as they progress in their ability to think and reason statistically (Broers & Imbos, 2005). Students must develop effective cognitive schema in relation to statistical ideas and methods. According to Broers and Imbos, the appropriate use of self-explanations is the key to enhanced learning. Students need to answer questions correctly but also be able to explain their underlying thinking and reasoning relevant to the completed problem. To assist struggling students, teachers should break down their lectures and examples into discrete elements that guide students through relevant steps and concepts. Initially, students' knowledge is fragmented but through directed teaching, students may come to develop integrated schemata and informed self-explanations. Melvin and Huff (1992) recommended that students learn to ask themselves whether their answers make sense. Students, as part of the self-explanatory process, need to develop the conceptual understanding that enables them to recognize absurd answers.

Gardner and Hudson (1999) found that students had difficulty knowing what and when certain statistical analyses were appropriate. They developed a quiz consisting of research scenarios representing different statistical concepts and potential analytic procedures. Students found the selection and justification of their choices to be a difficult task. Gardner and Hudson noted the inclusion of words identified with particular procedures stimulated incorrect answers— a measure of surface learning. For example, if the scenario included the word "association," students often appeared to have simply guessed "correlation" despite this answer being an incorrect response. They recommended the use of concept maps, portfolios, a focus on the identification of variables, workshop exercises, experimentation, and appropriate examples as a way to foster deeper levels of conceptual learning and selection skills.

In addition to rote memorization, students may attempt to develop rules that do not rely on underlying statistical reasoning. Unfortunately, rule-based as opposed to reason-based learning will often produce incorrect answers (Hubbard, 1997). Often students using a rule-based approach will ask for a series of additional problems to practice their rule-based learning. Unfortunately, high effort may not result in greater learning or better performance.

Guttmannova et al. (2005) argued that instructors should only teach statistics using definitional formulas to enhance students understanding of concepts and reasoning abilities. Unfortunately, Guttmannova et al. found, in a review of 12 commonly used introductory statistics texts, that each emphasized the computational formula when introducing various statistical techniques.

## Active learning

"Learning is situated in activity. Students who use the tools of their education actively rather than just acquire them build an increasingly rich implicit understanding of the world in which they use the tools and of the tools themselves" (Bradstreet, 1996, pp. 73–74). Students learn statistics best when they are engaged in active learning—they learn by doing as opposed to being passive recipients of information (Begg, 1997; Christopher & Marek, 2002; Moore, 1997; Sedlmeier, 2000). Active learning can take many forms, including the development of concept maps, the use of examples and demonstrations, and student involvement in research projects. Learning moves the focus from teacher as fountain of all information to learner as active educational participant. Petocz, Gordon, and Reid (2006) presented a model with lecture at the teacher-centered end and conceptual change at the learner-centered end of a continuum. They proposed that active learning is a balance between the two. Instructors direct student learning but allow for the exploration of topics. According to Miserandino (1999), "active learning demands changing our role of sage on stage to guide on the side" (p. 110).

Sedlmeier (2000) reported that students learned best when actively engaged in exploring topics. However, this research supported the hypothesis that the highest and most robust degree of learning occurred when students were engaged in active learning that included diagrams or other forms of pictorial representation (e.g., grids). This finding suggests that a visual or graphical representation of data may be important component to include in active learning exercises.

Active learning is a fundamental corollary to authentic assessment (Barr & Tagg, 1995). Begg (1997) asserted that assessment begins on the first day of class with discussions of what students want to learn; what their interests are; and what ideas and perhaps, misconceptions, they already have about the topic. The integration of students' interests and ideas on that first day of class, with active learning throughout the semester, can be a powerful motivational tool. Teachers can also use active learning for both formative and summative assessments (Moore, 1997). However, it is imperative that active learning exercises be well designed with goals and methods of assessment considered before implementation (Miserandino, 1999).

Instructors often express two concerns related to active learning. First, active learning may take more time in the classroom and, second, active learning approaches may be difficult with large classes. Moore (1997) noted that although the teacher may cover less material in a class using active learning techniques, students actually learn and retain more information. Zacharopoulou (2006) noted that large class sizes do not preclude the use of active learning. Group work with peer teaching and many demonstrations work best with large numbers of students (e.g., teaching random sampling). Additionally, instructors may benefit from large class sizes to generate data for use in demonstrations (ASA, 2005).

## Real data

Data and statistics do not exist in a vacuum. Students need to learn to reason about data as opposed simply to learning how to compute formulas (Cobb & McClain, 2004). Ideally, students will learn about the entire data-analytic process and discover that the numbers used in formulas do not just magically appear. Thus, statistics educators and researchers have argued for the use of real data as a means to enhance statistical reasoning and thinking skills (e.g., ASA, 2005; Cobb & McClain, 2004; Gourgey, 2000; Rumsey, 2002). The national curriculum guidelines related to the teaching of statistics in the United Kingdom, South Africa, Australia, and New Zealand all highlight the importance of using real data within a broader research context (Connor & Davies, 2002). Additionally, Holmes (2002) argued that real data should be integral to assessment as well.

The use of real data increases what Rumsey (2002) referred to as "data awareness" (p. 4). Data awareness involves three factors: (a) the omnipresent nature of data; (b) understanding the misuse of data; and (c) the importance of using data appropriately to ensure good decisions. Thompson (1994) described a class project in which students developed their own "Student Information Questionnaire" (p. 41). Students generated questionnaire items designed to obtain demographic and attitudinal information. Thompson stressed that each class may develop new questionnaire items based on their unique interests. This exercise not only generated real data but also got them thinking about the type and form of questions asked to generate appropriate data. Students may find such data particularly motivating due to the relevance to their own lives (ASA, 2005; Snee, 1993; Thompson, 1994). Jacobs (1980) suggested passing out a simple short questionnaire for students to complete the first day of class with items such as "how may brothers they have" and "how many children they would like to have" (p. 242). Collecting real data, particularly data directly applicable to students' interests, can serve to reduce anxiety and increase the desire to explore statistics (Harlow, Burkholder, & Morrow, 2006; Mvududu, 2003; Pan & Tang, 2005; Scuitto, 2002).

Gourgey (2000) stated, "Statistics is by nature an experimental discipline, and it should be taught that way as much as possible" (p. 3). By grounding a statistics course in the practice of statistical authenticity (e.g., real data and experimental studies), students see the connection of the data generation process to research and demonstrate greater levels of statistical reasoning (Derry et al., 2000; Groth, 2006). Cobb and McClain (2004) further asserted that students needed to engage in and recognize that researchers conduct data analyses within specific contexts. Students must understand that investigators aim research and accompanying analyses at specific audiences to address specific questions.

## Instructional Techniques

Despite calls for educational reform, many statistics instructors have been slow to change their teaching methods (Garfield, 2000). Indeed, some instructors use the same classroom methods as their teachers did creating a perpetuating pedagogical stagnancy (Lomax & Moosavi, 2002). Changing one's usual method of teaching a course can be a daunting task. Therefore, whether in relation to assessment or active learning, instructors may want to change their courses one step at a time (ASA, 2005; Chance, 1997; Garfield, 1994).

When thinking about change, instructors should consider carefully what active learning strategies they plan to use and why they plan to use them. As part of that process, instructors should consider their course objectives, proposed outcomes, and issues of assessment (Miserandino, 1999). Rossman and Chance (1999) provided a "top ten" (p. 297) list of teaching outcomes for statistics with a focus on the development of statistical reasoning. For example, they asserted that students should be able to differentiate between "no significant difference" and "no effect." Ideally, instructors may create their own "top ten" list of broad goals for the course and then create active learning exercises that will facilitate student development towards these goals.

## Lecture

According to Benjamin (2002), "lecture is the Velveeta of teaching methods" (p. 57). Like many comfort foods, lectures are secure, familiar, and predictable, and we often reach for this old standby in our refrigerator of instructional strategies. Unfortunately, lecture may not be the healthiest choice if not balanced by other methods (Garfield, 2000). Halpern (2004) argued that lecture does not lead to good transfer of learning. Therefore, although lecture may be the most popularly used statistics teaching method, it may be the least effective method.

Nonetheless, instructors can learn to use lecture quite effectively. Benjamin (2002) outlined some key elements of quality lectures. First, passion is critical to the lecture. The enthusiasm that a teacher has for the course material can be infectious. Benjamin commented that instructor enthusiasm and passion lead to greater student excitement about the material and increased course satisfaction. Second, teachers must carefully prepare their lectures using clearly delineated goals. These goals should be obvious to the student and the end of the lecture should include a summary of the main points. Finally, teachers should focus on depth as opposed to breadth in their lectures. More is not always better. Rumsey (2002) argued that instructors should only lecture on the most important concepts. Instructors may elect to make better use of valuable class time by omitting minor concepts, particularly those not fundamental to an understanding of the big issues.

In relation to statistics, instructors can transform lecture into an active learning experience using several strategies. Teachers can present problems and then change elements of the problems to examine the impact on the results and conclusions (Larsen, 2006). For example, instructors may change the probability level or the values used in the problems. The instructor should be prepared to think aloud and make mistakes when teaching. Thus, they demonstrate the use of active reasoning and thinking in front of the class. Consequently, students come to view statistics as a process and see themselves as part of a team and not distinct from the instructor (Bradstreet, 1996). Instructors also may convert note taking into an active learning experience by requiring students to turn in their notes for feedback. Students who exhibit poor noting behavior often perform less well on testing (Lambiotte, Skaggs, & Dansereau, 1993).

## The use of questions

Instructors may use questions as an important adjunct to the lecture (Larsen, 2006; Rumsey, 2002). Teachers should routinely ask students to apply concepts, explain how these concepts are important, propose solutions to problems, and provide rationales for their proposed solutions. In addition, instructors may ask directive questions that lead students towards self-explanations of concepts (Broers, Mur, & Bude, 2004). This process may lead students to correct answers and improved statistical thinking and reasoning. Although students may initially chaff at instructors selecting them to answer questions, the method of randomly asking students to respond to questions is pedagogically sound. McDougall and Granby (1996) found that compared to a group of voluntary questioners, students enrolled in an introductory statistics course in which the instructor would call on them at random to answer questions, read more of the required readings prior to class, demonstrated greater knowledge of the material, and were more confident when responding orally to questions.

It is not only important to ask questions but it is also important to listen to what students have to say (Wulff & Wulff, 2004). Dolinsky (2001) devoted several class periods to student-generated questions. She noted that it was important to let students attempt to answer and discuss the questions first as opposed to the teacher just providing the answers. Benedict and Anderton (2004) described the use of Just-in-Time Teaching (JiTT) as an approach to help students organize what they know and for instructors to be aware of what students need to know. The instructor posted questions online for students to respond to before class (at least 2 hours). They used the answers to assess what students knew and what additional information the instructors needed to stress again during class. Students could read the other students' responses and each student received a graded copy of their response. Thus, the JiTT served also as a means of formative assessment. Students who used the JiTT method performed better on the final exam and expressed satisfaction with the course. Unfortunately, Benedict and Anderton commented that this method required additional time on the part of the instructor and was difficult for some students who did not have easy access to the Internet.

## Practice problems and examples

Examples and practice problems are a mainstay in statistics education (Chew, 2007). Unfortunately, the traditional method of examples followed by practice problems may not be conducive to the development of underlying statistical schemas (Sweller, van Merriënboer, & Paas, 1998; van Merriënboer & Sweller, 2005). The increased cognitive load associated with learning a new statistical technique, learning how to use the formula, computing the problem, and interpreting the results may be too high, and hence, lead to decreased learning (Chew, 2007; Paas, 1992; Sweller & Cooper, 1985). Teachers may opt to present partially or fully worked examples to the class, thereby decreasing cognitive load. Students who work partially completed problems or study fully worked problems demonstrate greater conceptual learning of statistics and increased abilities aimed at transfer of learning to new problems (Paas, 1992; Sweller & Cooper, 1985).

Although instructors may want to know the best order to present information, the research findings are contradictory. Hong and O'Neil (1992) found that students learned best when teachers introduced conceptual information to students before procedural or quantitative information. Conversely, Kester, Kirschner, and van Merriënboer (2004) ascertained that students learned best when teachers presented procedural information first followed by supportive information during the working of problems. These seemingly contradictory findings may simply suggest that reducing cognitive load is important when teaching statistics and that examples and problems work best when the instructor teaches computations separately from the underlying concepts.

Quilici and Mayer (2002) reported that direct instruction (e.g., schema-building exercises and lecture) with completed examples highlighting the structural features of a problem aids with transfer of learning. They tested students by having them sort problems based on an identification of the appropriate statistical method for use with each problem. Students previously taught to ignore the story and focus instead on the structural elements of each example (e.g., type of study or variables) performed better on the sorting tasks than students who had not received such training. Teachers may facilitate transfer of learning by using highly variable examples (Paas & van Merriënboer, 1994; Quilici & Mayer). The use of varied examples forces students to move beyond surface learning towards an identification of underlying concepts and structural elements.

If instructors assign homework problems, it is imperative that they provide students with solutions to the problems and discuss why particular answers are incorrect or incomplete (Chance, 1997). Chance also noted that student presentations of homework problems to the class could further facilitate learning and discussion of statistical concepts.

Teachers also may use examples from the news media that may have high relevancy for students. Instructors may use these articles as examples in class, discussion starters on-line, or components of peer-reviewed projects. Additionally, instructors may use news articles to assess, either formatively or summatively, statistical thinking and reasoning (Chance, 1997; Watson, 1997). *The Journal of Statistics Education* has a regular feature entitled "Teaching Bits: Topics for Discussion from Current Newspapers and Journals" that may be useful to instructors looking for such items (see http://www.amstat.org/publications/jse/).

## Journal assignments

Instructors may also use the reading and evaluation of journal articles as a useful adjunct to any statistics course. Oldenburg (2005) found that 22.7% of undergraduate statistics courses included readings from primary sources. Christopher and Walter (2006) had students read and evaluate pre-selected student-published research articles. Their criteria for article selection included its relationship to the material discussed in class, whether the article was within the students' range of abilities, and the length of the selection. Christopher and Walter developed questions to guide students through the analysis of the articles. The assignment reinforced learning of the course material and drew immediate connections between the concepts learned in class and the world of psychological research.

Rossi (1987) had students find articles with summary information from which students could compute t-tests or ANOVAs. Students evaluated the articles and recomputed the statistics. On several occasions, students discovered that data analyses presented in the original article were wrong. Rossi used this information to promote the idea of researcher and statistician as detective and to highlight the importance of critically reading results sections in journal articles.

Ware, Badura, and Davis (2002) recommended having students evaluate statistical results from student-published research in journals such as the *Psi Chi Journal of Undergraduate Research*; *Journal of Psychological Inquiry*; and *The Journal of Psychology and the Behavioral Sciences*. They recommend these journals, as they tended to be more accessible and consisted of shorter studies or experiments, which instructors could easily translate for use in class. Moreover, the use of student-generated research may open the door for students to pursue their own research projects (Christopher & Walter, 2006).

## Activities and demonstrations

Instructors can include activities and demonstrations as a means to promote active learning. Gnanadesikan, Scheaffer, Watkins, and Witmer (1997) discussed information concerning an activity-based statistics course. They presented a range of activities that instructors could use to promote active learning on topics ranging from central limit theorem to factorial designs. For example, the authors described a method using coins of various value and minted year to demonstrate sampling distributions. The exercise was interactive and visual to enhance learning of the concept. Gnanadesikan et al. provided many examples of activity-based learning exercises using coins, beads, tennis balls, and a host of other ideas. They noted that each activity must be carefully thought out, constructed, and assessed or students may become bored, confused, or fail to see the point of the activity.

Many researchers have written articles or books inclusive of sample active learning exercises or experiments (e.g., Gelman & Nolan, 2002; Hunter, 1977; Scheaffer, Gnanadesikan, Watkins, & Witmer, 1996; Lindquist & Hammel, 1998; Mackisack, 1994; Smith, 1998). For example, Martinez-Dawson (2003) developed a lab manual that instructors can use with science majors in the teaching of statistics. Fischer (1996) described a lab-based statistics course for sociology students. Sowey (2001) provided 30 demonstrations catalogued by subject that instructors could use to make statistics learning memorable. Albert (2002) described a statistics course taught entirely from a baseball perspective.

Fiorini, Miller, and Acusta (1998) included an activity in which students placed a range of weights in cans and then studied the number of balloons needed to enable the cans to rise. Based on the data from the various weights and numbers of balloons, the students then predicted and tested the number of balloons needed to lift the instructor. The journal *Teaching of Psychology* regularly includes active learning exercises that instructors can integrate into a statistics course (e.g., Harlow, Burkholder, & Morrow, 2006).

Morgan (2001) used obituaries to teach a variety of concepts and facilitate active learning. She provided a set of approximately 50 obituaries for students to code and record (e.g., age, gender, number of children). Instructors may address a number of topics based on these data. For example, instructors may highlight the messiness of real data as obituaries often contain missing elements (e.g., age). Additionally, instructors may address the issue of outliers as the deaths of infants or children are outside the norm. Morgan suggested that teachers could introduce inferential statistics through an examination of gender and age of death. Students could also compute correlations between number of children and age of death. Morgan cautioned instructors to warn students about the use of obituaries in advance in case a student may have experienced a loss in recent weeks and suggested that perhaps obituaries from a different decade or city might prevent some of these issues.

## Writing assignments

Instructors may use writing as a process to help students learn (e.g., Nodine, 1999; 2002). However, many students might respond to a writing assignment with the following question, "You want us to write in a statistics class?" Students may have the underlying assumption that statistics is a math class comprised only of formulas and numbers. Although most students do not find introductory statistics mathematically difficult, the conceptually complex interpretations may leave students befuddled. Adding a writing component to a statistics course may facilitate students' deeper understanding of statistical concepts.

Beins (1993) tested the impact of writing on students' learning of statistics, specifically their computational abilities, conceptual understanding of the course material, and their interpretive skill in communicating the results of data analyses. He used three formats to teach students. In the traditional-emphasis class, students learned statistics without any added writing component. In the moderate-emphasis class, students spent time in class working on interpretation and explanation of the results of their data analyses. In the high-emphasis class, students had the opportunity of extra credit assignments involving the creation of a press release based on analyses performed in class. The goal of the press release was for students to communicate the results in a non-statistical format to a general audience. As part of the process, students may discover areas of knowledge about which they are unclear. Thus, instructors can build a self-monitoring component into the assignment. Although, the study found no differences among the groups on the final test of conceptual understanding, students in the writing intensive class performed significantly better at computations and demonstrated better interpretive skills.

Dunn (2000) recommended a unique writing assignment involving student letter exchanges. Dunn paired students with peers taking another section of the course and provided students with the following instructions:

> Your goal is to write a letter in which you explain one thing you have learned about statistics . . . that you find interesting, compelling, confusing, or otherwise noteworthy. Tell why it was important to have learned it, and explain why it is important for students of psychology to know it. Finally, discuss whether students outside of psychology would benefit from this knowledge, as well. (p. 129)

Students could write on a range of topics and send their letters by either hard copy or e-mail. Dunn instructed the peer receiving the letter to respond and the original sender could reply with further clarification. Dunn graded the letters based on quality of topic presentation, quality of writing, and peer interaction. The writing assignment provided peers the opportunity to "teach" by responding to letters providing feedback, clarification, suggestions, corrections, etc. The interaction was beneficial to both the initial letter writing and the peer respondent. Dunn commented that these peer communications also could take place via a class discussion list or chat room.

Dolinsky (2001) recommended the use of a learning journal. About every two weeks, Dolinsky asked students to respond to varying questions related to their attitudes towards the course, the learning of statistics, and their study strategies. The instructor used the journals to monitor students learning and difficulties. Additionally, students used the journals to monitor their own learning and course progress. Students can effectively use journals to begin and explore the process of self-assessment (Chance, 1997).

Sciutto (2002) described and studied the use of student portfolios. Sciutto provided students at the beginning of the term a list of required (e.g., measures of variability, one-way ANOVA) and optional topics (e.g., reliability and validity). For each topic, students wrote a maximum 3-page entry concerning material presented in lecture, readings, and laboratory assignments. The point of the assignment was for students to organize the material in a manner useful to them for future reference and potential research ideas generation. Sciutto did not allow students simply to reiterate the lecture or reword their notes. In fact, he rated the portfolios on "uniqueness" (p. 214) as well as readability and future value to the students. Sciutto found a positive correlation between ratings of the portfolio and performance on the final exam. In addition, he noted that, when reviewed regularly, the portfolio was an effective formative assessment tool to identify students who are having difficulty explaining concepts or have faulty reasoning and ideas. When students' writings resembled the book or lecture, Scuitto noted that students were less likely to have mastered the material. He commented that effective use of portfolios enhanced students' understanding of the material.

Gore and Camp (1987) had students complete research projects and presented their studies via poster sessions, which gave students the opportunity to communicate to others the entire context of their experiments including methods and results in text, table, and graphic form. Students were able to see the context of their statistics, explain their results to other students, and receive feedback. Chance (1997) also advocated for the use of lab write-ups and oral presentations. Dunn (1996) recommended the use of peer review of student-written articles both before the completion of a project and at the end.

Students may be concerned that there is a "correct" way to communicate statistical information and hence the statement, "I don't know how you want me to say this." Students should recognize that there is not an explicit set of rules for the communication of statistical results. Rather, instructors should teach students that the goal is to make analyses interpretable to individuals reading about a research project. Consequently, Dunn (1996) argued for the collaborative writing of studies. Such collaborations might enable students to share ideas, clarify areas of confusion, and learn from one another without the pressure of a right or wrong way to communicate ideas.

## Concept maps

Instructors may find concept maps to be particularly useful for students who are struggling with statistics or who have less developed verbal skills (Lambiotte, Skaggs, & Dansereau, 1993). Concept maps may help students develop a "connected understanding," which is fundamental to the development of statistical thinking and reasoning (Schau & Mattern, 1997, p. 91). Instructors should avoid discrete presentations of information as such methods may lead to disconnected learning and thinking. Fortunately, concept mapping can help detect the development of inaccurate schemas and serve as a method of formative assessment. Structural awareness is a necessary component in the development of concept maps or mental modeling (Quilici & Mayer, 2002).

Lambiotte et al. (1993) compared student learning and found a significant interaction between type of student and method of learning. Confident students performed better when provided lists of statistical ideas and concepts. These students tended to take good notes and included extensive annotations on their lists. Such behaviors correlated with good performance in the class. However, less confident students performed better with concept maps. Instructor-provided concept maps may give students an organizational framework for their thinking. Unfortunately, less confident students who took fewer notes and failed to annotate their concept maps still performed poorly on tests. Therefore, concept map use alone may not improve performance.

Hong and O'Neil (1992) presented students with varying conditions: separate or simultaneous training and descriptive information or diagrams in a study of mental models. Students given diagrams of various concepts learned better than with descriptive information. Moreover, students presented conceptual information before the introduction of the diagrams performed the best. The researchers hypothesized that students who learned the conceptual reasoning behind techniques followed by diagrams were better able to construct mental models. They noted that students demonstrated an ability to transfer the concepts they had learned to novel problems sets. Dyck & Mayer (1989) also found students learned best when instructors presented conceptual information first.

## Cooperative learning

Cooperative learning can greatly facilitate students' understanding of course material and concepts (Halpern, 2004). In relation to statistics, students in cooperative learning structured classes performed better on tests of learning in statistics than students in lecture-based courses, exhibited greater retention, and possessed better attitudes about the course (Dietz, 1993; Giraud, 1997; Keeler & Steinhorst, 1995; Potthast, 1999; Shaughnessy, 1977). Although Courtney, Courtney, and Nicholson (1994) did not find a difference in student performance, their research demonstrated improved attitude, increased motivation, increased cohesiveness within the group, and increased levels of self-efficacy. Additionally, Palincsar and Brown (1984) found that cooperative learning helped develop metacognitive skills associated with self-questioning one's knowledge, focused students' attention to the most salient feature under discussion, and highlighted areas of confusion.

Giraud (1997) randomly assigned students to one of two conditions: cooperative learning class and traditional lecture class. Within the cooperative learning class, the instructor randomly assigned students to learning groups to ensure that students at various levels were represented within each group. Across groups, students with greater conceptual understanding of the material were able to assist students at lower levels. Consequently, students in the cooperative learning class performed better on the exams. Most importantly, Giraud found that those cooperative learning students who were most at risk at the beginning of the semester had higher test scores at the end of the semester than at-risk students from the lecture class. Cumming (1983) reported that mixed ability groups were not necessarily beneficial for high functioning students but very beneficial for those students who had trouble with statistics.

Peer tutoring is a beneficial form of cooperative learning. Mill et al. (1994) found that tutorial sessions helped improve students' reasoning and critical thinking abilities compared to students in a lecture course. Finn (1983) reported that students responded positively to a peer tutoring method and that students felt a sense of pride at working with and helping others. Students who received assistance also responded positively as they did not feel the same levels of worry or self-consciousness about asking for help. Even with the use of individualized learning approaches such as the Personalized System of Instruction (PSI: Keller, 1968), Finn reported that peer tutoring groups fostered accountability and assisted students in avoiding procrastination.

Rumsey (2002) encouraged students to work in teams and rotated team membership during the semester. She found that over time, her students developed their own language and approaches to concepts that were different from the instructors but nevertheless correct. She argued that this added a richness and collaborative spirit to the class that more closely mimicked the workplace situation where individuals must work in teams. Perkins and Saris (2001) used a "jigsaw" approach to cooperative learning in groups. As many problems have multiple steps, the instructors assigned each group to work on a specific aspect of the problem. In the end, students brought the pieces together for completion of the overall problem. Perkins and Saris reported increased student learning of the material, better use of class time, and students commented that they benefited from the experience. For a variety of suggestions related to cooperative learning exercises in statistics, see Garfield (1993).

## Projects

Research projects are an invaluable means to increase both statistical authenticity and authentic assessment. To be effective, however, statistics projects must have carefully defined objectives (Starkings, 1997). For longer projects, instructors may subdivide and explain the steps of the task (Jolliffe, 1997). Additionally, Low (1995) reported that although data collection is important, continuous feedback concerning each step of the research process might be more important. The researchers placed students in continuous, partial, or no feedback conditions. Students in the continuous feedback groups performed significantly higher on a task measuring their understanding of statistical concepts than the partial or no feedback groups. Starke (1985) had students participate in a research practicum and reported that students liked the hands-on experience and collaborative process involved in serving as research assistants.

Instructors may be concerned that there is not enough time in class to cover the material, let alone conduct research projects. Gore and Camp (1987) provided two counterarguments to this concern. First, they argued that the projects themselves might increase students' understanding of statistics and thus, reduce the amount of time teachers spend in class re-explaining ideas. Second, they noted that the assignments could be relatively simple projects in terms of design and implementation. For example, Smith (1998) described his course in which students completed six projects and presented the results of their projects in both written and oral presentations. Smith provided a list of 20 projects that instructors could use to teach topics ranging from descriptive through inferential (ANOVA) statistics.

Instructors may effectively integrate projects into their statistics courses in myriad ways. Stallings (1993) described student research projects involving the growth of radishes. Radishes apparently grow quickly and student researchers do not need Institutional Review Board approval to study them. Bradstreet (1996) described a workshop-based course in which students worked together on projects to test notions such as whether "Ballpark Franks plump larger" (p. 74) and if pizza was an effective treatment for the chicken pox (it is not). Nolan and Speed (1999) described a model of integrated lab exercises they used to supplement classroom experience in statistics. They argued that such work is necessary for students to study the material in depth. Student feedback regarding the exercise was positive. In fact, some student reported using their lab reports as part of their submitted portfolios when applying for jobs.

Melton (2004) had students collect data about customer service at local fast food restaurants. The students created a list of variables and data they wanted to collect and determined whether to observe another person's or their own transaction. Melton commented that this method highlighted the role of variability in the data collection process. Consequently, he used these data throughout the class when discussing various analytic techniques.

Truran and Arnold (2002) added a service-learning component to their class and had students involved in statistical consulting projects with real clients. Students developed a listener questionnaire and survey method for a radio station. Students not only learned a real-world application but also came to understand that statistics is part of a process involving client meetings, study planning, data collection and analyses, and communication of the results back to the client. However, Truran and Arnold commented that this project required a great deal of time, communication, and effort on the part of the faculty member. Brakke, Wilson, and Bradley (2007) also advocated for a service-learning project with students. They paired statistics students with social psychology students who were required to complete a research project in their course. Students in statistics class gained valuable hands-on experience while the social psychology students received important assistance with their project. The authors described it as a "'win-win-win' situation" (p. 120). For more teaching statistics tips, including the use of minute papers, case studies, and simulations, see our Web site at www.teachstats.org.

## Assessment

Instructors should view assessment as both instructive and evaluative. Goals for assessment include improvement of instructional strategies, motivating students, providing feedback to students concerning areas of needed work and mastery, developing diagnostic tools to identify what the instructor needs to reemphasize, and measuring student performance (Onwuegbuzie, 2000). Traditional methods of quizzes and exams are unlikely to meet all of these goals. Therefore, instructors also should evaluate the context of the course, their pedagogical style, and course content (Onwuegbuzie & Leech, 2003). Such an evaluation will provide instructors the direction needed for the development of appropriate assessment tools.

Instructors may use a variety of alternative assessment strategies in their courses such as portfolios, reflective journals, peer writing, evaluation of research articles, group projects (research collected and presented), press releases, critiques of media articles, quizzes, exams, and other assignments. Garfield and Chance (2000) discussed several assessment strategies including "authentic tasks" and "concept maps" (p. 103). Garfield (1994) outlined 17 different methods of assessment ranging from quizzes to portfolios and projects. As with active learning techniques, instructors should incorporate only one new assessment technique at a time to their courses to enable better evaluation of the method and its effectiveness (ASA, 2005; Chance, 1997; Garfield, 1994).

### Principles of effective assessment

Instructors should integrate assessment methods throughout their courses. Moore (1997) argued that instructors should assess anything that they want their students to know or accomplish. Osborne and Wagor (2004) outlined a five-step process for the development of assessment methods within a course to promote assessment as an ongoing and developmental process (pp. 130–131):

1. Defining what skills and capacities students most need to acquire from the course or program.
2. Deciding what level of expectation there is for those skills and capacities.
3. Detailing what faculty will do to provide instruction in and practice with those skills and abilities and identifying what students will do to demonstrate those skills and abilities.
4. Discovering whether students are sufficiently demonstrating those skills and abilities.
5. Determining what changes to make if students do not demonstrate skills or abilities at desired levels.

Statistics education researchers have outlined general principles for the effective assessment of a statistic course (Begg, 1997; Chance, 1997; Colvin & Vos, 1997; Onwuegbuzie & Leech, 2003). First, instructors must outline and assess statistics education content. They should use assessment tasks that focus directly on the material taught. Second, instructors must develop assessment techniques that enhance learning. Third, instructors must use assignments that encourage student self-assessment and statistical reasoning. Fourth, instructors should use assessments that take into account individuality and the developmental levels of the learners. Fifth, instructors should use multiple assessments and a range of assessment methods. Sixth, instructors must work to insure that all methods of assessment are consistent, fair, and open.

Consistent with the principles outlined above, students should know the scoring criteria before they attempt any task and when the task is completed they should receive timely and responsive feedback. To facilitate this process, instructors should create rubrics to use in evaluating tasks, assignments, and projects (Colvin & Vos, 1997; Onwuegbuzie & Leech, 2003). For example, Bosack et al. (2004) outlined developmental levels that instructors could use to assess statistical reasoning.

## Mastery learning

Conners et al. (1998) recommended mastery learning as a possible technique to increase student motivation and success in statistics. Within the context of mastery learning, students learn the criteria associated with the successful completion of an information module and then study the module. When students believe that they have successfully mastered the content of that module, they take a test over the material. If the student does not pass the test demonstrating sufficient knowledge, teachers provide feedback about the student's performance highlighting what they know well and where there are knowledge deficiencies. The student, armed with this feedback, again studies the material, and then retakes the exam. This process continues until they have demonstrated a mastery of the information. Once completed, the student moves on to the next module of information. Conners et al. asserted that mastery learning worked to insure that students attempt no concept before fully understanding the statistical building blocks of the prior section. Moreover, students who experience evaluation apprehension associated with learning quantitative methods may particularly benefit from the mastery learning approach. Friedman (1987) also recommended the use of repeat exams as a means to master learning and reduce test-taking anxiety. Of course, multiple testing requires a time commitment on the part of the instructor to create and grade multiple versions of a test.

## Confronting Fear and Anxiety

Statistics anxiety is a multidimensional concept with many factors affecting students' anxiety levels including dispositional, environmental, and situational factors (Onwuegbuzie & Wilson (2003). Unfortunately, there is a negative correlation between statistics anxiety and performance in a statistics course (Lalonde & Gardner, 1993; Onwuegbuzie & Seaman, 1995; Zanakis & Valenza, 1997). Conversely, Vanhoof et al. (2006) found a positive correlation between positive attitudes towards statistics course and final statistics exam grades. With leaders in mathematics education recommending the inclusion of statistics at the pre-college level (e.g., National Council of Teachers of Mathematics, 2000), Mills (2004a) asserted that student attitudes might become more positive over time. Until that happens, instructors need to address issues of statistics anxiety in the classroom.

It is important to note that math anxiety and statistics anxiety are not synonymous concepts (Onwuegbuzie & Wilson, 2003) and researchers should study these concepts separately. For example, Townsend, Moore, Tuck, and Wilton (1998) found that students who worked in cooperative learning groups performed better and had more confidence in their ability to handle statistics problems but math anxiety remained unchanged. Fortunately, there are several measures of statistics anxiety and attitudes towards statistics. They include:

• Attitudes Toward Statistics (ATS) Scale – Wise (1985). Shultz and Koshino (1998) found the scale to be a reliable and valid measure for students' attitudes towards statistics. They cautioned that instructors and researchers should use different norms for undergraduate versus graduate students.
• Statistics Attitude Scale (SAS) – Roberts and Bilderback (1980).
• Statistics Anxiety Inventory (SAI) – Zeidner (1991).
• Survey of Attitudes Towards Statistics (SATS) – Gal et al. (1997).

Instructors may use these measures to assess students' attitudes before taking a statistics course or as a form of assessment following students' completion of a course.

Pan and Tang (2005) identified four factors that contribute to anxiety in statistic students. They are "math phobia, lack of connection to daily life, pace of instruction, and instructor's attitude" (p. 209). The authors tested and found three methods to reduce anxiety. First, instructors may use multiple methods of instruction and assessment, particularly those connected to real world data and direct relevance to students. Second, instructors may demonstrate real concern for and connection to the student. Third, instructors may eliminate traditional exams and elect for alternative testing and assessment strategies (e.g., mastery learning, projects, writing assignments).

In a cross-cultural study, Mvududu (2003) found that U.S. students particularly benefited from the teaching of statistics using real-world data. Students who learn using active learning techniques, the use of student-generated data, and data directly applicable to their lives experience reduced anxiety levels (Harlow et al., 2006; Mvududu, 2003; Scuitto, 2002).

Pan and Tang (2005) argued that instructors' attitude also plays a significant role in students' anxiety levels. They provided an orientation letter to students before the beginning of the semester. Students responded positively to the letter and reported that it gave them a sense that the instructor cared about them as individuals. Dillon (1982) argued for discussing anxiety with the class and presenting information specifically on the topic of anxiety management. Sgoutas-Emch and Johnson (1998) used journal writing as a means to reduce anxiety. Teachers instructed students in the writing group to keep a regular journal. As part of that journal, students wrote about their thoughts, feelings, concerns, and summarized each daily lecture. The instructor provided students class time each day to write in their journal. Students in the journal writing group reported lower anxiety levels and performed better on tests. Onwuegbuzie (2004) found that students with high anxiety tended to procrastinate more when completing assignments. Therefore, instructors may want to break up tasks to counter this trend in high anxiety students.

Assessment also can be a source of statistics anxiety. Researchers have found that learning activities (e.g., projects) are less anxiety-provoking than tests, with timed tests related to the highest levels of anxiety (Onwuegbuzie, 2000). Onwuegbuzie and Seaman (1995) found that both high and low anxiety students performed better on final exams when untimed. They randomly assigned high- and low-test anxiety students either to the timed examination condition or to an untimed exam condition. Both high- and low-anxiety students performed better in the untimed condition with the high anxiety students exhibiting the greatest benefit. In fact, the difference for high anxiety students was an entire letter grade. Onwuegbuzie and Seaman noted that statistics test anxiety might be greater than test anxiety for other courses. In statistics, the level of anxiety affects students' test performance, sense of self-efficacy and motivation, and overall attitude toward the course. Onwuegbuzie (2000) reported that untimed tests, open book tests, or tests that allow for some access to course material result in the highest levels of performance, lowest levels of anxiety, and greater demonstration of statistical reasoning. Consequently, Conners et al. (1998) argued for the elimination of exam pressure to reduce anxiety and for the use of peer tutoring. For more teaching statistics tips, including first day activities and the use of humor, see our Web site at www.teachstats.org.

## Conclusion

Johnson and Dasgupta (2005) surveyed students over a 5-year period who had completed an introductory statistics course. They found that students tended to prefer nontraditional courses (e.g., cooperative learning, active learning-based, distance learning) versus traditional courses. However, students who preferred large classes preferred lecture format. Therefore, Johnson and Dasgupta concluded that due to the variability in responses, it is best to use a myriad of approaches to teach statistics. Fortunately, there is an over abundance of novel ways that instructors can approach the teaching of statistics.

Some instructors, however, may find it unappealing or daunting to change their approach to teaching, particularly if they have experienced some student success in the past with their current methods. Therefore, the GAISE Report (ASA, 2005) suggested that instructors make changes slowly—implement one new teaching or assessment strategy at a time. Through gradual change, instructors may find educational reform less overwhelming and enable better assessment of the each newly added technique.

Regardless of what new strategies an instructor may implement in teaching statistics, it is evident that statistics education is improving due to reform efforts. Such efforts foster an active learning environment that is exciting and challenging for both the student and the instructor. Certainly, the classroom has come a long way since the time of Cohen and Firestone (1939) who wrote:

> The good teacher is half actor, half scholar. The competent statistician is rarely the sparkling captivator who keeps students from slumber through the sheer power of personality. Accordingly, the classroom becomes, more often than not, the abode of boredom, however conscientious the instructor may be. Timidity keeps the student from the temptation of asking a question to clear up a difficulty and terror ties his [sic] tongue if he is called upon to recite. The brilliant instructor sets the tempo of his class to the tastes of the clever students, while the slow learners lag dismally in their mire. The thorough teacher drills, pounds, and repeats until his [sic] incessant bombing penetrates even the thickest of skulls, but alas the clever chap chafes at the restraint. (p. 714)

# III

# Teaching Specific Statistical Concepts

III

# Chapter 5

# Descriptive Statistics and Bivariate Distributions

*There are three kinds of lies: lies, damned lies, and statistics. –*
*Benjamin Disraeli*[1]

Prior to setting out on a nature walk with a group of 6-year-olds, du
Feu (2005) wondered, "How old must children be before they can
learn about statistics?" (p. 34). Much to his surprise, he found that
the children were able to engage in statistical comparisons between
two species of flowers across different habitats. du Feu's experiences
mirrored the recommendations of the National Council of Teachers
of Mathematics (NCTM, 1989, 2000) which encouraged K-12
instructors to teach students to collect, organize, display, and analyze
data using descriptive and inferential statistics.

The NCTM (2000) justified the inclusion of the *Data Analysis*
*and Probability Standard* in K-12 mathematical education because
students needed to be able to reason statistically to make sense of
the massive amount of data available on any given topic. However,
instruction in descriptive statistics and bivariate distributions does
not end upon the completion of high school. Introductory statistics
instructors at the college level also need to remind students as to the
promises and pitfalls associated with statistics as they appear in real
world contexts. Specifically, instructors need to make students aware
that businesses, politicians, marketers, and other special interest

groups may misuse statistics to sway or misrepresent public opinion (NCTM, 2000; Weaver, 1989).

For example, Kosslyn (1994) provided a chapter in his book on graph design devoted to lying with graphics. He provided numerous examples of misleading graphs and discussed the principles that helped explain why these graphs were "successful" at projecting misinformation. Hertzberg (2003) reported that President George W. Bush had asserted that his economic stimulus package, which contained numerous tax cuts and incentives, would result in Americans saving an average of $1,083. Hertzberg pointed out that the typical American taxpayer would only get a few hundred dollars whereas the richest would receive well over $300,000. Clearly, it pays to understand the impact of outliers on measures of central tendency.

Statistical educators have consistently cited the importance of developing a thorough understanding of statistical concepts and applications (Weaver, 1989). Students need to develop the ability to reason logically about statistical concepts before engaging in memorizing computational formulas or tables (Anastasi, 1985). To achieve lasting comprehension of statistical concepts such as descriptive statistics and bivariate distributions, statistics scholars have encouraged instructors to use hands-on activities.

## Graphing Data

The effective use of graphs is an essential tool for communicating research results (Cleveland, 1984a; Pittenger, 1995). Well-constructed graphs can convey descriptive information, quantitative patterns, trends, relationships, and are critical tools for understanding main effects and complex interactions. According to Latour (1990), graphs are powerful due to the fact they are easily understood, amenable to a variety of phenomena, readily manipulated (i.e., scale can be changed) to convey novel connections, easily transported and reproduced, and most importantly, extremely persuasive.

Although psychology textbooks regularly expose students to graphs, there is a paucity of literature on teaching students how to create, read, and interpret graphs (Pittenger, 1995). In addition, textbooks only present students with the most common, and sometimes least effective, means of presenting data. For example, Peden and Hausmann (2000) found that only five types of graphs were present in their sample of introductory psychology textbooks—with line and bar graphs being most common. Butler (1993) reported that text-books contain mostly pictures, journals tend to have an abundance of data graphs, whereas conceptual graphs (e.g., Venn diagrams) are largely absent from psychological literature. Moreover, most text-books only review a limited set of graphing options, without any substantive discussion of the qualities that make graphs effective (Pittenger, 1995).

The ability to create effective graphs has become an increasingly important skill given the availability of computerized data and the ability of statistical software to conduct more sophisticated and complex analyses. Software applications (e.g., Microsoft Excel) have made the creation of graphs much simpler—students are merely a point and click away from a polished graph. However, Goldman and McKenzie (2002) remarked that such applications "make it all too easy for the neophyte to produce a striking but often misleading or unhelpful display" (p. 96).

Over 20 years ago, Cleveland (1984a) proposed five areas in the field of graphical communication that lacked sufficient empirical support: (a) evidence of how people use graphs; (b) guidelines for effective graphs; (c) how people process graphical information; (d) the types of graphing methods available; and (e) development of graphing software. Although there has been modest growth in these areas since Cleveland's seminal paper, very little of this research has found its way into lecture or statistics textbooks—particularly in the behavioral and social sciences (Friedrich et al., 2000; Pittenger, 1995; Wilkinson, 1999).

## The use of graphs in science

Graph use varies throughout the sciences. For example, Cleveland (1984a) examined the fraction of journal space devoted to graphical communication among 57 journals from 14 disciplines, including four psychology journals. He found that journals in the natural sciences tended to devote more space to graphical communication than journals in the social sciences. For example, *Journal of Geophysical Research* had a fractional graph area (FGA) of .310 whereas the *Journal of Experimental Psychology* was approximately .08.

To explore further this relationship, Smith, Best, Stubbs, Johnson, & Archibald (2000) rated the "hardness" of the disciplines and examined whether graph usage varied as a function of disciplinary hardness. They found results similar to those reported by Cleveland

(1984a). Journal articles from the "hard" sciences (e.g., chemistry, physics) contained a higher FGA than those in the "soft" sciences (e.g., sociology, psychology). Smith et al. (2000) then examined whether the FGA in 25 APA journals differed as a function of the hardness attributed to each psychology subfield. Those journals that represented areas of psychology that raters had designated as hard psychology subfields (e.g., *Behavioral Neuroscience*) had a higher FGA than soft psychology subfield journal articles (*Journal of Counseling Psychology*).

However, Smith, Best, Stubbs, Archibald, and Roberson-Nay (2002) noted that the lack of graphs within the softer areas of psychology did not correspond to a deficiency in quantitative information. In fact, they reported an inverse relationship between statistical procedures and the hardness of the psychology subfield. Softer areas in psychology were more apt to use inferential statistics than harder subfields. Smith et al. asserted that these findings support the notion that "graphs constitute a distinct means of inference in their own right and thus represent an alternative to statistical inference, not a mere complement to numerical methods" (pp. 757–758). Indeed, Wilkinson (1999) provided an excellent overview of graphical exploration, inference, and presentation in counseling psychology.

## Elements of good design

Cleveland (1984a) conducted a detailed analysis of every graph published in one volume of the journal *Science*. He focused on four types of errors: poor construction, degraded image, poor explanation, and difficulty discriminating between graph items. Cleveland's analysis revealed that 30% of the graphs in that particular volume had errors. Unfortunately, it is highly unlikely this error rate was unique to *Science*.

To assist researchers create effective graphs, the American Psychological Association (APA) recently published two practical guides to creating tables (Nicol & Pexman, 1999) and figures (Nicol & Pexman, 2003) as companion pieces to the APA *Publication Manual* (2001). Nicol and Pexman's (1999) guide for creating tables provided sample tables for virtually every statistic a researcher might utilize. Examples ranged from tables appropriate for descriptive statistics, correlations, chi-squares, and ANOVAs to tables for complicated statistics such as factor analysis, logistic regression, MANOVA, and structural equation modeling.

Nicol and Pexman's (2003) guide to creating figures provided numerous examples of bar graphs, line graphs, plots, and pie graphs. They also provided a set of general guidelines to assist researchers in producing effective figures that comply with APA style guidelines. First, all figures must play a key role in the manuscript. Second, images need to be as clear and simple as possible. Cleveland (1984a) asserted lines and lettering should be large enough to survive reduction for publication. Third, graphs should have clear concise labels with font consistent with the manuscript text. Fourth, quantitative information and units of measurement should be readily apparent. In addition, Wilkinson and the Task Force on Statistical Inference (1999) recommended that all figures include confidence intervals. Fifth, unless the graph is for a poster or PowerPoint presentation, authors should avoid the use of color because the vast majority of scientific journals are printed in black and white. Sixth, figures need to contain all the necessary information to interpret the figure without distracting from the image itself.

Instructors should consider adding these guidelines to their lectures on graphing. Additional guidelines, plus good and bad examples of a variety of graphs from actual research studies, are available in numerous books (e.g., Cleveland, 1993, 1994; Kosslyn, 1994; Nicol & Pexman, 1999; Nicol & Pexman, 2003). Instructors should also consider examining current journal volumes for interesting articles with poorly constructed graphs to present in class.

## Human graphical perception

"Reading graphs is a skill that requires practice, not unlike riding a bicycle. Once acquired, such skills can be performed quickly and with little cognitive effort, however 'cognitively complex' they turn out to be in the laboratory" (Smith, Best, & Stubbs, 2003, p. 819). According to Cleveland (1993), the process of creating a graph involves the transformation of quantitative and categorical information into the chosen graphical medium. The accuracy with which the reader decodes the graph's content is the measure of success. However, some graphical mediums are easier to decode than other displays.

Over the past 20 years, there has been a growing body of research on graphical perception. For example, researchers have concluded that line graphs, scatter plots, and dot charts are easier to interpret than bar, histogram, and pie charts (Cleveland, 1984b; Cleveland, 1994; Cleveland & McGill, 1984; Kosslyn, 1994). Similarly, Carswell and Ramzy (1997) found that when participants interpreted visual displays, line graphs were superior to other graphing methods (e.g., table, bar graphs) regardless of the size of the data set. Cleveland (1984b) encouraged researchers to use dot charts instead of bar graphs (particularly when presenting error bars), full scale breaks over partial breaks, and consider using multibased logarithmic transformations when applicable.

Meyer and Shinar (1992) reported that the inclusion of a regression line in a scatter plot draws the reader's attention to the data and increases the likelihood that the viewer will perceive a correlation between variables. Furthermore, they found that correlation estimates were higher for shallow regression line slopes as opposed to steeper slopes. Meyer and Shinar theorized that the increased density of the data points for the shallow slope biased their participant's responses. Consequently, instructors may want to demonstrate the effect of slope on perceived correlation.

Computer software has made it easy to create three-dimensional graphs to capture readers interest (Wilkinson, 1994). Although such graphs are tempting, research suggests that participants exposed to two-dimensional graphs were more accurate and confident in their data interpretations than participants exposed to three-dimensional graphs (Barfield & Robless, 1989). The deficits associated with three-dimensional graphing were most apparent with line graphs (Carswell, Frankenberger, & Bernhard, 1991). Shah and Carpenter (1995) found that undergraduate and graduate student participants were generally unable to integrate information about three continuous variables projected onto a three-dimensional line graph.

## Available graphing methods

According to Pittenger (1995), textbook authors tend only to include a handful of graphs in statistics textbooks: bar graphs, histograms, line graphs, and scatter plots. Pittenger also noted that text coverage of this topic is typically descriptive with little attempt to go much beyond a cursory discussion of graphing techniques. Wilkinson et al. (1999) discussed the need to have more boxplots, stem-and-leaf plots, and kernel density estimates in psychological research. Yet, less than 40% of the instructors surveyed by Friedrich et al. (2000) spent more than one hour discussing these specific topics. Fortunately, several educators have published activities and material for introducing graphs into the classroom.

For example, Callaert (2000) presented students with a particularly poor graph of European Union socioeconomic data (something his Belgium students were interested in examining) and then discussed how the graph could be improved—eventually deciding on a dot plot. Marshall and Swan (2006) reported that students could use M & Ms to visualize graphs. The authors placed students into groups of four and provided each group with 50 M & Ms. Students then created several different graphs (e.g., bar graph, pie graph) plotted as a function of M & M color. Although this exercise was originally designed for children, the demonstration could also be used to reduce anxiety (i.e., everyone loves M & Ms) and introduce the concept of graphing to college students.

Statistics educators have also published material related to the teaching of specific graphs. For example, Perks and Prestage (2000) provided a means to introduce students to the concepts of scale and proportion when creating bar and pie charts. Farnsworth (2000) presented an exercise to encourage discussion of the limitations and pitfalls associated with the histogram. Perry et al. (1999) proposed that instructors use collectable stuffed animals called Beanie Babies to teach stem-and-leaf plots. Students looked up the "birthdays" of their favorite Beanie Babies and created a stem-and-leaf plot. Following the creation of the stem-and-leaf plot, students compared this plot to other graphs (e.g., pie graph, bar graph). Several authors have focused on newer exploratory data analysis graphing tools. For example, Benjamini (1988) discussed several variations of the boxplot to convey information about the density of the values in a data set. Doane and Tracy (2000) introduced beam-and-fulcrum displays as a complement to the boxplot and Cohen and Cohen (2006) discussed the sectioned density plot as a means to combine the abilities of the boxplot with the histogram.

## Software design

There are numerous software applications available for the production of statistical graphs. Although some statistics educators have created their own graphing applications and modules (e.g., Chambers, Cleveland, Kleiner, & Tukey, 1983), the majority of researchers and educators use commercial statistical applications (e.g., Excel, Minitab, SPSS). However, these software packages are not uniform in their ability to generate appropriate graphs. For example, Frigge, Hoaglin, and Iglewicz (1989) noted that various computer applications (e.g., Minitab, SAS, SPSS, SYSTAT) all produced boxplots in a slightly different fashion. Consequently, they urged increased standardization across these statistical packages. Until that happens, Frigge et al. urged users to investigate which algorithms each program used to create graphical displays.

Goldman and McKenzie (2002) examined the displays generated by Microsoft Excel, Minitab, and SPSS to determine which program was most effective at generating effective graphs. They detailed exactly what types of one-, two-, and three-dimensional displays were available through each of these applications and assessed the extent to which each display followed the guidelines established by Cleveland and McGill (1984) and Tufte (2001). Goldman and McKenzie concluded that researchers and instructors should use software specifically designed for statistical analysis (Minitab and SPSS). They reported that the display options in Excel often "violated principles of good graphical practice" (p. 99). Goldman and McKenzie recommended that software developers: (a) better organize the graphing commands; (b) include sophisticated guidance based on accepted guidelines; (c) provide more associated categorical displays; and (d) enable users to customize displays to better fit their needs.

## Normal Distribution

Students need to develop an understanding of the relevance and use of the normal distribution in order to succeed in an introductory statistics course. Batanero, Tauber, and Sánchez (2004) asserted that a thorough understanding of the normal distribution is important because various types of phenomena from the natural and social sciences can be modeled using the normal distribution. In addition, when there is a large enough sample, the central limit theorem can assure a normal distribution even when the samples are from a non-normal population distribution. Investigators can also use the normal distribution to approximate other distributions such as the $t$ distribution under certain conditions. Finally, many statistical procedures require the normal distribution.

Although there is uniform agreement as to the importance of the normal distribution in teaching statistics, there has been a paucity of research investigating students' understanding of the concept. Much of the existing research has examined students' misperceptions about the normal distribution. For example, Huck, Cross, and

Clark (1986) presented two errors regarding students' conceptions of the normal distribution as related to $z$-scores. They found that some students believed all $z$-scores would lie between $-3$ and $+3$. Other students believed that there was in fact no limit to the size of $z$-scores. In these cases, students likely overgeneralized from textbook examples (e.g., figures showing a curve with $-3$ to $+3$ range) and lecture material (e.g., distribution tails are asymptotic) regarding the normal distribution. Wilensky (1997) presented a case study of graduate students with extensive statistical knowledge exhibiting confusion regarding the normal distribution. He termed this confusion "epistemological anxiety" (p. 172). The individuals he interviewed could solve textbook problems regarding the normal distribution but could not explain why they used the normal distribution versus some other concept.

Batanero et al. (2004) conducted research to examine students' understanding of the normal distribution by assessing student performance on five different tasks that employed the normal distribution. Students had to fit a curve to a histogram, approximate the binomial distribution, and find the sampling distribution of the mean. Researchers tested them on their use of symbols, words, and graphs to represent the normal distribution using paper-and-pencil, verbal, and computer tools. Students also computed probabilities, standard scores, and critical values; provided definitions of statistical concepts related to the normal curve; and demonstrated an understanding of relevant informal arguments and proofs. Batanero et al. concluded that the normal distribution is a truly complex concept. Student success was dependent on their ability to integrate previously learned statistical concepts such as probability, spread, skewness, and histograms. As was the case with previous research, Batanero et al. reported that students had difficulty differentiating between theoretical models and empirical data.

There are limited published demonstrations devoted to illustrating the normal curve. Shatz (1985) used a simulated Greyhound bus strike to illustrate normal and skewed distributions. He assigned groups of students to represent either the labor or the management positions in the strike. Shatz provided each group with salary data for the employees as well as drivers from three rival companies. Students used the data to create a basis for each of their positions. After the exercise, students reported that they felt that the demonstration enabled them to make use of the statistical concepts they had learned in a fashion that was more than just computing statistics.

Weaver (1999) used medical growth charts to illustrate the $z$-scores and the normal distribution (many different growth charts are available online). Some charts plot the weight of newborns from birth to 36 months, others combine height and weight plots, and still other charts include head circumference. Weaver had students compare the weights of newborns with 36-month-old toddlers and determine weights associated with certain percentiles using $z$-scores. Fernald and Fernald (1990) had students flip 15 pennies and chart the number of times they obtained heads. They encouraged instructors to use other variables to create a normal distribution such as height, time estimation, and academic ability. For more exercises related to the teaching of the normal distribution, see our Web site at www.teachstats.org.

## Measures of Central Tendency

Elementary, middle school, and high school teachers are increasingly teaching students about measures of central tendency (Konold & Pollatsek, 2002). According to the National Council of Teachers of Mathematics (NCTM, 1989, 2000), instructors should expose elementary school students to informal conceptualizations of central tendency. By the time students complete high school, they should be adept at using measures of central tendency. Unfortunately, as many instructors can attest, some introductory statistics students have retained only the most basic information about central tendency (e.g., how to compute the mean) from their high school education.

There are numerous proposed explanations to account for the inability of some elementary and secondary school students to retain statistical knowledge regarding central tendency. For example, Quinn (1996) asserted that the teaching methods used by K-12 mathematics teachers might be partly to blame. He suggested that the current group of mathematics teachers tend to use the same approach that was used when they were taught statistics—the traditional computational method (e.g., cookbook approach). Indeed, Lappan and Zawojewski (1988) suggested that many junior high school students have only mastered the computational process and have not achieved the depth of knowledge necessary to understand the conditions under which this statistic is the appropriate choice. For example, Lappan and Zawojewski felt it was unlikely that these students understood the impact of outliers on the median and mean.

In addition, textbook authors tend to focus on computation versus comprehension. Interestingly, some authors have asserted that the existing conceptual material available in textbooks may not be completely accurate. For example, von Hippel (2005) described a common rule of thumb presented in statistics textbooks regarding the positioning of the mean, median, and mode in skewed distributions. He demonstrated that this heuristic was unreliable under a variety of conditions (e.g., discrete data).

Since the NCTM (2000) recommended that K-12 instructors teach central tendency measures and related concepts, there has been a critical examination of the methods used by statistics instructors. Konold and Pollatsek (2002) discussed the four primary means by which instructors introduce measures of central tendency. The fair share approach (e.g., how to divide fairly quantities of an item that someone previously distributed unequally) is common in elementary school. Instructors typically do not refer to the mean when presenting the solution to the fair share approach. The typical value approach is more common in secondary schools and suggests that the mean is a tool to find out how most people would respond in a particular situation.

According to Konold and Pollatsek (2002), during high school and into college, the data reduction strategy is prominent. In this approach, educators are introducing measures of central tendency as tools to reduce a set of numbers down to one value. However, Konold and Pollatsek recommended that instructors introduce measures of central tendency as the signal (i.e., stable feature) within the noise (i.e., variability) of individual data points. They asserted that this signal in noise approach is suitable for students age 8 and above. Implicit in this strategy is the notion that variability is equally as important as central tendency. Konold and Pollatsek reported that students taught using this perspective developed a richer, much more nuanced view of central tendency that is more adaptable to situations removed from the original learning environment.

Statistics educators have also been calling for increased use of activities, simulations, and other active learning approaches to facilitate student understanding of these concepts beyond mere computation. For example, Tyrrell (2003) described a novel way of illustrating income data—he linked an individual's height to their income level. Tyrrell represented someone making the average income as being almost 6 feet tall. Someone making the minimum wage was only 9 inches tall as opposed to the richest individuals who stood at over

230 feet tall. Tyrrell used a public UK income database and images available through Microsoft Excel to create this illustration. He reported that the technique proved useful when he discussed the impact of outliers on income data.

Bakker and Gravemeijer (2006) encouraged instructors to learn about the historical phenomenology of the mean and median prior to addressing the topic of teaching central tendency in class. The authors charted the evolution of the mean and median beginning as far back as 500 BC and proceeding up through modern times. Bakker and Gravemeijer then used those historical examples to design instructional activities. For example, they used stories from Thucydides' *History of the Peloponnesian War* (e.g., Homer's battleship crew estimates) to challenge students to develop and use intuitive measures of central tendency. As a result, students were able to walk in the footsteps of these historical figures to aid in their conceptualization of central tendency.

Bragger and Freeman (1999) used a discussion of research ethics to illustrate measures of central tendency. They presented students with five controversial psychology studies, such as Milgram's (1963) obedience study, and then asked them to rate the costs and benefits of each study on separate 100-point scales. Students then computed the average student opinion of the costs/benefits for each study and discussed the role of the Institutional Review Board in making those decisions. Following the completion of the exercise, students reported that the exercise was an effective means to help them understand central tendency and recommended that the instructor continue to use the exercise to teach statistics in the future.

Schumm et al. (2002) described how instructors could use publicly available data on three historical events—the 1986 space shuttle *Challenger* explosion, the attack at Pearl Harbor in WWII, and the sinking of the *Titanic* in 1912—to teach descriptive and inferential statistics. For the *Challenger* disaster, students could examine the temperature at the time of launch and the rate of O-ring failure from previous shuttle launches. Students could also examine the year of commission for U.S. Naval vessels destroyed at Pearl Harbor versus those sent away prior to December 7, 1941, to explore the revisionist hypothesis that the U.S. government had advance warning of the attack and only acted to get the newest ships out of danger (e.g., Stinnett, 2000). Finally, students could explore whether *Titanic* survivors and casualties varied as a function of gender and social class. According to Schumm et al., students rated the course very highly, appreciated the hands-on learning, and evidenced lowered anxiety because of these exercises. For additional exercises related to the teaching of central tendency, see our Web site at www.teachstats.org.

## Measures of Variability

Variation, or variability, is a critical component in statistics education (Ben-Zvi, 2004). Indeed, "if there were no variation in data sets, there would be no need for statistics" (Watson & Kelly, 2002, p. 1). Unfortunately, statistics courses tend to overemphasize central tendency and minimize the importance of variability (Reading & Shaughnessy, 2004). Indeed, Gould (2004) remarked, "The conceptualization of data as 'signal versus noise' . . . teaches students that the central tendency, however it's measured, is of primary importance and variability is simply a nuisance. A noisy one at that" (p. 7).

Despite the tendency for some instructors to emphasize measures of central tendency, variation is a fundamental component of several models of statistical thinking and reasoning (e.g., Moore, 1997; Pfannkuch & Wild, 2004). For example, Wild and Pfannkuch (1999) included consideration of variation as one of five types of statistical thinking. They introduced four aspects of variation: (a) noticing and acknowledging the omnipresence of variation; (b) measuring and modeling variation for the purposes of prediction, explanation, or control; (c) explaining and dealing with variation to examine its impact on design and sampling; and (d) investigative procedures to examine the properties of variation.

Reading and Reid (2005) mapped the above components of variation onto four organizing themes (e.g., exploratory data analysis, probability, sampling distributions, and inferential statistics) from an introductory statistics course and assessed the impact of Wild and Pfannkuch's (1999) variation-oriented approach on student learning through an examination of minute papers (i.e., short in-class papers that focused on the curriculum themes). Following the completion of the course, the vast majority of students reported that their understanding of variation had improved since the beginning of semester.

To facilitate student understanding of statistical concepts such as variation and measures of variability, statistics educators have encouraged instructors to move beyond teaching mere calculation and develop instructional strategies that promote the concept itself (Ballman, 1997). Unfortunately, the majority of instructors continue to emphasize computation over comprehension (delMas & Liu, 2005). However, there is some good news. The recent adoption of the National Council of Teachers of Mathematics (NCTM, 1989, 2000) standards has focused increased attention on teaching variability in primary and secondary schools. Instructors should consider applying many of these teaching strategies aimed at younger students to the discussion of variability in college classrooms.

For example, Weaver (1999) encouraged instructors to use medical growth charts to illustrate the concept of variability. Prior to introducing the growth chart, Weaver asked students to find out their own birth weights and then estimate the range of weights for newborns and 36-month-old children. He then asked whether newborns would have a larger distribution of weights than those of the older children. Weaver reported that most students felt that older children had the most variability. He then distributed a simple weight growth chart and discussed the fact the newborn weights are in fact more variable. Students rated the exercises very high with respect to purpose, presentation, and interest level.

Lillestøl (2000) had students examine data from an actual fraud case at a supermarket where a cashier deliberately entered the wrong amount into the register, had a manager unknowingly correct only a portion of it, which allowed the cashier to pocket the remaining amount. Lillestøl presented students with the actual data and had the class compute means and standard deviations for the 16 cashiers—including the criminal cashier. The class then had to estimate how much the criminal cashier stole from the supermarket. Given there was no way of determining the exact sum (i.e., the cashier was less than forthcoming about the amount she stole from the supermarket), the class used the normal distribution and standard deviations to plot probable amounts. In the actual case, the prosecutor examined the various estimates provided by Lillestøl and chose one that seemed most appropriate.

Several educators have presented examples in which the students were key components in the exercise. For example, Connor (2003) proposed that instructors use students' bodies and the physical layout of the classroom to illustrate variability. Students positioned themselves on a numbered line according to how they responded to an opinion question (e.g., how do you feel about chocolate?). Connor asserted that this exercise helped make the concept of variation more concrete, which would in turn improve student retention of the material. Similarly, Barbella and Siegel (2001) had students simulate standing in line at a bank teller to determine which line strategy (e.g., one line for all tellers vs. a line for each teller) would result in the shortest wait for customers. The instructor assigned each student a time to arrive and indicated how long the transaction should take to complete. Barbella and Siegel reported that students first focused on the mean time it took for them to receive service. However, with some prodding, the students began to appreciate the information they could glean from the standard deviation.

There are also numerous articles regarding the computation of the standard deviation. For example, Hurlburt (1993) developed eyeball-estimation techniques for standard deviation to enable students to get a general sense of their data prior to beginning calculations. He reasoned that such techniques: (a) allowed students to demonstrate they understand the statistic; (b) permitted students to explore the data prior to computation; (c) were inherently interesting; (d) were much faster than statistical computations; and (e) could enable a student to spot their mistakes. In addition, Primavera and Gorman (1994) presented a thorough analysis of the formula for computing variance and the standard deviation. Croucher (2004) and Petocz (2005) presented rules of thumb that students could use when determining whether their calculation of the standard deviation was accurate. Finally, Joarder and Latif (2006) discussed how one could compute variance without a calculator if the sample size was small (e.g., 3 or 4 data points) and observations were integers. For more exercises related to the teaching of variability, see our Web site at www.teachstats.org.

# Correlation

Correlation plays an important role in scientific inquiry (Goldstein & Strube, 1995). Consequently, it is critical for instructors to provide students with the necessary knowledge to understand how correlation coefficients measure the degree to which two variables are related. In addition, instructors need to review the situations when the correlation is not the appropriate statistical analysis, given the data and stated research goals. Unfortunately, correlation coefficients may be so popular precisely because:

[T]hey eliminate the need for having any sense of direction in the research. They allow the investigator as well as the statistical consultant, to avoid making any decisions about whether y depends on x or vice versa. The investigator is then liberated from doing any scientific thinking. (Freeman, 1977, p. 308)

As instructors, we need to ensure that students are engaging in statistical thinking and reasoning when considering the use of correlations to explore the relationship between two variables. Indeed, the NCTM (2000) recommended that instructors provide students with the tools to understand the relationship among variables, including scatterplots for younger students (e.g., grades 6–8) and correlation and regression for older students (e.g., grades 9–12).

Goldstein and Strube (1995) indicated that when they discuss correlations in class they review some of the issues that affect the size of the correlation (e.g., curvilinear relations, outliers). Chance and Rossman (2001) asserted that any lecture on correlation coefficients must include a discussion of the distinction between causation and association. Unfortunately, the scientific literature, news outlets, and the popular media are replete with examples of individuals, many of whom should know better, inferring causality when reporting correlations (Rigby, 2000). Consequently, statistics educators have encouraged instructors to develop "hands-on and minds-on" exercises that promote active learning to better assist students develop an understanding of correlation coefficients and the situations in which they are appropriate tools for data analysis (Goldstein & Strube, 1995, p. 205).

For example, Quinn (2006) proposed a correlation example that utilized several publicly available statistics associated with golfers on the Professional Golf Association (PGA) tour. He suggested that students examine the relationships between driving accuracy and driving distance, putts per round and putting average, and putts per round and greens in regulation. In addition, he recommended that students examine how some of the above factors affect adjusted scoring average. Finally, Quinn provided a personal account of how these variables played out on his recent trip to the greens.

Rajecki (2002) encouraged instructors to use personal advertisements in the local newspaper as a convenient means of illustrating correlation. Specifically, Rajecki had the class examine whether men and women prefer partners who are similar to their own age. The majority of students reported that the personal ads increased their understanding of the $r$ statistic. In addition, over 90% of the students were successful on the computational portion of the final exam. Dollinger (2004) used data generated by his students to illustrate the relationship between personality traits and behavior. Earlier in the semester, he had students complete a personality measure (Big Five Personality model) and a 15–20-item checklist of behaviors a student may engage in at some point in their college career (e.g., pulled an all-nighter to complete an assignment). When it came time to discuss correlations, Dollinger instructed students to form groups and predict the behavioral correlates of the personality traits. Following this discussion, he provided students with a correlation matrix based on the behavior checklist and the Big Five Personality measure. The class then examined the results, explored any erroneous predictions, and discussed anomalous findings. Students reported that they enjoyed the interactive aspect of the exercise and felt it enhanced their understanding of the material.

Several educators have reported examples that used the students themselves to illustrate correlations. For example, Connor (2003) created a human scatterplot to illustrate correlation and regression. She had students position themselves in a row according to their height and then move forward until they reach the point on the second variable that corresponded to their shoe size. Connor reported that she typically did this exercise separately for men and women. After the scatterplot was complete, the class discussed the results, noted any outliers, and formulated a regression line. Similarly, Sullivan (1993) reported forming a human scatterplot using measurements from students' own bodies—width of the shoulder and length of one's arm.

The teaching literature is also a good source for finding demonstrations or techniques designed to highlight a particular element critical for computing Pearson's $r$. For example, Peden (2001) described an activity in which he provided students with four data sets with identical correlation coefficients to illustrate the role scatterplots play in data analysis. Students entered the data into SPSS, calculated Pearson's $r$, generated scatterplots, and wrote a paragraph on each data set discussing the appropriateness of conducting Pearson's $r$. Although each of the four data sets had identical correlation coefficients, plotting the data revealed only one was appropriate for a correlation analysis—the others were curvilinear or contained influential outliers. Meyer and Shinar (1992) provided a detailed examination of the ability of individuals to estimate correlations from scatterplots. They concluded that perceptual cues (e.g., regression line) biased participant estimates. In addition, formal statistical training did not influence estimates. For more exercises related to the teaching of correlation, see our Web site at www.teachstats.org.

Statistics educators have also reported numerous exercises designed to illustrate mistakes or misconceptions associated with correlations. For example, Cramer and Jackson (2006) illustrated the association between the winner of the U.S. Presidential election and the home-game winner of the Washington Redskins professional football game just prior to the election. Prior to the 2004 election, there was a perfect correlation between these events. Whenever the Redskins won the home game prior to the election, the Presidential incumbent won. Cramer and Jackson hypothesized that this relationship would be an effective means to capture students' attention, discuss the distinction between causation and prediction, and illustrate the fact that some relationships merely exist—there is no explanation. Similarly, Matthews (2000) examined the folk tale that storks deliver babies to the expecting household. He found that, at least in Europe, there is a statistically significant relationship ($r = 0.62$) between the number of breeding pairs of white storks and the birth rate of children across 17 European countries. Interestingly, Wirth (2003) proposed that Matthews' finding might be due to the influence of extreme observations. Specifically, Poland and Turkey have very large stork populations. When he removed these outliers, the relationship was no longer significant, dashing the hopes and dreams of all fairy tale enthusiasts.

## Simple Linear Regression

Jones, Hagtvedt, and Jones (2004) remarked that simple linear regression is anything but simple to many introductory statistics students because they must grapple with several challenging concepts (e.g., slope, intercept, true residuals, observed residuals) in order to develop a sophisticated understanding of the procedure. To avoid overwhelming students early in the course, Chance and Rossman (2001) recommended that instructors introduce regression using descriptive methods to lessen the computational burden. Similarly, Stanton (2001) suggested that instructors begin the section on regression with a brief history of how Galton originally derived and applied linear regression to heredity.

To assist students with the computation of linear regression, Weldon (2000) recommended that instructors make use of computational shortcuts (e.g., standardized variables) to reduce student anxiety and increase comprehension. For example, Chance and Rossman (2001) suggested that instructors present the formulas for the least squares slope and intercept using means, standard deviations, and the correlation coefficient between the two variables. Gibson (2000) suggested that instructors introduce the "three Rs of regression" when discussing this analysis. The first R is the importance of *randomizing* the data collection process to ensure there is not any systematic bias that would confound the results. The second R refers to the importance of *replicating* the experiment to establish the reliability of the results. The third R is the importance of conducting a thorough analysis of the *residuals* to ensure that they are consistent with the model.

Lorenz (1987) stated that most introductory statistics courses and textbooks only included a cursory discussion of regression assumption violations—nonlinearity, heteroscedasticity, and outliers. Although these are important issues, Lorenz felt that educators needed to place greater importance on influential data points. He recommended that instructors utilize Cook's distance D (Cook, 1977; 1979) as a summary measure of influence. Lorenz asserted that Cook's distance is both conceptually and computationally easy to introduce and is available as part of SPSS and SAS. To illustrate the effect of influential data points, he recommended that instructors take advantage of Anscombe's (1973) classic set of four data sets that each produced the same correlation coefficient but very different scatterplots. In fact, two of these data sets illustrate an outlier and extreme data point. In his conclusion, Lorenz highlighted the importance of good examples and effective graphical displays for highlighting the process and issues surrounding simple linear regression.

Statistics educators have devised a number of exercises to illustrate linear regression. For example, Richardson and Gabrosek (2004) presented a classroom activity that examined the relationship among the frequency of letters in the English language, the percentage of Scrabble game tiles that corresponds to each letter, and the points that each Scrabble game tile is worth. To find the frequency of letters in the English language, students examined journal articles of 300 words to count the frequency of each letter of the alphabet. Students then constructed a scatterplot illustrating the relationship between the frequency of letters in the English language and the percentage of scrabble tiles for those corresponding letters. Richardson and Gabrosek suggested that instructors then have students construct a regression line and use this equation to predict the percentage of scrabble tiles associated with letters not mentioned in the previous lecture (e.g., L and W). Richardson, Gabrosek, Reischman, and Curtiss (2004) presented a similar exercise that examined the relationship between a letter's frequency in English text and International Morse Code units.

As discussed earlier, Connor (2003) proposed that instructors form a human scatterplot to illustrate the relationship between shoe size and height. She then had the class create a regression line by having students at relevant points on the scatterplot raise their hands. The class was then able to use the human scatterplot and regression line to predict the shoe size for an individual of a particular height. Connor suggested that instructors with small classes try this activity using different opinion questions (e.g., the number of hours per week they watch sports on television). Armero and Ferrándiz (2002) provided a simulation exercise using data collected by groups of students to illustrate the least squares approach to regression. du Feu (2001) provided the blueprints for a physical apparatus to illustrate a least squares regression line using a pin board, thumbtacks, a magnetized rubber band, and a metal rod for the regression line.

The literature on teaching regression includes several articles in which educators have created a means to illustrate a specific aspect of linear regression. For example, Barrett (2000) introduced a strategy for teaching students the nature of the coefficient of determination as it applies to correlation and regression (i.e., $r^2$ and $R^2$). Samaniego and Watnik (1997) presented an illustration of the separation principle using a Major League Baseball (MLB) example whereby the number of wins for MLB teams is regressed against team payrolls. Dunn (1989) encouraged instructors to emphasize graphical methods when teaching regression. He recommended this approach because: (a) recent developments in statistics have emphasized the role of graphics in data analysis; (b) the graphical approach is easier for students to comprehend; and (c) it empowers researchers to engage in interactive and exploratory data analysis. Marasinghe, Duckworth, and Shin (2004) presented a collection of highly interactive instructional modules to assist students and instructors discuss regression analysis. The teaching literature also offers methods to introduce alternatives to the popular OLS approach to regression. For example, Eisenhauer (2003) introduced regression through the origin (RTO) and discussed the situations in which this analysis is an appropriate alternative to the OLS approach. For more exercises related to the teaching of linear regression as well as regression to the mean, see our Web site at www.teachstats.org.

## Computer Applications

There is a growing body of literature demonstrating that technology (e.g., spreadsheets, Java applets, statistical software), if used appropriately, can enhance student understanding of statistical concepts and applications. For example, Morris, Joiner, and Scanlon (2002) examined what specific aspects of computer-based activities contributed to students' overall understanding of statistical concepts. They found that computer-based activities that involved the direct manipulation of data were most beneficial to students—particularly for measures of central tendency. Wender and Muehlboek (2003) demonstrated that animation diagrams were particularly useful for explaining abstract concepts. However, instructors need to be cautious when using technology to teach statistics. For example, Wender and Muehlboek suggested instructors not to use too many animated graphics during a lecture as they might become a distraction and might actually inhibit student performance.

Several comprehensive computer applications exist that are directly applicable to teaching descriptive statistics and bivariate distributions. For example, Fathom (Key Curriculum Press, 2007a), TinkerPlots (Key Curriculum Press, 2007b), FISH (Brooks & Raffle, 2005), and ESTAT (Britt et al., 2002) are all designed to assist students learn introductory statistics material. Morris (2001) described the computer application *Link*, which she created to assist students in their understanding of correlation. The application utilized data from actual research studies in psychology to address student misconceptions about correlations. To assess the effectiveness of *Link*, Morris compared pre- and post-test scores for those students exposed to *Link*, presented with paper-based instructional materials, and a control group. She found that the use of *Link* helped in students' conceptualization of correlation. The addition of the *Link* program also ameliorated misconceptions about correlations for some of the students.

Statistics educators have also encouraged instructors to use commercial data analysis programs such as Matlab, Minitab, SPSS, and

SYSTAT to illustrate introductory statistical concepts such as graphics and linear regression (Armero & Ferrándiz, 2002; Dunn, 2004; Hubbard, 1992; Laviolette, 1994). Many commercial applications include interactive visualization tools that enable students to see the shape and the impact of manipulating data for themselves. For example, Hammerman and Rubin (2004) explored the use of TinkerPlots (Key Curriculum Press, 2007b) in the classroom. They found that students gained a better understanding of statistical concepts such as variability. However, they cautioned that instructors needed to experience these programs as learners to prepare themselves for the types of questions they will no doubt receive as instructors. Bajgier, Atkinson, and Prybutok (1989) introduced LINEFIT, a software application that enabled students to fit a regression line to a data set displayed as a scatterplot. Students were also able to compare their regression line to that created by the program using OLS criterion. Bajgier et al. asserted that the LINEFIT program improved student learning and retention.

Statistics educators are also advocating the use of spreadsheets as a tool for teaching descriptive statistics, the normal distribution, correlations, and regression analyses (e.g., Forster, 2006, 2007a; Hall, 1995; Hubbard, 1992; Whigham, 1998; Wood & O'Hare, 1992). For example, Jones et al. (2004) developed VisualRegression, a Visual Basic for Applications (VBA) tool that runs within Microsoft Excel. The application enables students to enter relevant parameters (e.g., min/max sample size, standard deviation), examine the resultant scatterplot, and view the OLS regression line. In addition, the program can resample the data using the initial parameters each time the student presses a key. After using the tool, students responded that the application was a user-friendly, valuable teaching tool, which enabled them to understand OLS regression. Jones et al. commented that another benefit of using Microsoft Excel was the fact many students were already familiar with this program due to the ubiquity of the Microsoft Office suite.

Instructors can also turn to the Internet to find Java applets to illustrate a wide range of topics from graphing, correlation, and regression (Briggs & Sheu, 1998; Wender & Muehlboeck, 2003; West & Ogden, 1998) to trend analysis (Forster, 2007a, 2007b). Indeed, Forster (2006) reported that dynamic graphs created through Java applets were particularly useful for teaching least squares regression. Statistics educators have also created their own computer simulation programs using programming language (e.g., BASIC, FOR-TRAN, C++) to illustrate a statistical concept or application (e.g., Bradley, Hemstreet, & Ziegenhagen, 1992; Goldstein & Strube, 1995; Hassebrock & Snyder, 1997; Mitchell & Jolley, 1999). For more simulation exercises related to descriptive statistics, see our Web site at www.teachstats.org.

## Conclusion

The adoption of the National Council of Teachers of Mathematics (NCTM, 1989, 2000) *Principles and Standards for School Mathematics* has increased the likelihood that introductory statistics students at the college level are knowledgeable about proper graphing techniques, measures of central tendency, variability, the normal distribution, correlation, and regression. Unfortunately, there is variability in the level of instruction students receive during K-12 mathematics courses (Lappan & Zawojewski, 1988). Specifically, K-12 instructors may have focused solely on computation versus comprehension. Consequently, it is imperative that college introductory statistics instructors ensure that students receive exemplary education in these areas of statistics education.

There is a growing body of literature devoted to assisting instructors create the best possible classroom environment to ensure students have every opportunity to develop a thorough understanding of descriptive statistics and bivariate distributions. For example, numerous articles on teaching correlation and regression exist for instructors at all levels of academia. However, there is a paucity of material related to the teaching of the normal distribution. Curiously, there is a rich body of literature on statistical graphing, but much of it exists in the mathematics and statistics fields—very little has entered into more psychologically-orientated introductory statistics textbooks. Similarly, the concept of variability has been the subject of numerous articles and models on statistical literacy and reasoning. However, much of this material has not yet found its way into the psychological literature. Statistics textbook authors and instructors in the field of psychology need to reach out to other fields (e.g., statistics, sociology, education) to develop teaching material related to descriptive statistics and bivariate distributions.

## Note

1  Scholars have attributed this phrase to Walter Bagehot, Leonard Henry Courtney, Cornelia Augusta Hewitt Crosse, Benjamin Disraeli, Robert Giffen, William Abraham Hewitt, Henry Du Pré Labouchère, and Holloway Halstead Frost. A complete analysis can be found at www.york.ac.uk/depts/maths/histstat/lies.htm

# Chapter 6

## Teaching Hypothesis Testing

*Do not put your faith in what statistics say until you have carefully considered what they do not say. – William W. Watt*

Students in today's society are living in an era characterized as the "age of information" where an ability to conceptualize, manage, and evaluate statistical data is no longer a luxury (Higgins, 1999). They are likely to encounter scientific research findings through a wide array of print and online sources (Utts, 2003). In addition, an increasing number of media outlets are presenting sophisticated statistical results. Unfortunately, "most citizens, and even many reporters, do not have the knowledge required to read them critically" (Utts, 2003, p. 74).

Although the majority of students will never actually analyze their own data, instructors should be preparing students to read, understand, and analyze published research (Lauer et al., 2006; Utts, 2003). The Task Force on Undergraduate Psychology Major Competencies (APA, 2006), appointed by the Board of Educational Affairs (BEA) of the American Psychological Association, recommended that instructors work to ensure that students understand how to interpret statistical results, distinguish between statistical and practical significance, describe effect size and confidence intervals, and critically examine the conclusions presented in research studies.

Several researchers, using a variety of methods, found that the majority of surveyed departments required statistics as part of their psychology curriculum (e.g., Friedrich et al., 2000; Perlman & McCann, 1999). Unfortunately, when Friedrich et al. examined the content of statistics courses offered in psychology undergraduate programs, they found that the majority of courses continued to stress "traditional approaches" to data analysis—specifically the analysis of variance (ANOVA). Instructors often provided little more than cursory coverage to themes and techniques, such as confidence intervals, effect size, and meta-analyses, highlighted in the American Psychological Association's Task Force on Statistical Inference (Wilkinson & the Task Force on Statistical Inference, 1999).

Rossman and Chance (1999) created a "Top Ten" list to assist instructors teaching statistical inference. They encouraged instructors to present $p$-values versus rejection regions, promote the use of confidence intervals, and discuss the importance of non-inferential techniques. In addition, they recommended that instructors discuss the distinction among significant, insignificant, and no effect when examining research results. They also suggested that instructors remind students: (a) to consider elements of good experimental design and utilize effective visual displays; (b) to encourage students to present research findings in scientific and lay terms; and (c) to assist students explore the interconnections between statistical inference techniques and concepts.

Statistics educators have consistently encouraged instructors to utilize hands-on demonstrations to convey basic ideas of inference and use technology to explore the properties of inference. There are many books devoted, at least in part, to teaching statistics (e.g., Albert, 2003; Gelman & Nolan, 2002; Moore, 2001b; Ware & Brewer, 1999; Ware & Johnson, 2000). Unfortunately, many of these texts provide demonstrations related to inferential statistics in piecemeal format (i.e., a compilation of previously published demonstrations) without the range or depth of topics typically covered in a psychology statistics course. We have organized this chapter according to the commonest topics discussed within the inferential statistics portion of an introductory statistics psychology class.

# Samples, Sampling Distributions, and the Central Limit Theorem

The central limit theorem is the foundation for statistical inference (Pierce, 1983). Indeed, students who gain a thorough understanding of this principle can more readily grasp statistical sampling, hypothesis testing, and other core statistical concepts (Aberson, Berger, Healy, Kyle, & Romero, 2000; Dambolena, 1984). Statistics educators have examined the best strategies for teaching these topics for K-12 (e.g., Watson, 2004), undergraduate (e.g., Chance, delMas, & Garfield, 2004), and graduate students (e.g., Fecso et al., 1996). The National Council of Teachers of Mathematics' (NCTM) Principles and Standards for School Mathematics (2000) stated that as students move through the grade levels, they should be increasingly able to define a sample, collect data, and make reasonable inferences from the data. Specifically, the NCTM recommended that children in grades 3–5 should begin learning about statistical inference and students in grades 6–8 should address the ideas of sample selection. Eventually, students should leave high school as critical consumers of research data.

The process of educating students about the importance of scientific sampling does not end with high school. Indeed, most psychology undergraduates are required to take a course in statistics—the vast majority of which cover statistical sampling and the central limit theorem. Wybraniec and Wilmoth (1999) asserted that the ability to differentiate between population, sample and sampling distribution is a key step in developing an understanding of inferential statistics. Unfortunately, students do not always grasp the importance of sampling (Dimitrova, Persell, & Maisel, 1993; Zerbolio, 1989) and many have difficulty understanding the central limit theorem (Chance, delMas, & Garfield, 2004; Johnson, 1986).

Wybraniec and Wilmoth (1999) reviewed 25 introductory statistics textbooks from the social sciences, education, and statistics to examine how each author approached sampling. They found most texts introduced the topic with figures and explanatory text. Very few provided techniques that promoted active learning. Wybraniec and Wilmoth also found that only a paucity of research existed on techniques for teaching sampling techniques, distributions, and the central limit theorem within academic teaching journals. However, a more recent review of the literature revealed several demonstrations relevant to these topics. For example, Zerbolio (1989) described how he used imaginary marbles, chips, and bags to teach students about populations, samples, and sampling distributions. First, he depicted a raw score population as a bag of marbles. Instructors can also discuss probabilities and $z$-scores using the same initial bag of marbles. To create a sampling distribution, Zerbolio repeatedly scooped out a glass full of imaginary marbles from the fictitious bag of marbles. Next, he determined the mean number of marbles in each glass and noted this on a chip. Finally, he placed all of the chips in a new imaginary bag labeled the sampling distribution of the mean. The author described similar procedures for the distribution of the difference between independent means as well as correlated means. Zerbolio did not recommend the use of actual bags, chips, and marbles because their use would "imply a finite limit to theoretical populations" (p. 209).

Although several researchers have cited Zerbolio's (1989) demonstration as a useful technique, most have commented that students would benefit from a more hands-on approach (e.g., Dyck and Gee, 1998). Wybraniec and Wilmoth (1999) asserted that sampling demonstrations should have the following characteristics: (a) involve students in the process of sampling, calculating means, and verifying the sampling distribution; (b) take into consideration the needs of small and large classes; and (c) take place in a single class period.

For example, Singleton (1989) asked students in his research methods class a series of questions (e.g., number of siblings, gender) and then used the data set to illustrate the distinction between populations and samples, create a sampling distribution, and compute the standard error. He also used the data set to illustrate types of sampling strategies such as stratified random sampling. Dyck and Gee (1998) used M & Ms to illustrate the concept of the sampling distribution of the mean to students. Midway through a lecture on the sampling distribution of the mean, they gave one class the M & Ms demonstration, and the other class received the textbook demonstration. The authors asked students taking part in the M & Ms demonstration to open their candy packages, record the number of candy pieces of each color, and then consume the M & Ms. Dyck and Gee then randomly chose five students, asked each to reveal the number of blue M & Ms in their candy package, and instructed the class to compute the mean for the five students. They repeated this process 20 times and then had the students compute the mean of the sampling distribution of the mean. Accordingly, Dyck and Gee reported that the mean of the population was typically very similar to the mean of the sampling distribution of the mean. Following the exercise, students who experienced the M & Ms demonstration reported that they learned more, enjoyed the class more, and felt more positive about the demonstration than did students exposed to the textbook illustration.

Wybraniec and Wilmoth (1999) provided students with a bag of numbered wooden blocks, had each student draw samples from the bag, and calculate the mean and standard deviation of their sample. After all samples were drawn, the class computed the mean of the sampling distribution of the mean and discussed the importance of the central limit theorem. Similar demonstrations have appeared in the literature using slips of numbered paper in place of wooden blocks (e.g., Johnson, 1986; Potter, 1995). Although student test scores did not significantly change as a function of this exercise, Wybraniec and Wilmoth noted that students performed better in class and on the written portion of the exam—suggesting a more intuitive understanding of the material.

Ryan (2006) presented an exercise in which students constructed null-true and null-false sampling distributions by selecting samples (numbered slips of paper) from a series of bags containing populations in which the null hypothesis was either true or false. According to Ryan, previously reported exercises designed to facilitate student understanding of sampling distributions (e.g., Dyck & Gee, 1998; Johnson, 1986) did not provide students the opportunity to create null-true and null-false sampling distributions. He reasoned that students given the opportunity to create both sampling distributions would better understand the distinction between a distribution of scores and a distribution of sample means. Following the exercise, the majority of Ryan's students reported that they understood sampling distributions better because of their participation in the exercise. Furthermore, students who took part in the exercise achieved higher exam scores than students in the control condition. For more exercises related to the teaching of samples, sampling distributions, and the central limit theorem, see our Web site at www.teachstats.org.

## Confidence Intervals

Confidence intervals have become increasingly popular as criticism regarding null hypothesis significance testing (NHST) has grown.

Callahan and Reio (2006) stated that confidence intervals "offer researchers and laypersons a rich source of information in addition to the simple yes/no dichotomy of NHST" (p. 166). Wilkinson et al. (1999) recommended that researchers present effect sizes and confidence intervals when reporting research results in psychology journals.

However, Callahan and Reio (2006) asserted that simply encouraging researchers to use confidence intervals when presenting results was not enough to create enduring change. Instead, they stated that statistics instruction needed to involve teachers who are committed to presenting this material in a coherent and unbiased fashion. Textbook authors also need to explain the use and misuse of null hypothesis significance testing, effect sizes, and confidence intervals. Unfortunately, the "authors of introductory statistics textbooks have largely ignored the 1999 Task Force report and the 2001 APA *Publication Manual* recommendations regarding confidence intervals" (Kirk, 2007, p. 35).

The concept of confidence intervals is often difficult for students to understand. According to Robinson-Cox (1999), the root of student difficulties lies in the fact that confidence intervals address our "confidence in a process rather than the interval produced" (p. 81). Consequently, students need engaging examples and activities to help them understand what it means to have confidence in a process. To help students understand this concept, Gelman and Glickman (2000) suggested that instructors ask students at the beginning of class to write their weight on a slip of paper. After all of the papers have been collected, each student selects four slips at random and computes a 90% confidence interval for the average weight of all students in the class. The instructor presents the resultant confidence intervals on the board as horizontal segments with a vertical line representing the average weight of the class (of course, asking for a student's height to the nearest tenth of an inch might be less threatening). Anderson-Cook (1999) used a similar approach for illustrating confidence intervals by having students provide subjective, followed by objective, confidence intervals in response to various demographic questions (e.g., percentage of the U.S. population in cities). She reported that students responded positively to the demonstration and were better able to verbalize these concepts on the exam.

To achieve a more interactive version of this exercise, Gelman and Glickman (2000) adapted a demonstration first reported by Johnson (1997), in which students play volleyball with an inflatable globe in an attempt to estimate the proportion of the earth covered by water.

However, for this version, the teacher instructs students to toss the ball around, strike the globe with their index finger, and shout "water!" or "land!" depending on where they struck the globe. Students then used the results to construct a 90% confidence interval for the proportion. Gelman and Glickman encouraged instructors to discuss how to interpret the interval, the role of sampling variability in the results, possible biases in the sampling procedure, and the applicability of this procedure to other practical situations.

Robinson-Cox (1999) suggested that instructors take a chalkboard covered with a film of chalk dust and have students toss tennis balls at a vertical line (i.e., population mean) on the board. After all the tosses have been made (e.g., five), each student creates an interval by extending a 15 or 20 cm line to the left and right of the center of the mark created by each tennis ball. According to Robinson-Cox, instructors can use this exercise to stimulate a discussion of the means by which the class could improve the accuracy of the procedure (e.g., automating the process, reducing the distance to the board, extending the interval width).

Richardson and Haller (2003) reported a similar interactive activity to illustrate the properties and construction of confidence intervals using Hersheys Kisses. For this activity, the instructor divides students into groups, hands them 10 Hershey Kisses in a plastic cup, and assigns the group several tasks. Each group tosses (i.e., spills) the cup of kisses 5 times onto a table and records the number of chocolate kisses that land on the base (i.e., the flat portion of the kiss). Following the end of the exercise, each group constructs a 90% confidence interval for the proportion of base landings from all five tosses. The instructor then collects the class set of confidence intervals and displays the data on an overhead transparency with the baseline of 35% (based on previous data) as the comparison line. Richardson and Haller recommended that instructors ask the class to compute 80% and 99% confidence intervals for the proportion of base landings and write statements addressing the impact of raising or lowering the confidence levels.

## Introduction to Null Hypothesis Testing

An introductory statistics course would not be complete without an introduction to hypothesis testing. Indeed, Maret and Ziemba (1997) asserted that "early exposure to statistical hypothesis testing as a rigorous method of comparing experimental results to predictions helps students understand the role of statistics in science" (p. 285). The introduction of hypothesis testing in a statistics course provides a useful gateway for the discussion of more sophisticated concepts in inferential statistics. When presented discretely, without proper context, advanced concepts such as $p$-values, effect size, power, and error rates, are difficult for student to master and apply (Seier & Robe, 2002). Consequently, researchers have recommended that educators introduce a real-world example or research question to frame subsequent discussions of hypothesis testing and related advanced topics in inferential statistics (Seier & Robe, 2002). Not only can this approach highlight the interrelatedness of these concepts, it may also serve to reduce anxiety and facilitate active learning (Goernert, 1995; Wiseman, 2004).

For example, Goernert (1995) motivated student interest in hypothesis testing by making use of a popular television advertisement where consumers took part in a blind taste test. The advertisement reported the percentage of individuals who chose a particular product —but not the sample size. Goernert had students conduct significance tests using several potential sample sizes (e.g., 100, 1000) to demonstrate the role of sample size in hypothesis testing. Students reported that the exercise enhanced their understanding of this concept and demonstrated the relevance and application of statistical procedures to everyday issues. Magel (1998) presented two class exercises using different brands of chocolate chip cookies to illustrate hypothesis testing. In the first exercise, students counted the number of chocolate chips in each cookie to determine if the amount of chocolate chips varied as a function of brand. In the second exercise, students examined whether there were any taste differences between the brands of cookies. Following each exercise, students analyzed their results using a computer software package and then answered questions (e.g., regarding assumptions, statistical results) on accompanying worksheets. Magel reported that students enjoyed the activities, practiced statistical analyses on the computer, and interpreted their results correctly.

Nordmoe (2004) described how instructors could utilize material from Milne's (1928) *The House at Pooh Corner* to create a classroom discussion of hypothesis testing, significance, and $p$-values. Specifically, he described passages from the book where Pooh devises an experiment to examine which fir cones will travel the fastest down a river. Nordmoe took the trial data described in the book, developed null and alternative hypotheses, examined the data using a one-sample $z$-test, and discussed some of the data limitations.

In another creative use of literature to illustrate hypothesis testing, Revak and Porter (2001) adapted an exercise originally designed by Simons and Irwin (Bolt, 1996) to demonstrate the effect imagery has on memory. In the Revak and Porter version, the instructor assigned students to rate a series of vivid sentences (e.g., The lanky leprechaun wore lavender leotards) on: (a) how easily they can pronounce these passages to themselves or (b) how easily they can form a vivid mental image of the portrayed event. Students were blind to the conditions. After the instructor read aloud a list of 20 sentences, students answered a series of questions designed to assess memory (e.g., Who wore lavender leotards?), calculated relevant statistics, determined whether there were significant differences, and displayed the data accordingly. Revak and Porter encouraged instructors to build in time for class discussion of the experimental design, sampling techniques, and whether statistical assumptions were met for this sample.

Hong and O'Neil (1992) conducted a mental model analysis for hypothesis testing to determine the most effective way to teach this concept. They found that students performed better on a subsequent skills test when given conceptual material prior to procedural instruction rather than a combined approach. Furthermore, participants performed better and developed fewer misconceptions if the researchers utilized a diagrammatic presentational style versus a descriptive presentational style. In other words, students did best when the instructor discussed conceptual and procedural material separately using a visual presentational style. For example, Loosen (1997) used a frame containing wooden curves, each on separate axes, to represent the distributions associated with the null hypothesis, alternative hypothesis, and the true state of reality. Additionally, he used vertical rods to define specific rejection region(s) and convey the interconnectedness of these concepts. Instructors wedded to Microsoft PowerPoint may feel uncomfortable using a physical apparatus to teach statistics. However, Loosen asserted that his device is more flexible, easier to use, and more visually appealing than comparable computer programs. He also reported that students were more enthusiastic, motivated, and developed a greater understanding of the basic concepts when this apparatus was utilized. For more exercises related to introducing the null hypothesis, see our Web site at www.teachstats.org.

# Additional Introduction to Hypothesis Testing Concepts

Many of the statistical concepts associated with inferential statistics are difficult for some students to understand (Looney, 2002). Although the vast majority of introductory statistics textbook authors discuss the concept of power, effect sizes, and Type I and II errors, the depth of coverage varies. Textbooks designed for introductory classes tend to provide a more cursory discussion (e.g., Spatz, 2008) whereas more advanced textbooks offer theory and computational guidance (e.g., Howell, 2007). Consequently, difficulties regarding power, effect size, and Type I and Type II error are some of the most frequent issues that instructors and statistical consultants hear about from students and researchers in the social sciences (Kraemer, 1985; Looney, 2002). The reason for these queries, according to Kraemer, is quite simple—students and researchers have received too little training. For example, Friedrich et al. (2000) found that the majority of instructors surveyed reported spending only an hour or less of class time on power analysis and effect size.

## Power

The reason why so little time is devoted to a discussion of more advanced inferential concepts, such as power, lies in the time constraints inherent in an introductory statistics course. Kraemer (1985) asserted that, "it is difficult enough to introduce researchers to the uses of the normal, central-$t$, $\chi^2$, and $F$-distributions essential to use of standard statistical tests, much less those of noncentral distributions necessary to power calculations" (p. 173). Her solution to this issue was to take the multiple power tables presented in Cohen (1988) and distill them into one multiuse table. She suggested instructors teach power: (a) by introducing the general concept; (b) by presenting students with the single power table; and (c) by reinforcing the concept and use of the table through exercises and problem sets.

Additional shortcuts to the computation of power are available for use in the classroom. For example, Cohen (1992) offered some simple rules of thumb for power analyses and provided a table detailing the sample sizes needed to achieve sufficient power (e.g., 80%) for small, medium, and large effects sizes. Dunlap and Myers (1997) provided additional shortcuts for simple correlations, tests of the difference between two group means, and chi-square analyses for $2 \times 2$ contingency tables. However, given the difficulties associated with hand calculations, Gatti and Harwell (1998) argued that, "students who are learning to estimate power are better served by using computer software designed for this task than by the more traditional Pearson and Hartley power charts" (para 24). Pittenger (2001) created a free program, Power Calculator, which instructors and students can use to conduct power analyses on a host of statistical tests and procedures (e.g., correlation, multiple regression, chi-square, two-sample independent groups $t$ ratio, ANOVA). The program will also calculate critical values for various inferential statistics, generate random numbers, convert inferential statistics into indices for use with meta-analysis, and conduct Monte Carlo studies of the ANOVA.

Regardless of the means by which researchers conduct power analyses, it is imperative that instructors convey that such calculations should take place prior to data collection for planning purposes (Wilkinson et al., 1999). Unfortunately, "there is a large, current literature that advocates the inappropriate use of post-experiment power calculations as a guide to interpreting tests with statistically nonsignificant results" (Hoenig & Heisey, 2001, p. 19). The authors asserted that the inappropriate use of these calculations ignores several major shortcomings associated with the use of power analyses as data analytic tools (e.g., observed power, detectable effect size). Hoenig and Heisey called for introductory statistics instructors to reduce this confusion by emphasizing the appropriateness of power analyses in the planning stage, encouraging the use of confidence intervals, and deemphasizing the importance of hypothesis testing.

Wiseman (2004) presented an exercise to assist instructors when conveying the interrelationships that exist among level of significance, sample size, and power. He took advantage of a common advertising technique whereby one product brand asserts superiority over another competing brand (e.g., Pepsi vs. Coke). The major networks have research and documentation standards that advertisers must meet prior to the broadcast of any commercial that makes superiority claims. For example, NBC requires that for comparisons between two products there needs to be a minimum of 300 subjects tested and that a statistically significant proportion (95% confidence level) of the sample must prefer the advertised product (NBC, 2007). Wiseman provided students with the basics of these standards and instructed students to determine the sample size needed to find significant differences among hypothetical product comparisons, the likelihood a researcher could substantiate superiority claims given various sample sizes and true percentage differences, and the costs that would be incurred by the advertising company to achieve these differences.

In a more hands-on demonstration of power, Gelman and Glickman (2000) had two student volunteers each throw 20 tennis ball into a trash can to determine which student is the better shooter. The authors reported that the difference between the shot percentages was typically not significant. However, according to Gelman and Glickman, the lack of significance provided the ideal opportunity to introduce the notion of statistical power (i.e., how many tries are necessary to get significance). After the class completes the requisite power calculations, the instructor may open up the discussion to explore the implications of making important conclusions based on small sample sizes (e.g., medical research) or large sample sizes (e.g., census data).

Nguyen (2005) used chicken soup to demonstrate the role of sample size when determining the accuracy of a public opinion poll or survey. First, he provided students with several public opinion polls, with random samples between 1,000–1,500 participants, and then asked the extent to which the students believed the polls were accurate representations of the population (e.g., U.S. adult population, voters in a city). As expected, most students indicated that the sample size was too small—particularly when examining a large population. Next, he assigned students to cook chicken soup for varying numbers of guests (e.g., 4, 14, 40) using one of three different size pots (e.g., small, large, very large). Following the demonstration, he found that students accurately concluded that regardless of the amount of soup produced, a tablespoon of soup, if the cook properly stirred the pot, would be a sufficient means to test the quality of the soup. In other words, the absolute sample size (i.e., tablespoon of soup) is more important for determining the accuracy of a poll than relative sample size (i.e., the ratio between the teaspoon of soup and the amount of soup in the pot).

## Effect sizes

The lack of instructional coverage devoted to effect sizes (Friedrich et al., 2000) is surprising given the increased popularity of meta-analyses, for which effect sizes form the foundation (Callahan &

Reio, 2006; McGrath & Meyer, 2006). In addition, researchers have called for the use of effect sizes to differentiate between statistical, practical, and clinical significance (e.g., Thompson, 2002a).

Cohen's (1988) operationalization of small, medium, and large effect sizes has made it much easier for researchers to use effect size to compute power and compare obtained results to previous findings. Unfortunately, instructors may be simply presenting students with Cohen's basic rules of thumb and ignoring the complexity underlying the use of effect sizes (Thompson, 2002b). The rigid use of Cohen's effect size benchmarks is problematic because the most effective means to understand effect sizes is within the context of underlying theory, previous research findings, and the current sample (Callahan & Reio, 2006; Thompson, 2002b). In addition, the choice of an effect size index (e.g., Cohen's $d$ or Hedge's $g$) is a critical decision given the fact that each statistic is differentially sensitive to the base rate or variance of the relevant variables (McGrath & Meyer, 2006). Indeed, Kirk (2005) recently published a list of 72 measures of effect magnitude. Clearly, students need to understand the complexity of effect sizes; they "cannot be understood in a vacuum" (McGrath & Meyer, 2006, p. 399).

## Type I and Type II errors

Like many of the concepts associated with hypothesis testing, Type I and Type II errors are difficult for many non-statisticians to grasp (Hauptman, 2004). Consequently, several statistics educators have proposed the use of analogies to assist student understanding of these concepts. For example, Looney (2002) encouraged instructors to use hypothetical student test scores plotted on a continuum from strong to weak knowledge about the subject matter. By manipulating a pass/fail cutoff (e.g., 70/100), the instructor is able to demonstrate the relationship between alpha levels and the likelihood of a Type I or Type II error.

In our classes, we use a courtroom analogy similar to that provided by Looney (2002) in which the jury is charged with rendering a guilty or non-guilty verdict for a capital crime based on the evidence provided. We often use the "ripped from the headlines" approach popularized on the long-running NBC series *Law and Order* to find criminal examples with which students can readily identify during our discussion. In some situations, the jury is given very stringent instructions for determining guilt or innocence (e.g., only convict if an extremely reliable eyewitness was present at the crime). In other scenarios, the judge provides the jury with a less stringent set of instructions (e.g., convict if the evidence is even marginally convincing). By manipulating the judge's instructions to the jury, students are able to get a better understanding of the interconnectedness of Type I and Type II error rates.

# Analysis of Variance

A sizable body of literature exists devoted to the teaching of analysis of variance (ANOVA) in introductory statistics. Educators have developed this material with the goal of making ANOVA understandable to introductory students through the use of real-world analogies and active learning exercises (e.g., Johnson, 1989; Rajecki, 2002; Refinetti, 1996). However, a handful of articles (e.g., Eisenhauer, 2006; Saville & Wood, 1986) found primarily in mathematics and statistics journals have introduced teaching strategies to illustrate the relationship between multiple regression and ANOVA—establishing analysis of variance as a part of the general linear model (Keith, 2006). Unfortunately, according to Cobb (1984), "this comparatively transparent approach seems too abstract for many biologists and social scientists who need to learn ANOVA but whose mathematical background does not go much beyond high-school algebra" (p. 120). Indeed, Friedrich et al. (2000) found that the majority of surveyed introductory statistics instructors in psychology did not devote any class time to discuss the relationship between ANOVA and regression. Nonetheless, the vast majority of advanced statistics instructors reported spending at least an hour of class discussion to the general linear model. In time, this approach may trickle down to introductory level courses.

## Introduction to ANOVA

Several statistics educators have proposed methods to introduce students to the analysis of variance. For example, Johnson (1989) described a technique to increase student understanding of between- and within-groups variance for a one-way ANOVA. Following a standard introduction to the analysis of variance, Johnson presented students with a series of four data sets. Each data set was composed of small numbers (e.g., 1, 2, 3). By manipulating the data within each hypothetical data set, Johnson illustrated between- and within-groups variability as well as the effect of these concepts on the $F$ ratio. Students reported that the instructor should use the technique again in future classes. However, students also reported that they "had doubts as to whether their understanding of ANOVA would ever be 'considerable'" (p. 68). Although Johnson dismissed these student concerns, they are consistent with arguments stating that such disconnected presentations of data can lead to faulty reasoning (e.g., Gal, 2004; Pfannkuch & Wild, 2004).

Rajecki (2002) proposed that instructors use personal advertisements as a convenient sample to examine the relationship among a variety of variables using statistical analyses. Specifically, Rajecki had the class examine whether men and women, from different age-based cohorts (e.g., 20s, 30s), have different age preferences in their prospective partners. Previous research (Rasmussen et al., 1998) had suggested that men preferred younger partners, whereas women preferred older partners. However, these differences disappeared as individuals aged resulting in both sexes seeking younger companions. Rajecki used subjective (e.g., student opinion questionnaires) and objective measures (e.g., exam scores) to assess whether this exercise enhanced students' understanding of ANOVA. The majority of students reported that the personal ads were interesting subject matter (88%) and increased their understanding of the $F$ statistic (63%). In addition, over 90% of the students were successful on the computational portion of the final exam. Rajecki suggested that instructors should consider having students examine additional aspects of personal ads (e.g., appearance, personality) for use in a classroom exercise.

## Violating ANOVA assumptions

In addition to presenting the mechanics of the analysis of variance, instructors have a responsibility to describe the conditions under which the use of the analysis of variance is appropriate. Unfortunately, according to Buck (1990), there was little coverage of this topic in statistics textbooks. A decade later, Friedrich et al. (2000) reported that the majority of surveyed instructors devoted only an hour or less to this issue. Nonetheless, a growing number of statistics educators have proposed exercises to illustrate the consequences of violating the assumptions necessary for conducting an analysis of variance. For example, Refinetti (1996) presented a demonstration designed to illustrate the effect of non-normality and heterogeneity of variance on the analysis of variance. At the heart of the demonstration was a software program, developed by Refinetti, which would conduct 1,000 ANOVAs on various hypothetical data sets. Each data set consisted of three groups with 10 data points per group. Data sets varied in the extent to which they violated the assumption of normality and heterogeneity of variance. As expected, the ANOVA is generally robust enough to handle violations of normality and heterogeneity of variance when groups have equal numbers of participants. However, groups with unequal numbers of participants resulted in a significant number of Type I errors. Rheinheimer and Penfield (2001) obtained similar results when they examined the ability of the analysis of covariance to handle non-normality and heterogeneity of variance. Refinetti suggested that working firsthand with the data better enabled students to understand the impact of assumption violations on the analysis of variance.

## Factorial ANOVA

The factorial ANOVA has become a fixture in introductory statistics courses in the behavioral and social sciences. Indeed, the majority of introductory statistics textbooks include a chapter on factorial ANOVA (see online Appendix B at www.teachstats.org). According to Friedrich et al. (2000), most statistics instructors devoted at least one hour of instruction time to factorial between-subjects ANOVA designs. In addition, statistics educators have introduced several teaching strategies and illustrations to facilitate student understanding of the factorial ANOVA.

For example, Cohen (2002) presented an alternative formula for calculating the factorial ANOVA. In contrast to the traditional raw score method, which relied on individual scores, his approach only required the mean, standard deviation, and cell size. Cohen asserted that his formula was easier for students to calculate, provided instructors with an excellent teaching tool, and enabled students to determine effect sizes when reading published research. To produce data for use in a factorial design, Simonite (2000) developed an exercise for which data collection was quick, real, and the resultant outcome was interesting to students. Participants completed two quizzes, each consisting of 20 questions, about pop music in the 1960s and 1990s. She found a significant interaction between participant age (student vs. staff) and music era (1960s vs. 1990s). She felt that students found the task entertaining and educational. Indeed, one student responded, "It was good to take part rather than just being given results" (p. 60).

Developing an understanding of main effects and interactions is an integral part of becoming an educated research consumer. Unfortunately, students sometimes have difficulty grasping the concept of an interaction. Sturm-Beiss (2005) introduced a Java applet to assist students visualize a two-way ANOVA. The applet enabled students to explore the features of a factorial ANOVA by manipulating parameter values and viewing the impact of these changes on significance levels for main effects and interactions. Richardson and Segal (1998) created an interactive computer program to help students understand factorial ANOVAs. For each problem, the program provided students with a summary table, factorial matrix, and graphs. In addition, students had the option of running the program in the Demo (examples of several factorial ANOVAs), Quiz Me (students are quizzed on the analysis), or What If (witness the cumulative impact of changes to the design or data) modes. Strube and Goldstein (1995) introduced a similar interactive program, written in QuickBASIC, which allowed students to become familiar with the differences between main effects and interactions.

## General linear model

Most basic statistics textbooks introduce the ANOVA as an extension of the $t$-test (Eisenhauer, 2006). However, few introductory statistics textbooks designed for psychology students conceptually tie the ANOVA to regression. Three approaches for introducing students to the general linear model appear in the literature. Some statistics educators suggest teaching students the mathematical theory underlying the general linear model (e.g., Saville and Wood, 1986). Other researchers advocate primarily for the use of applied examples to illustrate the connections between regression and ANOVA (e.g., Eisenhauer, 2006). Still other researchers, mindful of the diverse mathematical background of students, but driven to provide a theoretical foundation, encourage instructors to find an approach that bridges theory with application (e.g., Cobb, 1984; Gaito & Shermer, 1985). For additional discussion on teaching the general linear model, see our Web site at www.teachstats.org.

# The Debate Surrounding Null Hypothesis Significance Testing

Although null hypothesis significance testing (NHST) has been dominant in psychology for well over 70 years, there has been continuing discussion as to the logic and usefulness of this approach (e.g., Cohen, 1994; Falk, 1986; Federer, 1978; Loftus, 1993). Nickerson (2000) captured much of this debate in his excellent historical review of the topic. He described the major positions in the debate, discussed common misconceptions, and provided alternative procedures and supplements to NHST.

According to Schmidt (1996), it is apparent that researchers have begun to shift away from NHST and towards newer quantitative methods such as casual modeling, confirmatory factor analysis, and meta-analysis. However, Schmidt noted, "Our younger generations of upcoming researchers are still being inculcated with the old, discredited methods of reliance on statistical significance testing" (pp. 127–128). Indeed, Friedrich et al. (2000) found instructors still teaching traditional inferential statistics at the expense of newer quantitative methods. In addition, Kirk (2007) noted that only 25% of the introductory statistics books he sampled mentioned the NHST controversy. Consequently, the call for change at the instructional level has become more vocal (e.g., Estes, 1997; Falk, 1986; Schmidt, 1996; Taylor & Muncer, 2000).

# Nonparametric Statistics

Most statisticians would point to the late 1930s and 1940s as the formative years for the development of nonparametric statistics (Noether, 1984). During that time, Hotelling and Pabst (1936) introduced rank correlation, Wolfowitz (1942) coined the term nonparametric statistics, and Scheffé (1943) proposed the theoretical framework and submitted a list of statistical procedures for consideration as nonparametrics. Although the field of nonparametric statistics had grown considerably, many still viewed the procedures as "synonymous with shortcut, rough-and-ready, and quick-and-dirty methods" (Noether, 1984, p. 176). Psychology has been particularly slow to accept nonparametric measures despite the fact that psychological data are often nominal or ordinal in nature (Buckalew,

1983). Indeed, Siegel remarked that nonparametric statistics were "uniquely suited to the data of the behavioral sciences" (Siegel and Castellan, 1988, p. xv).

Recently, however, a growing number of statisticians have embraced nonparametric statistics, introductory textbooks traditionally include a chapter on the field, and 50% of surveyed psychology statistics instructors reported spending two or more hours lecturing on the chi-square test (Friedrich et al., 2000; Noether, 1984). In addition, Coakley (1996) provided a nonparametrics course template, including an annotated bibliography, course schedule, list of projects, and Minitab macros. Although these developments are noteworthy, there still exists the perception that nonparametric techniques are "inferior alternatives to more desirable tests" (Buckalew, 1983, p. 448). For example, the majority of text authors place the nonparametric chapter at the end of the book, fail to integrate nonparametric statistics with earlier material, and focus on only a few well-known tests used for hypothesis testing (Buckalew, 1983; Noether, 1984). Similarly, the majority of surveyed psychology statistics instructors spend less than an hour of instructional time on nonparametric tests other than the chi-square such as the Mann-Whitney U test (Friedrich et al., 2000). Buckalew asserted that "Modern psychology, in its push for enhanced respectability and reliance on tradition, has continued viewing as inferior the use and efficacy of nonparametric treatments" (p. 447).

Despite the reluctance of modern psychology to embrace nonparametric statistics, statistics educators have provided instructors with lecture suggestions and materials. For example, Katz and Tomazic (1993) identified several primary and supplemental textbooks, conceptual and applied journal articles, and computerized statistical packages (e.g., SPSS) that instructors can use to augment their discussion of nonparametric statistics. The best examples are those that simultaneously tap into previously learned, discipline-specific knowledge and promote active learning. For example, Kneidel (1996) introduced a chi-square demonstration for biology students that used dihybrid corn that scientists had bred to produce different yields (e.g., purple smooth, purple wrinkled). By coupling previously learned material (e.g., Mendelian genetics) with good visual stimuli (e.g., frequency distributions), Kneidel was able to introduce the chi-square table, discuss $p$-values, and describe Type I and Type II errors.

Allen (1981) proposed that instructors use Weber's Law, a concept that ideally should be familiar to psychology students, to introduce the Pearson $\chi^2$ statistic for testing goodness-of-fit. He encouraged instructors to begin discussion by describing absolute thresholds and difference thresholds. Next, to set the stage for the Pearson $\chi^2$ statistic, he recommended that instructors introduce Weber's Law expressed as a ratio, and provide an example for students to complete. Allen's students readily followed the progression from difference thresholds, which measure differences in magnitude, to the Pearson $\chi^2$ statistic, which detects the difference between observed and expected event frequencies. The introduction of each respective formula also enabled students to see the similarities and differences between the two concepts. Allen found that students exposed to the Weber's Law ratio were more apt to remember the chi-square formula.

White (2001) presented students with a sports-related exercise to demonstrate the chi-square test of independence. He used a hypothetical basketball team's win/loss record to demonstrate if the team's performance was independent of whether it played at home or on the road. In addition, by manipulating the number of games played, White demonstrated the impact that a larger sample would have on the significance levels. However, according to Suich and Turek (2003), instructors need to go beyond simple coverage of the chi-square test of independence and discuss the distinction between the concepts of independence and prediction. They found that surveyed students were confused as to the meaning of independence between categorical variables. Suich and Turek attributed much of this confusion to a "misunderstanding between the concepts of independence and predictive association" (p. 88) and recommended that instructors introduce proportional reduction in error measures (PRE) such as the Goodman-Kruskal gamma to clarify this distinction (Suich & Turek, 1989; Turek & Suich, 1999).

Despite the inclusion of an increasingly wide variety of nonparametric statistics in textbooks, there is still a paucity of research devoted to the teaching of nonparametric statistics other than the chi-square statistic. For example, psychology instructors interested in developing methods to teach the Mann-Whitney $U$ and/or Kolmogrov-Smirnov tests need to look to the field of quantitative geology to find teaching suggestions. Kemmerly (1990) introduced geology students to these statistical procedures by describing the two procedures and applying them to various geological samples. Next his students selected a published study that employed these techniques. Students then answered a series of questions regarding the study methodology, sampling techniques, assumptions, reasons the author chose a nonparametric statistic, and the conclusions that the author drew from the results. Although Kemmerly's article is specific to geology, instructors can apply the above methods to the teaching of introductory statistics for psychology students.

## Computer Applications

Instructors have numerous computer applications at their disposal to augment the teaching of hypothesis testing within the classroom or as a student supplement. For example, Lee (1999) developed the PACE (Projects-Activities-Cooperative Learning-Exercises) approach to statistical education that provided a framework for incorporating active learning projects and computer exercises (e.g., Minitab, SPSS) into introductory statistics courses. However, statistics educators have begun to recognize that the mere use of computers in the classroom is not sufficient to enhance student comprehension or statistical reasoning. For example, Meletiou-Mavrotheris, Lee, and Fouladi (2007) reported that students exposed to the PACE method were more motivated, had more exposure to the practical applications of statistics, and reported appreciating statistics more than those students who were exposed to a traditional class environment. Unfortunately, the researchers also found that students in the PACE environment were not significantly different from their traditional counterparts with respect to their understanding of statistical concepts. According to Meletiou-Mavrotheris et al., these results suggest that the mere introduction of computers into the classroom may not be "effective in building student intuitions and fundamental statistical ideas such as sampling distributions and statistical inference" (p. 77). However, the use of computer applications in the teaching of statistics is not a bankrupt approach. Researchers are constantly developing new programs that emphasize active student learning over rote calculations.

For example, Fathom (Key Curriculum Press, 2007a) is a dynamic classroom statistics package that students can use to explore simulations, create sampling distributions, conduct data analyses, and display the results. Meletiou-Mavrotheris (2003) conducted an in-depth qualitative analysis of five introductory statistics students using this program to explore whether the use of Fathom in the classroom encouraged the construction of a coherent mental model of key concepts related to statistical inference (e.g., sampling distributions). Dynamic programs such as Fathom differ from traditional data analysis packages (e.g., Minitab, SPSS) by virtue of the fact that they promote statistical learning versus simply enabling students to conduct statistical analyses. Meletiou-Mavrotheris suggested that the use of Fathom enabled her students to develop a "fairly coherent mental model" of statistical inference concepts (p. 265).

The literature contains several computer software applications designed by educators to address specific statistical procedures (e.g., sampling, central limit theorem, confidence intervals). For example, Dimitrova et al. (1993) created ISEE (Introduction to Sampling Error Experiments) to assist instructors who sought to add a computer application to enhance student understanding of sampling errors. Chang, Lohr, and McLaren (1992) designed SURVEY, a computer program that creates population data, including nonresponsive households, for a fictitious county in the United States. The program allows students to access population data, create samples using a variety of strategies (e.g., simple random, stratified), and apply the resultant data set to class assignments and exams.

Java applets have become an increasingly popular means to demonstrate various statistical procedures. For example, Aberson et al. (2000) endorsed the WISE (Web Interface for Statistics Education) Java applet tutorial as an effective means to assist students in developing an understanding of sampling distributions. The authors stated, "Interactive computer-based tutorials can provide an effective supplement, or even replacement, for traditional classroom lectures" (p. 291). Several researchers have used Java applets to facilitate student understanding of a variety of statistical analyses. A list of representative Java applets is available at online Appendix C at www.teachstats.org.

The ubiquity of Microsoft Excel has made this application an attractive option for instructors who desire to add an interactive component to their course. Educators have reported using Excel to demonstrate Type I and Type II errors (Hauptman, 2004) and statistical power (Horgan, 1999). Mitchell (2002) suggested that instructors take advantage of the many features unique to Excel (e.g., open-endedness, formulas, design tools) to create an active learning environment in which students can create learning playgrounds. Students created these playground tutorials in order to teach novices about a specific statistical procedure—the ANOVA. According to Mitchell, students found that the exercise was engaging, fun, and an excellent opportunity to channel their creativity. However, most importantly, students felt that the exercise enabled them to develop a deeper understanding of ANOVA procedures.

Mills (2002) provided a review and critical analysis of computer simulation methods (CSM) used to teach a wide variety of statistical concepts. She concluded that instructors used CSMs to teach statistical concepts that range from introductory (e.g., frequency histograms) to more advanced procedures (e.g., ANCOVA). Furthermore, the vast majority of authors suggested that these CSMs appeared to facilitate students' understanding of the material. Unfortunately, Mills reported that there is very little empirical evidence demonstrating the effectiveness of computer simulation models and recommended future research focus on determining whether CSMs offer any measurable advantages over traditional classroom approaches.

## Conclusion

Hypothesis testing is a major element of any introductory statistics course in the behavioral and social sciences (Friedrich et al., 2000). Consequently, it is imperative that psychology students become well versed in the theory, computation, and applications of these procedures. Unfortunately, students often view the introduction to statistics course with a mixture of fear, anxiety, and uncertainty. It is against this backdrop that instructors need to find a way to get students excited, involved, and ultimately knowledgeable about hypothesis testing.

The literature reveals a growing body of material devoted to enhancing student understanding of hypothesis testing using engaging demonstrations, simulations, and computer applications. However, there are still areas of concern. First, much of the material published on the teaching of inferential statistics is not empirical (Becker, 1996). For example, few statistics educators have attempted to compare whether students exposed to demonstrations and active learning techniques have a greater chance of success than classmates exposed to a more traditional approach to teaching hypothesis testing. Second, there is uneven coverage of inferential statistics concepts in the literature. For example, although there was an abundance of information available on ANOVA procedures, there was a paucity of material on the teaching of ANCOVA and post-hoc analyses. Third, introductory statistics textbook authors and instructors need to incorporate criticism of null hypothesis significance testing into the discipline (Schmidt, 1996). Fourth, instructors need to incorporate statistical software applications, Java applets, and other computer simulations into statistics courses alongside other active learning techniques to maximize their impact on students (Hawkins, 1997). Nonetheless, there are numerous exciting approaches to teaching hypothesis testing available for instructors who wish to overhaul their introductory statistics course.

# IV
# Advanced Topics and Approaches

# Chapter 7

# Data Analysis in Statistical Education

*During my 18 years I came to bat almost 10,000 times.*
*I struck out about 1,700 times and walked maybe 1,800 times.*
*You figure a ballplayer will average about 500 at bats a season.*
*That means I played seven years without ever hitting the ball. –*
*Mickey Mantle*

Scholars in the field of statistics have been calling for a change in both the content and delivery of statistical education for several years (e.g., Cobb, 1992; Moore, 1997; Snee, 1993). On the content side, the consensus among experts is that statistical education should emphasize statistical thinking used in solving real-world applications versus mathematical and probabilistic computations (Snee, 1993). When it comes to the delivery of statistical education, instructors across disciplines have begun heeding the calls of their respective national organizations to employ active learning techniques when teaching statistics. For example, in 1992, the joint curriculum committee of the American Statistical Association (ASA) and the Mathematical Association of America (MAA) recommended that instructors emphasize statistical thinking through active learning, utilize more actual data and statistical concepts, and rely on computers rather than computational recipes (Cobb, 1992).

The strongest impetus for the shift from traditional lecture-based statistical instruction to more interactive teaching strategies has been technological advances in statistical analysis software (Forsyth, 2003; Moore, 1997). Instructors now have the ability to use statistical software within the classroom. Moreover, students typically have ready access to statistical or spreadsheet software tools such as SPSS, SAS, Minitab, or Excel to work on statistical problems outside of the classroom (e.g., home, library, or on-campus labs). Indeed, many of these programs come bundled with statistics textbooks or are preloaded on computers.

Increasingly, statistics teachers are taking advantage of software tools in their courses. For example, in their analysis of 243 statistics courses, taught in a variety of disciplines, Garfield, Hogg, Schau, and Whittinghill (2002) found that approximately one-half of the surveyed faculty required students to use a statistical software program to complete course-related material. In addition, Garfield et al. reported that two-thirds of respondents planned to make moderate to major revisions in their course. The most common change cited by instructors was increased use of technology in course content. Garfield et al. also found that the majority of faculty respondents anticipated future changes in their courses as technology changed or became more available.

The increased use of sophisticated statistical software tools for the classroom has resulted in calls for assessment (e.g., Forsyth, 2003; Garfield, 1995). Unfortunately, there is relatively little empirical research investigating the effectiveness of statistical instruction. In her review of the ERIC, PsycINFO, and ACAD databases, Becker (1996) found that only 30% (N = 56) of the available research cited in these databases (N = 171) was empirical—the rest was largely anecdotal. Regrettably, an even smaller percentage of empirical (3.5%) and non-empirical (18%) research examined by Becker were devoted to computer software evaluation. The lack of empirical research on statistical software is worrisome given Moore's (1997) assertion that "software designed for doing statistics is not necessarily well structured for learning statistics" (p. 131). Fortunately, in the decade since Becker's analysis, researchers have begun to investigate the effectiveness of the various major software packages for use in the classroom.

## Teaching with Statistical Software Tools

The late 1960s and 1970s saw the emergence of several statistical software programs (e.g., BMDP, Minitab, SAS, SPSS, SYSTAT) for use on mainframe computers. The initial use of these programs in statistics education was primarily limited to computer-based data analysis courses (e.g., Thisted, 1979). However, the introduction of affordable personal computers in the mid-1980s made it easier for instructors to use computer programs within the classroom to teach basic statistical concepts (e.g., Lehman, 1987; Ware & Chastain, 1989). In a regional analysis of computer use by undergraduate psychology departments, Stoloff and Couch (1987) found that over 50% of psychology departments used computers in their course offerings. Couch and Stoloff (1989), in a national survey of academic psychologists, found that 66% of departments reported using computers in statistics courses. Additionally, 31% of departments required students to use a statistical package such as SPSS.

The trend towards increased computer use within introductory statistics instruction became more pronounced after the release of Microsoft Windows 95 compatible statistical data analysis programs (e.g., SPSS/PC), the increased availability of less expensive student versions of software programs (often packaged with introductory statistics texts), and the use of Microsoft Excel for statistical analyses. For example, Bartz and Sabolik (2001) recently surveyed psychology departments and found that almost 70% of departments that offered their own introductory statistics course used computers—and the majority (59%) utilized SPSS.

However, there is evidence suggesting that not all statistics instructors are enamored with using data-analysis programs to teach basic statistical concepts. Bartz and Sabolik (2001) reported that 31% of departments did not use data analysis software within their introductory statistics courses even though 90% of the departments sampled used such programs somewhere else in their curriculum. Chris Spatz, in an interview published in *Teaching of Psychology*, suggested that professors might be "reluctant to have beginning students rely on computers because they think it will thwart students' understanding of statistical tests" (Dillon, 1999, p. 234). Rosen, Feeney, and Petty (1994) used SPSS/PC in an introductory statistics course and found that students believed there was too much emphasis placed on computers and not enough time spent discussing theory. In addition, students indicated that the introduction of the computer did not reduce their anxiety and they were somewhat ambivalent about the helpfulness of the computer.

In contrast, supporters have asserted that using statistical software to teach statistical concepts has enormous benefits. First, students are freed from "computational drudgery" (Smith, 2003, p. 276) and are instead able to spend more time learning statistical theory (Forsyth,

2003). Lehman (1987) reported that the introduction of the computer into his statistics and research design course allowed him to expand coverage of traditional topics and introduce advanced topics without any negative impact on student performance. In fact, students gained an appreciation of the role of statistics in research, experienced greater confidence in their computer skills, and were satisfied with what they learned in the course. In addition, Lehman argued that the use of computers in introductory classes allows instructors the freedom to use examples more representative of reality (e.g., data sets with over 100 cases) versus more artificial problems with restrictive samples due to the time constraints imposed by hand calculations.

Second, students learn data analysis skills in computer-enhanced classes that will be useful later in their academic and professional career (Oswald, 1996). Tromater (1985) asserted that students in traditional statistics courses have difficulty applying material learned in earlier classes to subsequent advanced classes such as experimental psychology. According to Tromater, their "recall is poor and their computational skills worse" (p. 225). However, Rosen et al. (1994) stated that students do not yet have the sophistication and background to appreciate fully the importance of computer-assisted data analysis when taking their first statistics course. Consequently, some researchers have advocated the use of two interdependent courses that integrate statistical instruction and data-analysis techniques (Hewett & Porpora, 1999; Tromater, 1985). Although this approach increases the number of courses that students need for graduation, supporters suggest that students develop a deeper understanding of statistical theory and application.

Third, students become more familiar with computers and computer-assisted data analysis. For example, Ware and Chastain (1989) found that students who used a mainframe computer in their introductory statistics course developed a more favorable attitude towards computers and statistics than did those students in traditional statistics courses.

# Data Analysis Packages

## SPSS

Statistics instructors currently have a wide variety of statistical software programs to use for instructional purposes. However, the majority of published research examining the utility and effectiveness of statistical software programs have focused on SPSS. For example, soon after the introduction of SPSS for Windows, Karp (1995) provided several pedagogical tools (lectures, papers, presentations, and SPSS exercises) for incorporating SPSS into an upper division statistics course in sociology. Karp asserted that the introduction of SPSS into the classroom provided students with a tool that "enhances their learning experience by allowing them to engage the material actively and analytically" (p. 240).

Dolinsky (2001) reported several strategies using SPSS to encourage active learning in an introductory statistics course. First, she encouraged students to examine data using SPSS. The goal was to give students the opportunity to independently discover and master statistical principles using real-world data. Second, the class spent time completing inductive reasoning exercises such as understanding SPSS-generated scatterplots. Third, all assessment measures (e.g., exams, assignments) required that students examine and interpret a meaningful set of data. Students reported that they spent less time memorizing facts and more time understanding the material. In addition, students reported increased self-confidence due to their ability to solve statistical problems using SPSS.

However, not all courses that benefit from SPSS are statistical in nature. For example, Anderson (1990) utilized SPSS to enhance his introduction to sociology course. He created six assignments designed to accent specific aspects of the course (e.g., sex role differences, attitudes towards abortion, urbanization). By creating a custom shell and BASIC interface, Anderson minimized the learning curve associated with this early version of SPSS. After three semesters of this course, Anderson found that students had less computer anxiety and were more apt to create innovative variable analyses when given unstructured assignments.

One of the primary reasons why instructors attempt to incorporate SPSS into their introductory statistics courses is the desire to create an active learning environment. However, this goal can be difficult to achieve. Instructors need to spend considerable time and effort creating assignments, finding data sets, and developing class exercises designed to foster active learning. Fortunately, educational software developers have created programs designed to assist instructors meet these goals. ActivStats (www.datadesk.com/products/mediadx/activstats/) is a multimedia software package on CD-ROM designed for introductory statistics students. The creators have designed the program to complement any introductory statistics course that also requires a data-analysis package such as SPSS, MINITAB, Excel, or JMP (a division of SAS). The CD-ROM contains interactive activities using narratives, animation, video, simulation, and the Web to encourage active learning.

Mills and Johnson (2004) reviewed *ActivStats for SPSS* using some of the same criteria (content, computing technology, and exercises) utilized in the statistics education literature (e.g., Cobb, 1987; Harwell et al., 1996; Huberty & Barton, 1990; Morris, 2001). They concluded that *ActivStats for SPSS* was an "engaging multimedia software presentation" that supported the "goals of the statistical reform movement" (p. 257). Mills and Johnson felt the program was appropriate for students as a supplement to the introductory course or as a tutorial for students in need of review. Taub (2003), in his review of *ActivStats for SPSS*, concluded that the program was a "worthwhile investment for the instructor who is interested in using multimedia instruction to facilitate students' learning" (p. 293).

## Microsoft Excel

The ubiquity of the Microsoft Office suite (Hamm, 2006), plus the steep learning curve associated with using commercial data analysis packages such as SPSS and SAS (Ostrowski, 1988; Tabachnick & Fidell, 1991), has led some instructors to implement Excel into their introductory statistics courses. Mitchell (1997) utilized Excel to incorporate active learning into a graduate-level education course on computer-based approaches to learning statistics. He required students to create six educational worksheets, each designed to instruct a novice about specific statistical procedures, over the course of the semester. According to Mitchell, the use of Excel enabled students to: (a) utilize multiple representations of statistical measures; (b) create mini-simulations to demonstrate a statistical procedure; and (c) create a story line using text, sound, and graphics. Although this approach may be better suited for more advanced statistics courses, Mitchell asserted that "asking students to teach others seems especially useful as a method for increasing student understanding and maintaining high student motivation to learn" (p. 221).

Warner and Meehan (2001) used Excel in their introductory statistics course because (a) students need data analysis and spreadsheet skills for future employment; (b) the intuitive nature of Excel enables students to focus on the material versus the software program;

(c) students can send assignments electronically; and (d) most students have ready access to Excel without incurring additional cost. Warner and Meehan had students complete five Excel assignments during their introductory statistics course. Students rated the assignments as useful, not too demanding, but important for the development of creativity and critical thinking skills. Christensen and Stephens (2003) obtained similar results when they incorporated Excel into a probability and statistics class for high school juniors and seniors.

Instructors can also utilize spreadsheets, such as Microsoft Excel, as a teaching aid by providing individualized tasks or assignments for student assessment (Hunt, 2005). In addition, instructors can take advantage of Excel and other spreadsheet programs to illustrate concepts and procedures such as the central limit theorem, confidence intervals, Type I and II errors, probability, correlation, linear regression, and ANOVA (Ageel, 2002; Bradley, 1989; Johnson & Drougas, 2004; Lee & Soper, 1986; Mills, 2003a). However, before Excel users can take advantage of the statistical features of the program, they need to install the Analysis Toolpak (this free add-in program comes with Excel). The Analysis Toolpak enables the user to perform descriptive statistics, correlation, regression, $t$-tests, single and two factor ANOVAs, as well as some graphing functions.

Despite the promise associated with using Excel in the classroom, there has been growing concern that the program itself is flawed (e.g., Nash & Quon, 1996). McCullough and Wilson (1999) tested the reliability of the statistical procedures used in Excel 97 across three areas—estimation, random number generation, and statistical distributions. Given Excel's performance in all three areas was inadequate, the authors concluded, "persons desiring to conduct statistical analyses of data are advised not to use Excel" (p. 27). In a subsequent analysis, the authors reported many of the same problems from Excel 97 still existed in Excel 2000 and Excel XP (McCullough & Wilson, 2002). In fact, the authors reported that some of the fixes put into place by Microsoft actually made the initial problems worse. Additionally, Goldman and McKenzie (2002) reported that display options (e.g., table, figures) in Excel often "violated principles of good graphical practice" (p. 99), suffered from poor documentation regarding the creation of displays, and offered relatively few display options as compared to SPSS and Minitab.

In their review of Excel 2003, McCullough and Wilson (2005) reported mixed results. Microsoft addressed some of the earlier complaints, did not fix other problems, and in some cases, introduced new problems. McCullough and Wilson concluded, "Excel 2003 is an improvement over previous versions, but not enough has been done that its use for statistical purposes can be recommended" (p. 1244). Apigian and Gambill (2004–2005) reached a somewhat different conclusion in their review of Excel 2003. They compared Excel 2003, Excel XP, Minitab 14, and SPSS 11.5 using the three areas originally proposed by McCullough and Wilson (1999). Apigian and Gambill concluded that Microsoft had adequately addressed many of the problems associated with Excel XP and that Excel 2003 generated results comparable to the other statistical packages they examined. However, the authors did find examples of statistical inaccuracies and noted that Excel 2003 is still lacking more complete data analysis tools (e.g., factor analysis).

## Other commercial data analysis programs

There is a paucity of research on teaching statistics with commercial data-analysis packages other than SPSS. Although we found a few articles that discussed SAS and SYSTAT (e.g., Walsh, 1991, 1993), they primarily dealt with very specific applications (e.g., constructing questionnaire data using SAS) rather than an analysis of teaching introductory statistics with that particular software program. The lack of literature on these programs may in part be because the majority of departments that offered their own computerized introductory statistics course utilized SPSS (Bartz & Sabolik, 2001; Tabachnick & Fidell, 1991).

There is some research investigating the use of Minitab in teaching statistics—primarily in mathematics and business journals. Spinelli (2001) reported that students who took a Minitab enhanced statistics course were more likely to find Minitab helpful in understanding statistics, preferred taking the exams in the Minitab lab (where they were able to use the program), and were more likely to choose the same type of class in the future than students who took the traditional statistics class. Hubbard (1992) reported that Minitab was particularly well suited for the classroom because it is an educational aid rather than a data analysis tool. Consequently, instructors can easily use Minitab to generate simulations and demonstrate statistical concepts and procedures. Webster (1992) examined the strengths and weakness of Minitab as compared to textbook-related software such as *Easystat* and found that Minitab performed as well as the textbook-related software programs.

## Comparing data analysis programs

Instructors can utilize many commercially available data analysis programs in their classrooms. However, choosing a program that best fits your needs can be difficult. SPSS is the most popular data analysis program but a well-cited liability is the program's complex user interface (Bartz & Sabolik, 2001; Ostrowski, 1988). Excel is probably most familiar to your students but has limited data analysis capabilities and there are questions about the reliability of the results (McCullough & Wilson, 2005; Warner & Meehan, 2001). SAS, SYSTAT, and Minitab are good data analysis programs but do not appear to be widely used in the social sciences, resulting in little support material. Which one should you choose? Fortunately, several researchers have compared how well these programs work in the teaching environment.

Lock (1993) examined the student versions of SPSS, Minitab, SYSTAT, Execustat, and Statistix. He found that "under the right circumstances, any of the five packages . . . might be just what you need" (p. 145). The author recommended the student version of SPSS for students who will likely be using similar packages in the future and Statistix was most useful for instructors seeking an easy menu-driven package. According to Lock, the student version of SYSTAT was best suited for instructors concerned about cost and Minitab was typically associated with good textbook support. Lock reported that Execustat was a nice program for graphics. Unfortunately, Wadsworth has not distributed a new version of Execustat since the mid-1990s.

Proctor (2002) examined the impact of two popular statistics programs (SPSS and Excel) on student conceptual knowledge, computational knowledge, and student perceptions of statistical understanding within an introduction to statistics course for criminal justice students. Proctor randomly assigned students (N = 22) in a summer statistics course to a lab session using either SPSS or Excel. Students exposed to Excel scored significantly higher on all three of these measures than those students who used SPSS in lab sessions. Proctor attributed these differences to the ability of Excel to replicate hand calculation procedures.

Prvan, Reid, and Petocz (2002) examined SPSS, Excel, and Minitab within the context of a statistics laboratory used by introductory statistics students. They examined how well the packages performed on three specific laboratory tasks: descriptive statistics, inferential statistics, and linear regression. Aspects examined included frequency tables, cross-tabulations, graphics, data manipulation, and the ability to perform requisite tests. The authors concluded that Minitab and SPSS were better packages for statistical testing but Excel had superior spreadsheet capabilities. Prvan et al. recommended that Minitab would be best for most students, particularly those in science, engineering, and medicine. Excel was best suited for business students given the fact that Excel is the spreadsheet program students will encounter often in their profession. The authors recommended SPSS as a primary statistics package for those students in psychology, social science, or education. However, despite the differences among the packages, the authors concluded, "All three packages could be used successfully within an introductory statistics course" (p. 74).

Feinberg and Siekpe (2003) compared the student user-friendliness of SPSS and Minitab by measuring three criteria: self-efficacy, engagement, and perceived disorientation. Over a two-day period, instructors introduced students to SPSS and Minitab during an introductory and intermediate business statistics class. The order of package presentation was counterbalanced. There were no significant differences between SPSS and Minitab on student user-friendliness as measured by these criteria.

In summary, SPSS appears to be the dominant data-analysis package in the social sciences (Bartz & Sabolik, 2001; Prvan et al., 2002). In addition, the student version is readily available for use in the classroom (and may already come bundled with the course textbook). Excel appears to be a useful tool for teaching introductory statistics—particularly in business (Proctor, 2002; Prvan et al., 2002; Warner & Meehan, 2001). However, there is a growing body of literature questioning the accuracy and utility of the program (Goldman & McKenzie, 2002; McCullough & Wilson, 2005; Warner & Meehan, 2001). Minitab is popular in math and science-based statistics courses. The program has good data analysis capabilities (Prvan et al., 2002), visual displays (Goldman & McKenzie, 2002), and is well suited for classroom instruction (Hubbard, 1992). However, the decision as to which data-analysis software program is best suited to your classroom ultimately depends on your own assessment of ease of use, capabilities of the program, and institutional support (Butler, 1986).

## Data Analysis Software Textbooks

The increased popularity of data analysis software packages in introductory statistics courses has resulted in the growth of supplemental books aimed at introducing students to these software applications. Mills (2003b) surveyed teachers and researchers who were members of the American Educational Research Association as to their statistical software and software textbook selections. Of the 37 respondents, 81% reported using SPSS in the classroom with almost half (40%) using a supplemental software textbook. The remaining respondents reported using their own SPSS handouts. Approximately, 53% of teachers reported using the supplement to teach mechanics, 40% of respondents indicated that they used the SPSS text to reinforce statistical concepts, and 13% indicated using the SPSS text to teach concepts.

Given the popularity of SPSS, Mills (2003b) examined 11 SPSS textbooks. She reported that all the authors appeared to follow the recommendations of the American Statistical Association (ASA) and the Mathematical Association of America (MAA) that instructors emphasize active learning, incorporate more actual data and statistical concepts in the classroom, and rely on computers rather than computational recipes (Cobb, 1992). Mills reported that the majority of books provided systematic instructions and illustrations for topics typically presented in an introductory statistics course. In addition, all the textbooks often provided guidance for interpreting data analysis output.

Mills (2003b) evaluated each text on three criteria (mechanics, content, and classroom activities) based on previous reviews of introductory statistics textbooks (Cobb, 1987; Harwell et al., 1996; Huberty & Barton, 1990). Although Mills did not provide a ranked listing of best to worst SPSS supplements, she did report the strengths and weaknesses of each text. The most popular book among the teachers and researchers was by far (40%) Green and Salkind (2003). Approximately, 13% reported using Kirkpatrick and Feeney (2003) and 13% adopted Norusis (2002). Online Appendix D at www. teachstats.org contains a representative listing of data analysis software texts and supplemental materials.

There are also a few supplemental texts based on other data analysis programs—most notably Excel. Rosenberg's (2007) text entitled *The Excel Statistics Companion 2.0* comes packaged with a CD-ROM full of demonstrations, sampling experiments, and problem solving exercises. The accompanying manual contains traditional, albeit brief, content with links to the CD-ROM material. Rosenberg stated that he designed the manual/CD-ROM not to teach students how to analyze data with Excel but rather to use Excel as a tool to understand statistics. In contrast, Meehan and Warner (2000) designed a supplement entitled *Elementary Data Analysis Using Microsoft Excel* to allow introductory-level students the opportunity to concentrate more on concepts and applications and less on the mechanics of statistical analyses. However, they encouraged instructors to use SPSS for advanced courses that would benefit from a more sophisticated data analysis program.

## Using Data Sets in the Classroom

The use of data within the classroom is a technique that rarely works exactly as planned the first time around. According to Ballman (2000), "it is impossible to create the ideal example from scratch ... Furthermore, the success of an example is somewhat dependent upon the personality of the class" (p. 12). Nonetheless, Ballman offered several steps to develop an effective data-based example. First, identify the general goal of the assignment (e.g., explore the effect of an outlier on measures of central tendency). The goal needs to be broad enough to lend itself to several potential data sets. Second, select a data set that best matches your general goal. Third, develop subgoals to refine your search for an appropriate data set. Ballman stated, "subgoals are by nature more fluid than goals. Goals are more closely tied to the course syllabus, whereas subgoals reflect lessons that are important, but whose precise placement in the course is less critical" (p. 13). Fourth, once the data set is chosen, state all goals and subgoals that will be put into the lesson plan. Fifth, develop the background information and discussion questions to guide students through the process. Instructors should take care to ensure the process involves active learning for the students. Questions should emphasize relevant statistical concepts without stifling student discussion. Although the implementation of the data-driven exercise will take several trials to perfect, much of the success of the exercise depends on the data set. Fortunately, there are many resources available to assist in the selection of an appropriate data set. Online Appendix D at www.teachstats.org contains a listing of publicly available data sets.

## Artificial data sets for the classroom

Technological advances have given instructors the means to create their own artificial data sets with relative ease. For example, Carmer and Cady (1969) described eight FORTRAN programs that instructors could use to generate sets of data according to preset parameters thus eliminating the "tedious search for 'real-life' research data" (p. 33). Walsh (1992) described a FORTRAN program to generate nonnormal data sets. Cake and Hostetter (1986) encouraged the use of the DATAGEN program for assessment purposes (i.e., homework, lab exercises) in introductory statistics classes to generate a unique data set and accompanying text for each student. A similar approach was utilized by Vaughan (2003) using an Excel macro written in Microsoft Visual Basic.

As the technology improved, programmers have designed data set programs to produce data well suited for specific analyses. For example, Miller (1999) introduced AnoGen, a PC compatible program for automating the process of developing data sets for use in ANOVA problems. Using the program, the instructor is able to set the means, variability, and effect sizes associated with the subsequent analyses. Similarly, Strube and Goldstein (1995) described a QuickBASIC program that provided students with data sets to match different main effect and interaction combinations in a $2 \times 2$ design. Day, Marshall, and Rubin (1998) introduced DYASIM, a FORTRAN program that generates a large number of random dyads from an existing set of didactic data.

In his review of GENSTAT, a commercial data generation program, Halley (1991) cited several benefits associated with artificial data sets: (a) complete data sets without the confusion of missing cases; (b) the size of the data set is controlled by the instructor; (c) programs that generate artificial data can create unique data sets for students to use during exams; and (d) data sets can be tailored to produce significant results. In addition, artificial data sets, when coupled with simulation programs, can illustrate a variety of statistical concepts. For example, Bradley et al. (1992) reported that Datasim, a data simulator, was able to illustrate sampling distributions, the central limit theorem, Type I and Type II errors, power, the impact of violating statistical assumptions, and the distinction between orthogonal and nonorthogonal contrasts.

## Reality-based data sets

Despite the advantages associated with the use of artificial data sets, critics assert that the use of these simulated data sets does more harm than good. Singer and Willett (1990) cautioned that the use of step-by-step computational formulas coupled with contrived data sets perpetuates the misconception that statistics is dull and boring. Additionally, such approaches seduce students into believing that "statistical analysis was always confirmatory, never exploratory, and that it could be reduced to a set of predefined steps conducted by a robot" (p. 224). The use of artificial data sets removes students from the challenge of constructing a research design to answer a meaningful question, the thrill of collecting their own data, and the knowledge of how to interpret their results and apply them to other settings (Singer & Willett, 1990). Thompson (1994) asserted that the use of artificial data fosters the illusion that data collection and analysis are not interconnected. Consequently, although students may learn how to compute a statistical test, the use of artificial data sets makes it less likely that students will become passionate about data analysis.

There are several benefits associated with the use of an authentic data set. First, students working with real data sets tend to be more motivated due to the fact they find the data more intrinsically interesting (Singer & Willett, 1990; Thompson, 1994). Bradstreet (1996) asserted, "Students will remember the statistical methods as those that were used to solve a real world problem instead of memorizing a list of isolated formulas that they memorized for, and forgot shortly after, a test" (p. 71). Second, the use of real data sets in the classroom is an excellent instructional opportunity. Students can assume the role of the researcher, responding to issues that commonly arise (e.g., outliers, missing data) when preparing data for statistical analysis (Singer & Willett, 1990). Third, the use of authentic or student-generated data sets also serves to reduce anxiety associated with statistical instruction (Stedman, 1993). Fourth, active learning techniques, such as the use of real data collected by students, can improve student retention—particularly among students with average or below average scores (Kvam, 2000).

According to Singer and Willett (1990), a real data set needs to have several pedagogical characteristics to be effective. First, the data set should be authentic. Cobb (1987) stated that "a dataset should not only be real, it should feel that way" (p. 331). The use of authentic data may lead students to ask relevant questions regarding how the researcher collected the data, whether outliers were present, etc. These questions are critical when analyzing real data. Students are less apt to raise such questions when data are obviously artificial. Second, sufficient background information must accompany any presentation of real data. Although a good data set has a purpose that is readily apparent to students (Cobb, 1987), instructors should include supporting evidence, relevant hypotheses, participant demographics, methodology, and validity concerns (Singer & Willett, 1990).

Third, according to Singer and Willett (1990), instructors need to select a data set that enables students to address relevant research questions through a variety of statistical techniques. Not only do students learn the advantages and disadvantages of various statistical analyses, they also gain a better appreciation of the different insights provided by each analysis. Fourth, the data set should provide students with the opportunity to engage in substantive learning. By selecting data sets with a story to tell, students learn something new about the world around them, and consequently, may discover the importance of statistical analysis. "If you want students to look for meaning, you cannot give them data sets that feel meaningless" (Cobb, 1987, p. 332). Fifth, the data set must be interesting and relevant to students. Singer and Willett suggested that instructors seek out topical (e.g., racism on campus), controversial (e.g., effectiveness of stem cell research), or historical data (e.g., Cyril Burt's data on the IQs of identical twins).

## Finding appropriate reality-based data sets

In his review of statistics textbooks, Cobb (1987) hoped he had seen the last of "XYZ Corporation," "Hospitals A, B, and C," and patients "suffering from a certain disease," among the examples used by statistics textbook authors (p. 331). Fortunately, researchers have published many ingenious means to acquire and/or create real data sets. In addition to specific scholarly articles on the use of data in statistics education, several books, journal appendices, and Web sites containing real data are available. In addition, every issue of the online publication of the American Statistical Association, the *Journal of*

*Statistics Education*, contains a section devoted to interesting data sets that instructors can use in the classroom. Online Appendix D at www.teachstats.org contains a listing of publicly available data sets.

*Large public data sets.* A relatively simple means to use real data in the classroom is by accessing a large public data set. Many large data sets (e.g., State Lottery results, Census Bureau publications, Gallup Organization) are free or available for a nominal fee and easily accessed via the Internet (Pachnowski, Newman, & Jurczyk, 1997). For example, Holmes (2002) discussed the use of the large international CensusAtSchool program data set to introduce students to develop and evaluate students' statistical understanding. The CensusAtSchool Web site (www.censusatschool.ntu.ac.uk/) enables teachers and students to access data (e.g., demographics, physical measurements, opinion surveys) collected from children in the United Kingdom, Queensland, South Africa, New Zealand, South Australia, or Canada. Similarly, Brosnan, Eriksen, and Lin (2002) described how to teach research methods and statistics for nursing students using large public-use data sets available on CD-ROMs for a nominal fee ($20) from the National Center for Health Statistics (NCHS).

Most commercial statistics programs such as SPSS come with sample data sets. For example, using the SPSS sample data set, Dolinsky (2001) had her students explore who was most likely to watch X-rated movies. They were surprised to learn that the percentage of individuals who reported watching pornographic movies was lower than expected. Further analyses revealed that college-aged men were more likely to view X-rated films than older men and women.

Many peer-reviewed journal articles and published conference proceedings have relevant data sets included in the appendices. In addition, several authors have published collections of real data (e.g., Andrews & Herzberg, 1985; Hand, Daly, Lunn, McConway, & Ostrowski, 1994). Unpublished doctoral dissertations are also excellent sources of data. Singer and Willett (1990) provided an extensive annotated bibliography of published data sets in scientific journals and statistics textbooks.

*Ripped from the headlines data sets.* One means to engage students in statistics is to draw from real events that have publicly available data. Yu, Chan, and Fung (2006) used publicly available Severe Acute Respiratory Syndrome (SARS) data to introduce students to a variety of statistical techniques (e.g., descriptives, chi-square, linear regression) in three different statistics classes (introductory statistics, demography course, time series class). The authors provided six different exercises appropriate for students with varying statistical backgrounds. For example, students computed whether age was a risk factor in SARS, examined why Hong Kong had the highest fatality rates, and analyzed the economic impact of SARS. According to Yu et al., students who worked with the SARS data learned more about the event, engaged in active learning, and had the opportunity to use a statistical program (e.g., SAS).

Morgan (2001) collected approximately 50 obituaries from the local paper for use in her research methods class. The resultant obituary data set was rife with problems normally encountered when collecting "live" data such as incomplete information and outliers (e.g., children). In addition, students answered meaningful questions (e.g., gender x age of death comparisons) using a variety of statistical techniques. However, given the possibility of triggering an emotional backlash, Morgan noted that instructors should give students ample notice and opportunity to withdraw from taking part in the exercise. She also recommended instructors should consider drawing their obituaries from another city.

Professional sports are a ripe source of data for use in statistics courses. For example, Cholkar and Deshpande (2004) had students examine the results of the 10th Men's Hockey World Cup Tournament to illustrate correlations and explore questions such as whether the team that scores first has a better chance of winning the game. Wiseman and Chatterjee (1997) used Major League Baseball (MLB) salaries, regularly published in *USA Today* and online, to create a data set for use in an introductory statistics course. Students used the data set to examine measures of central tendency, variability, and the impact of outliers. Given the importance of statistics in the game of baseball, and the fact such data are readily available in the daily newspaper or via Internet rotisserie (i.e., fantasy) baseball leagues, it is only natural that instructors have used baseball to teach statistics. In fact, Albert (2003) has written a very creative book devoted to teaching statistics using baseball. The text demonstrates how to use box scores, individual batting (e.g., Cal Ripken) and pitching data (e.g., Roger Clemens), team statistics, and analyses of specific record-breaking events (e.g., Barry Bonds' single season home run record) to illustrate statistical theory (e.g., probability, statistical inference) and applications (e.g., correlations, regressions, Markov Chain).

*Case study approach.* Although many instructors would like to give students the opportunity to collect real data, time and/or resource constraints limit their options. Consequently, some instructors use a case approach for incorporating real data into their course. For example, Nolan and Speed (1999) incorporated published data into their statistics course by developing case studies for use in an undergraduate statistics laboratory. The authors provided students with background material, specifics on the data set, specific questions regarding the data, and statistical theory and applications relevant to the lab. Students reported that the labs helped them better understand statistical theory and see the relevance of the material to the real world. Carlson (1999) and Sharpe (2000) also used the case study method for teaching statistics to business and economics students with similar results.

*Student-as-participant data sets.* A popular procedure for collecting real data with which students are intimately familiar with involves having students become research participants (e.g., Hettich, 1974; Jacobs, 1980; Low, 1995). For example, Stedman (1993) divided his introductory statistics class into two groups based on their response to a questionnaire that assessed whether the students were morning or evening people. Over the course of the semester, the class calculated measures of central tendency, variability, and performed *t*-tests to determine if the groups differed on television watching, GPA, etc. Schacht and Stewart (1992) presented students with one of two hypothetical situations where a police officer pulls over a youth (delin-quent or preppy) in a stolen vehicle. Students then respond as to what punishment the youth should receive. After the exercise is completed, students examine the raw data, compute relevant statistics (e.g., measures of central tendency, variability, and *t*-tests), and discuss statistical concerns. Sullivan (1993) created seven exercises that addressed a variety of different statistical concepts (scales of measure-ment, probability, central limit theorem, correlation) by collecting data from fellow classmates.

Bolstad, Hunt, and McWhirter (2001) surveyed students in their introductory statistics class on issues that are of universal interest for college students—sex, drugs, and Rock n' Roll. Students were asked the number of past sex partners they had, the most recent time they smoked marijuana, and their choice of the greatest Rock n' Roll singer of all time. The authors protected student privacy by using an anonym-ous questionnaire coupled with a randomization procedure whereby students responded to either the real question or a dummy question (approximately one-third of the responses). Students were eager to participate, motivated to explore the data set, and gained an understanding of randomization techniques often used in clinical drug trials.

*Student-as-researcher data sets.* Students are typically not involved in the formation of the hypothesis, choice of measures, and collection of the data in the techniques described above. According to Thompson (1994), "To derive full benefit from real data, students must be the researchers (not the subjects in the study), and they must collect the data themselves or assist in the design of the data-collection instrument" (p. 41).

To facilitate the use of students-as-researchers, Thompson (1994) introduced the Student Information Questionnaire (SIQ) to provide a skeleton framework that both instructors and students can easily modify to fit their needs. After the class decided on a hypothesis, students modified the SIQ, collected the data from other classes, entered the data into a computer spreadsheet, and analyzed the data. Thompson reported that students preferred the SIQ data to hypothetical data whenever he introduced new statistical procedures during the semester. In addition, students noted that the use of the SIQ data made the class more interesting, and as a result, found it easier to learn statistics.

Halvorsen and Moore (2000) had students in small groups conduct their own research projects using publicly available data, observational data collection strategies, or experimental approaches. Students chose a research project, developed a proposal, collected data, conducted statistical analyses, and presented the results of their study. The authors asserted that this approach fosters active learning and kept students' interest because they were investigating topics they chose to examine. According to Halvorsen and Moore, students reported that although the project was "a lot of work," it was "one of the most useful parts of the class" (p. 32).

There is no end to the topics that students can investigate to generate data for use in the classroom. Smith (1998) provided a list of 20 projects (observational, survey, experimental) that students conducted within the confines of an introduction to statistics course. Hunter (1977) listed 32 experiments performed by students in his statistics course including investigations of the spreadability of caramel candy, how to knock down the most bowling pins, and the yield of popcorn kernels. Stern (1999) had students collect data from

10 men and 10 women to investigate the effect of gender on the number of shoes owned. After the class created an aggregated data set, students produced descriptive statistics, graphed the data, and tested for differences between means.

Marek, Christopher, and Walker (2004) created a theme-based research methods course with a statistics laboratory. The authors reported that the theme-based course was particularly well suited for small liberal arts schools with limited library resources and no subject pool. Over the course of the semester, the class became familiar with the theme-based material (e.g., procrastination, Protestant work ethic, and personality), developed hypotheses, discussed the relevant questionnaires, prepared an informed consent form, and proceeded to each collect data from five respondents (class data were later aggregated). During the statistics lab session, students learned to conduct data analyses using SPSS and created an APA-style results section that included a variety of statistical analyses (e.g., chi-square, $t$-test, ANOVA). Although the theme-based course did not give students the opportunity to develop their own research ideas, students evaluated the class favorably and recommended including a theme-based class project for future classes.

The School Spirit Study Group (2004) was a particularly exciting project that involved 21 different instructors from 20 different schools all working together to create a joint data set that allowed students to examine how their school compared to others on several dimensions. Instructors from each school had students in their courses collect data on school spirit such as (a) percentage of students wearing school uniform: (b) percentage of cars on campus with school stickers; (c) alumni donation rate; (d) spirit ratings by *The Sporting News*; and (e) attitudinal measures of pride. Participating instructors responded very positively to the project, commenting that the exercise enhanced students' conceptual and practical understanding of course concepts (94%), demystified the process of doing research (61%), increased student engagement (56%), improved student learning (39%), and enhanced their ability to teach statistics (39%).

## Drawbacks to using real data sets

Despite the advantages associated with using real data sets in teaching statistics, there are some drawbacks. According to Singer and Willett (1990), instructors need to be aware that finding or creating real data sets greatly increases the amount of time needed for class preparation. In addition to problems locating and acquiring data sets, instructors need to find manageable data sets that they can easily download and format for use on their preferred data analysis program (Sieber & Trumbo, 1991). Furthermore, using a real data set to illustrate specific statistical procedures necessitates that instructors conduct preliminary analyses to identify potential problems. Consequently, the instructor may need to examine several data sets before finding one that best illustrates relevant concepts or produces desired results.

Whenever collecting data from human participants, regardless of intent (i.e., research purposes or classroom exercise), instructors need to keep in mind the ethical issues that bear on the situation. Consequently, Stern (1999) recommended that instructors contact their school's Institutional Review Board (IRB) to determine the best course of action. Instructors need to plan their activities well in advance of the scheduled implementation date in the event of a delay in the IRB approval process.

Although collecting student data is a quick and easy way to get students invested in data analysis techniques, the procedure limits the type of analyses that students can perform on the data due to small sample sizes (Thompson, 1994). According to Singer and Willett (1990), the use of small data sets "creates a false impression as to what constitutes adequate sample size in practice" (p. 225). In addition, the desire to have a significant outcome when presenting students with a new analysis may result in the selection of data sets with large effect sizes. Unfortunately, this procedure "builds a false anticipation" (p. 225) of the likelihood of encountering such effect sizes in everyday life (Singer & Willett, 1990).

One means to avoid the problem of small sample sizes is to collect data from semester to semester using the same stimulus materials. Alternatively, instructors who teach at an institution with an introductory psychology participant pool might be able to access the collective data set for demonstration purposes. For example, Lutsky (1986) used previously collected data sets to demonstrate research methods and statistical procedures in his introductory psychology course. Using a five-page handout detailing the purpose, methodology, data analysis possibilities, and specific instructions for conducting analyses in SPSS, student were given two weeks to complete the assignment. Lutsky reported that students found the project valuable, were less anxious about statistics, and were more confident using a computer.

Similarly, instructors can use the American Psychological Association's Online Psychology Laboratory (OPL: http://opl.apa.org/) to enable students to take part in psychology experiments. Instructors can then access the data from their class, as well as data from other classes, to examine the results of the study. Instructors can download data into Excel spreadsheets or import the data into a commercial data analysis program such as SPSS.

## Conclusion

The emergence of sophisticated computerized data analysis tools, such as SPSS, has given statistics instructors the opportunity to better engage students in the process of learning (Ben-Zvi & Friedlander, 1997). Students in classes that use programs like SPSS are free from the drudgery of hand calculations (Smith, 2003), able to spend more time learning statistical theory (Forsyth, 2003), learning a skill that may be useful later in their academic and professional career (Oswald, 1996), and may develop a more favorable attitude towards computers and statistics (Ware & Chastain, 1989). However, the successful integration of data analysis programs into statistics courses is dependent on how we ultimately use these programs in the classroom. Hawkins (1997) cautioned, "Technology *can* enhance the processes of teaching and learning statistics. However, not all technology is fit for this purpose, and the use we make of this technology is not always appropriate" (p. 2). Consequently, instructors need to review all available software packages, design exercises that encourage active learning, and provide adequate support material.

Although there is controversy regarding the utility of integrating commercial data analysis programs into statistical education (Hawkins, 1997), scholars are generally unanimous in the assertion that interesting data can infuse life into any statistics course. Cobb (2000) proclaimed, "Almost any course in statistics can be improved by more emphasis on data and concepts, at the expense of less theory and fewer recipes" (p. 3). In addition, the overwhelming consensus in the statistical education literature is that instructors should use authentic or real data (Ballman, 2000; Cobb, 1987; Singer & Willett, 1990). According to Ballman, there are several advantages associated with the use of real data in the statistical education. First, instructors can use real data to convey the importance and practicality of statistics. The course is not just an academic hurdle on the way towards graduation. Second, real data can teach students new information about other subject matter that they normally may not encounter. In other words, they may learn something other than statistical theory. Third, real data are messy. There are outliers, incomplete cases, and biased responses in real data sets. By using real data, students may come to appreciate statistics is not simply doing calculations but rather involves critical thinking skills.

# Chapter 8

# Endings and Beginnings

*While nothing is more uncertain than the duration of a single life, nothing is more certain than the average duration of a thousand lives. – Elizur Wright*

Statistics instructors have a significant amount of information to cover in a single semester. Nonetheless, statistics educators have recommended that topics such as advanced data analytic techniques (e.g., multivariate), ethics, and diversity issues be integrated into the course. To accommodate high-level statistics, Brakke et al. (2007) encouraged instructors (a) to streamline their traditional introductory statistics course by removing material that psychology students are unlikely to encounter or (b) to offer a second course in statistical methods that addresses advanced topics such as multivariate statistics. Although students may receive more in-depth coverage of this material and other topics on the graduate level, statistics educators recommend that instructors offer at least a conceptual overview of additional topics such as ethics, MANOVA, structural equation modeling and meta-analysis (Friedrich et al., 2000; Lesser & Nordenhaug, 2004). This recommendation is particularly important because most students may take only one statistics course in their entire academic career (Giesbrecht et al., 1997).

# Multivariate Statistics

The advent of sophisticated statistical software has produced an explosion of multivariate statistics in social science research. Grimm and Yarnold (1995) examined the number of articles that used at least one multivariate analysis in the *Journal of Consulting and Clinical Psychology* (*JCCP*) and the *Journal of Personality and Social Psychology* (*JPSP*). They found that the number of such articles from 1976 to 1992 in *JCCP* increased from 9% to 67%. Similarly, the number of *JPSP* articles that used multivariate analyses rose from 16% to 57%. Sherman, Buddie, Dragan, End, and Finney (1999) examined the statistical techniques used in research studies published in *Personality and Social Psychology Bulletin* (*PSPB*) and the *Journal of Personality and Social Psychology* (*JPSP*). They noted a similar increase in multivariate statistical analyses (e.g., MANOVA, multiple regression, factor analysis, structural modeling) from the late 1960s to 1996.

The increasing prevalence of multivariate statistics in psychological research underscores the importance of advanced statistical education in psychology. Harraway and Barker (2005) surveyed students from New Zealand who had graduated with advanced degrees in psychology between 1995 and 2000 to determine how they were using statistics in the workplace. Graduates were most apt to use statistics to read about published research as well as to design, conduct, and write about their own research. In addition to basic descriptive and inferential statistics, psychology graduates also reported the moderate use of multiple, nonlinear, nonparametric, and logistic regression, MANOVA, factor analysis, power analysis, and meta-analysis techniques.

The burden of teaching multivariate statistical analyses has traditionally fallen to graduate programs in psychology. Consequently, there has been a rise in graduate-level teaching materials related to multivariate statistics. For example, there has been an increase in textbooks devoted to multivariate analyses (e.g., Keith, 2006; Kline, 2005; Tabachnick & Fidell, 2007; Thompson, 2004). Katz and Tomazic (1990) presented a list of source materials for an applied graduate course in multivariate statistics including several texts and relevant journal articles.

Unfortunately, researchers have reported that graduate institutions are not adequately preparing graduate students in the theory or application of multivariate statistics. For example, Aiken et al. (1990) surveyed PhD programs in psychology across the United States and Canada and found that few programs responded that most or all of their students were competent to perform a variety of multivariate statistical analyses: MANOVA (18%), alternative OLS regression analyses (3%), confirmatory factor analysis (2%), and other multivariate procedures (11%). Aiken et al. suggested that the potential inability of graduate students to perform multivariate analyses might be due to insufficient training. For example, 40% of the graduate programs that responded to Aiken et al's. survey reported that students had received no training in multivariate procedures. Muthén (1989) asserted that the poor training of past educational psychology graduate students in topics such as structural equation modeling (SEM) had resulted in a large number of poorly conducted SEM analyses in the scientific literature. Interestingly, Harraway and Barker (2005) found that graduate students were aware that they needed additional training in advanced statistical methods. They gave Masters and PhD students the opportunity to nominate courses or workshops they felt would be most beneficial for post-graduate employment— the top requested topic was multivariate methods.

To remedy the above deficiencies in multivariate statistical training for psychology graduate students, Aiken et al. (1990) suggested that graduate statistical education focus on "proficiency" for those statistics students will typically use and strive towards "acquaintance" with the underlying theory for those procedures that the student may encounter later in their given profession. "We should no longer assume that each graduate student must be trained to perform all of his or her own analyses" (Aiken et al., p. 731). Munley (2002) presented an approach to teaching multivariate statistics to graduate-level counseling students that emphasized conceptually versus computational-orientated readings. For example, as a supplement to the assigned research design text, Munley had students read selected material from Grimm and Yarnolds' (1995, 2000) conceptually-orientated multivariate statistics texts and discussed original research articles from the *Journal of Counseling Psychology*.

Despite the increased attention placed on graduate-level multivariate statistical education within psychology, relatively little attention has been paid to these techniques within an introductory statistics course at the undergraduate level (Alder & Vollick, 2000; Friedrich et al., 2000) which is unfortunate given the likelihood that students will encounter this material as undergraduates. In addition, more advanced training at the undergraduate level, even if only a conceptual overview of multivariate statistics, would greatly assist graduate-level instructors by reducing the need to provide remedial statistical instruction (Aiken et al., 1990; Friedrich et al., 2000).

However, introducing students to descriptive, inferential, and multivariate statistical analyses in one undergraduate course may be too much for students to comprehend, let alone retain following the completion of the course. Consequently, some statistics educators at the undergraduate level have recommended that instructors develop a second, more advanced, statistics course to supplement the traditional introductory statistics course. For example, Friedrich et al. (2000) suggested that educators consider offering a hybrid course that combines tests and measurement issues (e.g., reliability and validity) with sophisticated statistical techniques (e.g., general linear model, confidence intervals, power analysis, and exploratory displays). In addition, they advocated for the conceptual treatment of basic causal modeling and meta-analysis to assist students when they encounter these topics in current psychological research. A similar advanced course, proposed by Brakke et al. (2007), covered advanced ANOVA techniques and multiple regression but did not include other advanced statistical techniques present in the psychological literature (e.g., causal modeling, factor analysis, and meta-analysis).

Regardless of the approach, researchers have argued that instructors should not create an advanced statistics course with the sole intent of preparing undergraduates to go to graduate school in psychology. Although graduate school preparation is an important issue, advanced statistical instruction can also increase the likelihood that students will succeed in subsequent undergraduate coursework, research projects, community work, and career development (Friedrich et al., 2000).

## Multiple regression

There is a considerable amount of published literature on the teaching of multiple regression—much more so than other multivariate topics. For example, Timmerman (2000) presented an exercise designed to facilitate students' understanding of multiple regression research reported in the scientific literature. The focus of this activity was on comprehension versus computation. Following lectures on correlation, simple regression, multiple regression, and survey methods, Timmerman assigned students to an activity group or control group. He divided students in the activity group into small subgroups and asked each group to generate five questions that could predict individual performance on the previous exam. Timmerman combined the survey items generated by each subgroup into one questionnaire. After students completed the questionnaire, Timmerman calculated the relevant statistics, and the class discussed the results. Although there was no significant difference between the activity and control groups on the subsequent test, students in the activity group scored higher on the regression portion of the exam than did control group participants. Students reported that the activity was worthwhile and that the instructor should use it again in future sections of the course.

García and García (2004) presented a hands-on exercise for teaching multiple regression. Specifically, students predicted whether they would like an upcoming film using a regression equation based on published movie critic reviews of films they had seen and rated in the past. The students constructed several different regression models (e.g., forward, backwards, and stepwise) using SPSS. García and García suggested the same approach could work with other media such as books, songs, and video games. Sachau (2000) created a three-dimensional model using the classroom walls and floor as axes and fishing bobbers suspended from the ceiling as data points. Using the model, he was able to illustrate the centroid, multivariate normality, mahalanobis distance, and multivariate outliers. Students exposed to the model did well on a surprise quiz one week later, reported that the exercise helped them understand multiple regression, and felt the three-dimensional model was more effective than a two-dimension illustration. Sachau reported that this approach worked because it lowered anxiety and deemphasized the role of mathematics.

Several statistics educators have presented exercises designed to illustrate particular aspects of multiple regression analyses. For example, Kowalski (1995) provided an overview of moderated multiple regression and illustrated six steps that instructors might use to introduce students to multiple regression. Specifically, she recommended instructors: (a) introduce dummy coding for categorical variables; (b) discuss how the interaction term is calculated; (c) conduct the hierarchical multiple regression; (d) present how main effects of continuous and categorical variables are interpreted; (e) determine the form of significant interactions using conditional regression equations; and (f) conduct additional regression analyses as needed.

Aguinis, Petersen, and Pierce (1999) examined the incidence of violations of the homogeneity of error variance assumption for moderated multiple regression across three applied psychology journals during a 12-year period (1987–1999). They found that researchers violated this assumption in 40–60% of the moderated multiple regression analyses in which they were able to retest. To assist researchers and aid instructors, Aguinis et al. created a computer program to assess whether the data violated the error variance assumption and for computation of an alternative statistic, if necessary. Serlin and Levin (1985) presented a set of procedures designed to simplify the process of coding qualitative variables for use in multiple regression analyses. Vaughan and Berry (2005) presented an in-class Monte Carlo demonstration to illustrate the effect of multicollinearity on regression coefficients. For more exercises related to the teaching of multiple regression, see our Web site at www.teachstats.org.

## Logistic regression

Logistic regression has become the preferred tool for predicting dichotomous outcomes in the health and social sciences because it is more flexible than other related techniques such as discriminant analysis, multiway frequency analysis, and multiple regression (Tabachnick & Fidell, 2007). However, Lottes, Adler, and DeMaris (1996) contend that there is still confusion as to the conditions under which logistic regression is an appropriate choice. To assist instructors in teaching logistic regression, they encouraged instructors to highlight the similarities between ordinary least squares (OLS) and logistic regression, present contingency tables as illustrations, and utilize computer outputs in SPSS and SAS when discussing interpretation strategies. Walsh (1987) presented a simplified overview of the statistic including the rationale, examples, and guidelines for interpretation. To illustrate logistic regression, Morrell and Auer (2007) presented an in-class activity in which students examined the impact of three explanatory variables (distance, orientation of a trash can, gender) on the ability to toss a ball into a trash can (outcome measure). They encouraged instructors to use pre- and post- activity homework to ensure the activity was optimally effective.

Simonoff (1997) proposed that instructors could use data associated with the sinking of the *Titanic* to illustrate logistic regression. Specifically, he suggested students use published data to investigate the link between economic status, age, and gender on the likelihood of surviving the disaster. Simonoff (1998) also proposed instructors use the 1998 McGwire/Sosa home run race to illustrate logistic regression by modeling whether the probability of McGwire or Sosa hitting a home run varied as a function of other variables. Souhrada (2006) created a logistic regression example based on the season two episode *All's Fair* (#218–31) of the CBS series *Numb3rs* in which the main character, Charlie, used logistic regression to determine which criminal suspect would strike next. In the classroom activity, students use provided information to determine whether a suspect is male or female.

## Additional multivariate techniques

The bulk of the literature on teaching multivariate statistics comes from the mathematics and statistics fields. Much of this material is limited to advanced regression techniques such as multiple regression and logistic regression. However, researchers have numerous multivariate procedures at their disposal, such as structural equation modeling (SEM), meta-analysis, multivariate analysis of variance (MANOVA), canonical correlation, factor analysis, and path analysis. Unfortunately, there is a paucity of literature on teaching these advanced topics.

For example, structural equation modeling (SEM) has grown considerably over the past two decades into one of the dominant multivariate techniques in psychological research (Hershberger, 2003; Tremblay & Gardner, 1996). Unfortunately, the only resource available relevant to teaching structural equation modeling was Stapleton and Leite's (2005) analysis of SEM syllabi. They collected 55 syllabi of quarter or semester-long courses on SEM from the fields of education and psychology. They reviewed each syllabus and reported on the presence of a required text or recommended readings, the type of topics covered, software applications utilized, and assessment criteria.

There are several good background resources available for instructors wishing to introduce students to SEM. For example, MacCallum and Austin (2000) provided an overview of SEM, illustrated the many applications of SEM in psychological research, and discussed some lingering problems associated with SEM. Several good book chapters (e.g., Klem, 2000; Tabachnick & Fidell, 2007; Thompson, 2000c) and textbooks (e.g., Hoyle, 1995; Kline, 2005; Loehlin, 2004; Schumacker & Lomax, 2004) on SEM provide good

186 Endings and Beginnings

background information that may be useful for instructors. In addition, Hittner and Carpenter (1994) recommended resource material, such as background articles, textbooks, and representative research articles for teaching SEM.

Meta-analysis has also become an increasingly important tool in the behavioral and social sciences (Durlak, 1995; McNamara, Morales, Kim, & McNamara, 1998). A search of PsycINFO revealed over 2,000 meta-analyses examining a broad range of topics in psychology. Friedrich et al. (2000) reported that approximately half of those advanced statistics instructors surveyed reported spending an hour or more of class time on meta-analysis. Several good meta-analysis tutorials exist in journals (e.g., Chambers, 2004; McNamara, et al., 1998; Quintana & Minami, 2006; Robey & Dalebout, 1998). There are also several texts and book chapters devoted to meta-analysis (e.g., Becker, 2000; Durlak, 1995; Hunter & Schmidt, 2004; Lipsey & Wilson, 2001; Schulze, 2004). However, despite its popularity, there is little research devoted to teaching methods associated with meta-analysis.

Additional background materials are available for instructors who wish to incorporate other multivariate procedures such as MANOVA (Huberty & Olejnik, 2006; Weinfurt, 1995), canonical correlation (e.g., Thompson, 2000d), factor analysis (e.g., Henson & Roberts, 2006; Thompson, 2004), path analysis (e.g., Klem, 1995; Wolfle, 2003), and other multivariate procedures (e.g., Grimm & Yarnold, 1995, 2000; Tabachnick & Fidell, 2007) into a statistics course. However, as was the case with many of the multivariate techniques discussed above, there is a lack of published research related to the teaching of these topics. Future research needs to address this deficiency given the importance of multivariate statistics in the psychology literature. At the very least, students need to have a conceptual understanding of these topics to keep abreast of new developments in the field. As statistics instructors, we have an obligation to develop the best means to convey this information to students.

# Special Topics

The development of statistical reasoning and thinking skills is fundamental to a quality statistics education. Statistics educators and scholars have argued that an understanding of the big picture of research is a key component of such skills (Ben-Zvi & Garfield,

2004; delMas, 2002; Pfannkuch & Wild, 2004). Without an understanding of ethics and the impact of diversity on research, students'
reasoning and thinking skills will be incomplete.

## Ethics

Too often, the words "statistics" and "lies" appear in the same
sentence or even title of a book (e.g., Best, 2004; Huff, 1954).
Schield (2005b) argued that statisticians rarely lie but are more likely
to prevaricate—mislead by omission or the selective use of statistics.
He cited Aaron Levenstein, who compared statistics to beachwear in
that "what they reveal is suggestive, but what they conceal is vital"
(p. 1). In response to concerns regarding ethics, the American Statistical Association (ASA; 1999), the International Statistical Institute
(ISI; 1985), and the United Nations Statistical Commission (UNSC;
1994) each developed and passed ethics codes and guidelines. The
ASA's *Ethical Guidelines for Statistical Practice* (1999) also argued
that the ethical principles and guidelines apply to students regardless
of whether they consider themselves future statisticians or not. As
such, instructors need to introduce and discuss ethics in their statistics courses.

Ethics has long been an integral topic in research methods courses
at the undergraduate level. Indeed, educators have written exten-
sively in scholarly publications, textbooks, and teaching resources
concerning teaching ethics in a research context (e.g., Beins, 2004;
Brinthaupt, 2002; Kardas & Spatz, 2007). Unfortunately, many
instructors have not integrated a discussion of ethics into their statistics courses. The omission is most likely the result of two factors.
First, Lesser and Nordenhaug (2004) found that until recently, few
statistics textbooks included sections on ethics. Second, researchers
and instructors have not rated ethics as an important component of
a statistics course (Friedrich et al., 2000; Giesbrecht et al., 1997;
Landrum, 2005). Landrum and Giesbrecht et al. compiled lists of
statistical topics and terms based on an evaluation of research articles and statistics textbooks. The topic of ethics did not appear in
either list or article.

The American Psychological Associations' (APA) *Ethical Principles of Psychologists and Code of Conduct* (2002) does not directly
address the use of statistics. However, Section 8 in *Research and
Publications* made two essential points in relation to research
results. First, researchers have an obligation to be as accurate as

possible and should not fabricate data. Second, if a researcher should discover errors later in their reported results, they should make an effort to correct the problem. Additionally, instructors should consider introducing all of the ethical principles related to research outlined in the APA *Ethical Principles* (e.g., issues of confidentiality, deception, informed consent). Statistical scholars and researchers have argued that instructors must teach statistics within a research context and that students must understand the big picture of the questions they are asking (e.g., ASA, 2005; Cobb & McClain, 2004; Gal, 2004; Goddard, 2005; Pfannkuch & Wild, 2004; Rumsey, 2002). Ethics is an essential component of that big picture and context.

The ASA's (2007) mission statement enjoined statisticians to use the "discipline to enhance human welfare" (para. 2). Towards that aim, the ASA Board of Directors approved the *Ethical Guidelines for Statistical Practice* in 1999 and included two broad sections: Preamble and Ethical Guidelines. The ASA subdivided the Preamble into three sections: Purpose of the Guidelines, Statistics and Society, and Shared Values. Instructors may find the Preamble particularly useful in discussing statistical ethics with students. It highlights statistics as grounded in professionalism, ethics, morality, and emphasizes the social value of research. The ASA subdivided the Ethical Guidelines into eight categories with some of the categories directed primarily towards statistical practitioners and employers. Teachers may want to address the categories focusing on professionalism, publications, and responsibilities to both research subjects and colleagues. Instructors can find the full text of the ASA *Ethical Guidelines* at www.amstat.org/profession/.

The International Statistical Institute (ISI) adopted the *Declaration of Professional Ethics* in 1985. Instructors may find this broader statement of statistical ethics a useful adjunct in a statistics course. The Declaration extends its content beyond a discussion of ethics solely in relation to the work of statisticians to a broader analysis of statistics in a research context including information related to informed consent and confidentiality. Instructors may find the ISI Declaration and particularly, the extensive bibliography useful (http://isi.cbs.nl/ethics.htm).

In 1994, the United Nations Statistical Commission (UNSC) passed the *Fundamental Principles of Official Statistics*. This document outlined 10 principles for the ethical use of statistics in an official capacity and highlighted the essential role that official government statistics play in national and international decision-making and policy planning. The UNSC argued that compilers and users of official statistics have particular ethical obligations to ensure that researchers collect data professionally, accurately, and according to sound scientific principles. Moreover, the UNSC asserted that researchers must protect individuals' privacy and guard against the misuse of statistics. The *Fundamental Principles of Official Statistics* stated, "Official statistics provide an indispensable element in the information system of a democratic society, serving the Government, the economy and the public with data about the economic, demographic, social and environmental situation" (Principle 1). Instructors can find the full text of the Fundamental Principles of Official Statistics at http://unstats.un.org/unsd/methods/statorg/FP-English.htm. Selzer (2005) provided a good overview of ethics in relation to official statistics. He discussed the rationale for ethics in official statistics, important concerns (e.g., methodology and confidentiality), and responses to ethical abuses.

Lesser (2007) argued that instructors should teach statistics from a social justice perspective. He asserted that this perspective not only puts the issue of statistics within an ethical context but increased the relevancy of the statistics, which consequently enhanced students' motivation in the course (ASA, 2005; Snee, 1993; Thompson, 1994). Instructors can also highlight the role that statistics play when used to inform and educate a population on social justice concerns. For example, Lesser discussed issues such as racial discrimination, poverty and pay equity, consumer issues, and health care. He provided examples that emphasized the role of operational definitions, different measures of central tendency, graphs, and inferential statistics on policy decisions when researchers misused statistics. Lesser and Nordenhaug (2004) discussed the application of probability to issues such as the death penalty and racial profiling. To increase the appeal of this approach, Lesser (2007) provided useful suggestions for instructors teaching in environments that might not be open to a social justice approach to teaching statistics.

Instructors can also integrate ethics into statistics courses through a discussion of the historic misuses of statistics. For example, Seltzer and Anderson (2001) discussed the role that confidentiality plays in data collection. They noted that researchers should use care even with aggregated data, as some individuals or small groups may remain identifiable. In this discussion, they highlighted the role that official statistics have played in historical incidents of forced migration, internment, and genocide. Of course, within a broader research context, instructors can discuss the Tuskegee study (Jones, 1993) or the Nazi experiments in the concentration camps (Woolf, 2001) to highlight a host of ethical abuses.

Bragger and Freeman (1999) used an exercise to facilitate the teaching of both ethics and statistics. Students evaluated five commonly discussed social psychology experiments (e.g., Milgram, 1963) and had them rate both the benefits and costs associated with each study on a scale of 1 (no benefit or cost) to 100 (high benefit or cost). Students computed the means and standard deviations for each by gender and reviewed the results. This exercise afforded students the opportunity to work with meaningful data, the opportunity to explore ethical concerns, and to get a glimpse into the potential workings of an institutional review board.

Vardeman and Morris (2003) argued that we should teach statistical ethics as an extension of broader ethical concerns related to being a responsible human being. For example, instructors should highlight issues such as working only in areas within which one is competent, living up to one's commitments, fully exploring ideas, avoiding misrepresentation, and being willing to reach unpopular conclusions. In addition to avoiding misleading results, Goddard (2005) also argued that all researchers, whether student or professional, should carefully proofread all their data. Vardeman and Morris asserted, "At its core statistics is not about cleverness and technique but rather about *honesty*. Its real contribution to society is primarily *moral* and not technical. It is about doing *the right thing* when interpreting empirical information" (p. 21).

## Diversity

In 1998, the APA's Board of Educational Affair's Task Force on Diversity Issues at the Precollege and Undergraduate Levels of Education in Psychology authored a series of articles in the *APA Monitor* (www.apa.org/ed/divhscollege.html), which suggested that an effective approach to making psychology more inclusive would be to incorporate diversity issues within existing courses in psychology. Much like ethics, researchers have not listed diversity as an important component in statistics courses (Friedrich et al., 2000; Giesbrecht et al., 1997; Landrum, 2005). Statistics have the appearance of being very democratic and hence, perhaps, unaffected by issues of diversity. Yet, the development of statistical reasoning and thinking skills necessitates the understanding of statistics in context (Cobb & McClain, 2004; Gal, 2004; Pfannkuch & Wild, 2004; Rumsey, 2002). Therefore, it is incumbent on instructors to address issues of diversity in statistics courses.

Diversity is a broad-reaching concept that educators often conceptualize as including race/ethnicity, gender, sexual orientation, age, disability, cross-cultural, international, socioeconomic status, language, educational level, religion, marital status, social class/caste, computer literacy, and physical appearance. Mio, Barker-Hackett, and Tumambing (2006) noted that there is a recent trend towards greater use of qualitative approaches when examining issues of diversity or multiculturalism in psychology. Nonetheless, researchers still largely use quantitative methods when examining the majority of domains within psychology including the study of diversity.

Chang and Sue (2005) suggested that the current scientific paradigm, with its focus on experimental designs, has introduced a bias in psychology, specifically a focus on internal validity and a devaluation of external validity. They suggested that the overemphasis on internal validity (i.e., causality) has fostered several problems such as an overuse of college students as research participants and an overwillingness to assume research conducted on one population (e.g., white, middle-class, U.S. citizens) can be generalized to other groups and situations. This issue is important in a statistics course due to the positive relationship between internal validity and statistical conclusion validity (Shadish et al., 2001). Researchers may endeavor to achieve high statistical conclusion validity by using homogeneous samples with accompanying low error rates. However, the exclusion of diverse participants does not reflect the diversity of human experience. Instructors need to make students aware of external validity issues in relation to the results of their projects and data analyses.

Although Woolf and Hulsizer's (2007) discussion of diversity focused on teaching research methods, much of their discussion is applicable for use in statistics courses. For example, they presented issues of sampling, experimenter bias, methodological design concerns, construct validity, and informed consent—each of which are important topics relevant to development of statistical thinking as well as statistical ethics (ASA, 1999; Ben-Zvi & Garfield, 2004; delMas, 2002; ISI, 1985; Pfannkuch & Wild, 2004). They further discussed the effect of group definition and the impact of omission/exclusion of groups on research conclusions. Instructors might use gender data to highlight the difference between statistical significance and practical significance or include information concerning illusory correlations during discussions of correlation coefficients. By placing issues of diversity within the context of statistical thinking, teachers can assist students with learning the limitations and appropriate interpretation of data-analytic techniques and results. Quina and Kulberg (2003) also highlighted goals and objectives that accompany the integration of sociocultural context and multicultural awareness into experimental psychology courses.

For the development of statistical literacy, students must be able to understand data in context (ASA, 2005; Gal, 2004; Phannkuch & Wild, 2004). Students should be aware of their method of data collection and possible non-equivalency of data due to the effect of diversity. For example, Brislin (2000) asserted that researchers should understand the influence of three sources of nonequivalence—translation, metric, and conceptual—when conducting cross-cultural research. Translation equivalence is necessary when using an experimental measure developed in a different culture. Metric equivalence involves the ability to compare the specific scores on a scale of interest across cultures. Conceptual equivalence is the degree to which theoretical concepts or constructs are the same between two cultures. Instructors can highlight nonequivalence in a variety ways. For example, instructors can raise the issue of whether clinical or personality measures are equivalent cross-culturally. In addition, instructors can stress that even a demographic variable such as "age" may not be culture-free. For example, the Ju/'hoansi, also known as the !Kung, use a culturally specific age categorization system as opposed to thinking of age in chronological years (Hames & Draper, 2004). Instructors can also highlight the potential for nonequivalency. For example, researchers have rarely standardized measures of assessment used in research, particularly those related to personality assessment and psychopathology, for use with a disabled population (Elliott & Umlauf, 1995; Pullin, 2002). Instructors who highlight the context of numbers are facilitating the development of statistical literacy, thinking, and reasoning skills (ASA, 2005).

In January 2000, the Council of National Psychological Associations for the Advancement of Ethnic Minority Interests (CNPAAEMI) produced the *Guidelines for Research in Ethnic Minority Communities*. Five ethnic minority associations within the APA worked collaboratively to create a document reflecting issues relevant to research with African-American, Asian-American, Hispanic, and American

Indian populations. The *Guidelines* provided a wealth of information that statistics instructors might find useful as a course supplement. The *Guidelines for Research in Ethnic Minority Communities* (CNPAAEMI, 2000) invited researchers to learn more about the rich diversity among individuals defined as belonging to a particular race and avoid treating racial categories as homogenous groups. Instructors can encourage students to think of diversity as not just a variable of interest but also as a source of variability within seemingly homogenous populations.

## Online Statistical Education

Technological advances in online course delivery software, increasing student demand for accessible college courses, and administrative pressure to offer courses with lower direct and indirect costs have resulted in a steady increase in online education across academia (Institute for Higher Education Policy, 1999). Of course, distance education is not a new concept—only the medium has changed. In the past, distance educators have utilized radio, television, and more recently video to offer education to students (Stephenson, 2001). However, computer technology has allowed instructors flexibility in both the content and format of the course that was unavailable in previous manifestations of distance education. Computers facilitate the incorporation of multimedia applications (e.g., Java applets, PowerPoint, video) into a lecture—regardless of whether the course takes place in a physical or virtual classroom. Online education software also has enabled instructors to offer courses in "real time" (i.e., synchronous instruction) or at whatever time is convenient for students (i.e., asynchronous instruction).

Teaching in an online environment can be a challenge (Kreiner, 2006). Instructors should expect to spend considerable time converting their traditional course to an online environment (Finley, 2006). According to Harris, Mazoué, Hamdan, and Casiple (2007), instructors need to take care when selecting course management software (e.g., Blackboard, WebCT) and ancillary technologies (e.g., Tegrity Web Learner, Centra Symposium) to insure the course platform meets their pedagogical needs and student expectations. Following the creation of the course, Finley warned that instructors should expect to spend time maintaining links, learning to navigate the course management software, and interacting with students. Indeed,

Finley revealed she spent one-third more time interacting with her online students than with her traditional course students.

One of the primary arguments against online instruction is the concern that the medium negatively affects the academic rigor of the course (Brink, 2004; Eaton, 2001). However, Brink (2004) argued that a good learning experience depends more on the student–teacher interaction than the means by which the instructor conveys the material to the student. Indeed, Harris et al. (2007) recommended that instructors create online courses with an eye towards maintaining, as much as possible, equivalent processes and outcomes associated with traditional face-to-face classroom instruction.

Researchers have offered suggestions specific to teaching statistics in an online environment. For example, Tudor (2006) offered tips on creating tutorials, self-help quizzes, activities, and exams for the online environment. She also commented on the importance of group discussions, statistical software, and supplemental course materials. Tudor asserted that the key ingredients to a successful online statistics course are organization, active-learning opportunities, student-to-student communication, and meaningful interaction between student and instructor. Pedagogy is not medium specific (Markel, 1999). Grandzol (2004) asserted that he approached online instruction in much the same way he approached the topic in a traditional class setting. Indeed, some of the tips for teaching a traditional statistics course that Kirk (2002) presented were similar to the recommendations offered by online statistics instructors (e.g., increasing student–teacher interaction, employing active-learning strategies).

Several studies have compared fully online statistics courses to traditional statistics courses or hybrid classes (i.e., only a portion of the course is online). Unfortunately, research on the effectiveness of online statistical education has produced mixed results. For example, Summers, Waigandt, and Whittaker (2005) compared students' final statistics grades and course satisfaction ratings in an online versus traditional face-to-face statistics course. They found no difference in students' final grades between the two instructional approaches. However, students in the online course were less satisfied with the instructor, class discussion, class assignments, and grading than were students in the traditional statistics class. Harrington (1999) examined the relationship between final course grade, undergraduate GPA, and instructional medium (e.g., traditional or a fully online statistics course) for MSW students taking a graduate statistics course. She found that students with high undergraduate GPAs performed equally well regardless of instructional method. However, students with low undergraduate GPAs did significantly worse in the online course than comparable students in the traditional statistics course.

Utts et al. (2003) compared traditional and hybrid statistics courses to determine if there were any differences in student performance or satisfaction. They found no difference in student performance on test scores and grades, and no difference in overall student satisfaction with the course. However, students in the traditional course reported more satisfaction with the organization, pace, and expectations than those students in the hybrid course. Ward (2004) also found no differences in student performance and overall course satisfaction between traditional and hybrid statistics courses. However, she reported that students in the hybrid course perceived their instructor more favorably than did those students in the traditional statistics course. Cole and Cole (2005) examined whether students enrolled in an online or hybrid statistics course would differ as a function of problem-solving ability and class performance. They found that students in the hybrid course performed significantly higher on exams than did students in the online course. In addition, unlike students in the online course, students in the hybrid statistics class demonstrated an increase in their mathematical problem-solving abilities.

Although there is some inconsistency in the literature, it may be possible to draw some tentative conclusions regarding the effectiveness of online statistical education. Several of the studies found no differences in student assessment between these three teaching methods. However, student satisfaction seemed to be highest when students physically interacted with the instructor (e.g., traditional face-to-face statistics courses). Because online education remains a relatively new phenomenon, educational researchers need to examine more fully the conditions that lead to success with Internet-based statistics instruction and learning.

## Finishing up Any Statistics Course

Instructors need to attend as much to the end of the semester as they do the beginning of a term. This point is important not only to bring closure to a course but also to begin preparation for following terms. Consequently, departments and instructors might elect to engage in programmatic, summative assessment strategies to ensure that the course is meeting curricular needs (Garfield & Chance, 2000). Assessment and curriculum development can occur at any point in a term. Departments with many statistics sections may elect to engage in programmatic assessment before the beginning of a term to ensure consistency in student learning outcomes. Instructors may engage in collaborative assessment strategies during a term to test out new activities and teaching strategies. Finally, departments may engage in broader assessment to ensure that students meet the departmental learning goals and outcomes. Regardless of the strategies employed, Garfield (1994) asserted that instructors should not attempt to engage in assessment alone but rather should work collaboratively with colleagues.

Departments may elect to adopt general learning goals and outcomes for their majors to facilitate uniformity across sections of various courses if taught by different instructors. These defined learning outcomes and goals facilitate linkages among instruction, learning, and assessment (Colvin & Vos, 1997; Gal & Garfield, 1997; Garfield & Chance, 2000). In relation to statistics, Roiter and Petocz (1996) discussed four different approaches or paradigms relevant to the teaching of statistics. These approaches included teaching statistics as a branch of mathematics, a data-driven or laboratory approach, a research approach, and a problem-solving approach. They asserted that each of these approaches involves different teaching strategies as well as differing learning outcomes and goals. For example, a mathematically-based course would focus heavily on probability and derivation of formulas, be primarily lecture-based, and utilize traditional testing strategies. A research-based course would involve greater use of inferential statistics, be project and active learning based, and would use assessment strategies that include non-traditional exams, lab assignments, and research reports.

To begin the curriculum development process, Roiter and Petocz (1996) recommended that departmental faculty complete a short assessment quiz aimed at highlighting each instructor's underlying assumptions about the goals of a statistics course. Their questionnaire required instructors to rate, on a scale of strongly disagree to strongly agree, 10 items such as the importance of formula derivations, the role of course projects, the role of research article critiques, and the use of data sets. Instructors can use the scores from the questionnaire to ascertain whether they prefer a mathematical, problem-solving, research, or data-driven laboratory approach to teaching statistics. Although there is much overlap with each of these approaches, departments and instructors may find it valuable to assess their areas of commonality and difference with the goal of developing focused departmental goals, outcomes, and assessment strategies. Departments may also want to review the *APA Guidelines for the Undergraduate Psychology Major* (adopted in 2006). The second goal of the Report focused on the learning goal of research methods and included students' ability to compute and correctly interpret data analyses as a recommended outcome. This inclusion of statistical understanding as a key component of research methods suggests that educational leaders within psychology lean toward the "statistics as research design/experimental design" approach as described by Roiter and Petocz (p. 7).

Roback, Chance, Legler, and Moore (2006) presented an approach to collaborative study for instructors aimed at improved lesson plans and quality of teaching. In addition, instructors have successfully applied the Japanese Lesson Study approach to the teaching of mathematics (Curcio, 2002; Stigler & Hiebert, 1999). This approach includes four steps: regular collaborative meetings with instructors teaching the course; new lesson plan implementation with observers; follow-up meeting to discuss the teaching and learning experience; and revision of the course materials. The process is reiterative with each instructor benefiting from joint development of lesson plans as well as feedback. Roback et al. commented that the approach works best when there are 4–6 instructors who teach the same course and have comparable learning goals and outcomes. Teachers who took part in the process noted that it required a relatively large commitment of time but that the process had improved their teaching and sense of collaboration with colleagues. In addition, instructors found the approach particularly useful when testing out new active learning techniques in the classroom. Observers were better able to assess what worked and what didn't than the instructor. Ideally, the Japanese Lesson Study approach improves the curriculum, student learning, and enables instructors to use this method as a research tool (Garfield et al., 2002; Roback et al., 2006).

To facilitate overall assessment and improvement of the course, Holmes (1997) recommended the use of outside evaluators. He asserted that outside examiners might better evaluate the function of a course in relation to programmatic goals and outcomes. For example, as compared to the instructor, outside observers may be in a better position to recognize a discrepancy among the goals outlined in the syllabus, the structure and methods of instruction in the course, and models of assessment. Holmes described a program with learning outcomes and goals aimed at the development of statistical thinking that focused on learning formulas and discrete tasks. Once teachers implemented projects as a key component of the course, students experienced improved levels of statistical thinking.

Scepansky and Carkenord (2004) described a method of assessing students in their senior year for retention of material from statistics and research methods courses. Students completed a multiple-choice exam compiled from various research methods and statistics test banks. Scepansky and Carkenord found no significant reduction in retention of material suggesting that students had developed an internal schematization of the material from these courses. They also found no significant correlation between the amount of time spent studying and subsequent performance on the assessment measure, suggesting that students might have developed broader statistical reasoning and thinking skills as opposed to simply memorizing course materials.

Garfield and Chance (2000) highlighted two assessment techniques that instructors might use for either summative or program assessment—the Statistics Advanced Placement course materials and exam and the Statistical Reasoning Assessment (SRA; Garfield, 2003). Statistics Advanced Placement test materials from previous years are available for download at www.apcentral.collegeboard.com. Instructors must register with the College Board to have access to the materials but registration is free. Instructors may opt to not use the exam as presented but rather use it as a model—tweaking the questions to make them more applicable to psychology. Instructors can also administer the SRA to examine the development of students' statistical reasoning skills (Garfield, 2003). Depending on the goals of the program, instructors can administer the paper and pencil test as a pre- and post-test to evaluate the development of reasoning skills within a specific course. Departments also can use the test as part of an overall pregraduation evaluation to assess skill retention and student attainment of departmental learning goals and outcomes. For more information on approaches to teaching your last statistics class of the semester, see our Web site at www.teachstats.org.

## Final Thoughts

Between the two of us, we have taught well over 100 different sections of introductory statistics, which begs the question: How do you keep your course fresh? Lloyd (1999) noted there are many ways to keep a course exciting and new. Some of her suggestions work particularly well in a statistics course. First, instructors should regularly try out new things. Because statistics is fundamentally about application and reasoning, instructors can discuss recent news articles, conduct new experiments with students, and test out novel active learning techniques. Many statistics educators have written articles and books highlighting a host of activities and projects (e.g., Gelman & Nolan, 2002; Gnanadesikan et al., 1997; Hunter, 1977; Lindquist & Hammel, 1998; Mackisack, 1994; Scheaffer et al., 1996; Smith, 1998). Second, Lloyd argued that instructors should keep learning. Fortunately, statistics instructors will find a wealth of resources related to teaching that they can explore on a regular basis (e.g., journals and books). Indeed, the *Journal of Statistics Education* is introducing a new feature entitled "From Research to Practice" specifically aimed at the dissemination of statistics education research (Miller, 2007). Moreover, there are increasing opportunities for continuing education at conferences and programs aimed specifically at promoting teacher education in statistics. The International Association for Statistical Education makes most of its conference presentations available online at no cost to those participants who are unable to attend. In online Appendix E at www.teachstats.org, we provide a listing of books, journals, organizations, and relevant information for instructors who want to keep abreast the latest statistics education resources and opportunities.

In the end, we hope that both students and instructors will not only learn from, but also enjoy, their statistics courses. Although the knowledge of statistics is imperative for students pursuing an undergraduate and graduate degree in psychology, it is just as essential for informed citizenship in today's data-driven world. We recall the words of Sir Arthur L. Bowley (1907), "A knowledge of statistics is like a knowledge of foreign languages or of algebra: it may prove of use at any time under any circumstances" (p. 4). Now learn, teach, and have fun!

# References

Aberson, C. L., Berger, D. E., Emerson, E. P., & Romero, V. L. (1997). WISE: Web Interface for Statistics Education. *Behavior Research Methods, Instruments, & Computers, 29,* 217–221.

Aberson, C. L., Berger, D. E., Healy, M. R., Kyle, D. J., & Romero, V. L. (2000). Evaluation of an interactive tutorial for teaching the central limit theorem. *Teaching of Psychology, 27,* 289–291.

Adler, A. G., & Vollick, D. (2000). Undergraduate statistics in psychology: A survey of Canadian institutions. *Canadian Psychology, 41,* 149–151.

Ageel, M. I. (2002). Spreadsheets as a simulation tool for solving probability problems. *Teaching Statistics, 24,* 51–54.

Aguinis, H., Petersen, S. A., & Pierce, C. A. (1999). Appraisal of the homogeneity of error variance assumption and alternatives to multiple regression for estimating moderating effects of categorical variables. *Organizational Research Methods, 2,* 315–339.

Aiken, L. S., West, S. G., Sechrest, L., Reno, R. R., Roediger, H. L., III, Scarr, S., et al. (1990). Graduate training in statistics, methodology, and measurement in psychology. *American Psychologist, 45,* 721–734.

Albert, J. (2002). A baseball statistics course. *Journal of Statistics Education, 10*(2). Retrieved July 31, 2007, from www.amstat.org/publications/jse/v10n2/albert.html

Albert, J. (2003). *Teaching statistics using baseball.* Washington, DC: Mathematical Association of America.

Allen, G. A. (1981). The $\chi^2$ statistic and Weber's Law. *Teaching of Psychology, 8*, 179–180.

Althaus, S. L. (1997). Computer-mediated communication in the university classroom: An experiment with on-line discussions. *Communication Education, 46*, 158–74.

American Psychological Association. (2001). *Publication manual of the American Psychological Association* (5th ed.). Washington, DC: American Psychological Association.

American Psychological Association. (2002). *Ethical principles of psychologists and code of conduct.* Retrieved July 31, 2007, from www.apa.org/ethics/code2002.html

American Psychological Association. (2005). *National standards for high school psychology curricula.* Retrieved July 31, 2007, from www.apa.org/ed/natlstandards.html

American Psychological Association. (2006). *APA guidelines for the undergraduate psychology major.* Retrieved July 31, 2007, from www.apa.org/ed/psymajor_guideline.pdf

American Statistical Association. (1999). *Ethical guidelines for statistical practice.* Retrieved July 31, 2007, from www.amstat.org/profession/

American Statistical Association. (2005). *Guidelines for assessment and instruction in statistics education (GAISE) Project.* Retrieved July 31, 2007, from www.amstat.org/education/gaise/

American Statistical Association. (2007). *ASA vision, mission and history.* Retrieved July 31, 2007, from www.amstat.org/about/

Amstat News. (1999). ASA launches Undergraduate Statistics Education Initiative, *Amstat News, 270*, 3.

Anastasi, A. (1985). Psychological testing: Basic concepts and common misconceptions. In A. M. Rogers & C. J. Scheirer (Eds.), *The G. Stanley Hall Lecture Series* (Vol. 5, pp. 87–120). Washington, DC: American Psychological Association.

Anderson, R. H. (1990). Computers, statistics, and the introductory class. *Teaching Sociology, 18*, 185–192.

Anderson-Cook, C. M. (1999). An in-class demonstration to help students understand confidence intervals. *Journal of Statistics Education, 7*(3). Retrieved July 31, 2007, from www.amstat.org/publications/jse/secure/v7n3/anderson-cook.cfm

Andrews, D. F., & Herzberg, A. M. (1985). *Data: A collection of problems from many fields for the student and research worker.* New York: Springer-Verlag.

Anscombe, F. J. (1973). Graphics in statistical analysis. *The American Statistician, 27*, 17–21.

AP College Board. (2006). *AP calculus/statistics growth.* Retrieved July 31, 2007, from www.apcentral.collegeboard.com/apc/public/repository/ap05_calculus-statistics_growth.xls

Apigian, C. H., & Gambill, S. E. (2004–2005, Winter). Is Microsoft Excel 2003 ready for the statistics classroom? *Journal of Computer Information Systems, 45,* 27–35.

Armero, C., & Ferrándiz, J. (2002). Simulation in the simple linear regression model. *Teaching Statistics, 24,* 12–16.

Bajgier, S. M., Atkinson, M., & Prybutok, V. R. (1989). Visual fits in the teaching of regression concepts. *The American Statistician, 43,* 229–234.

Bakker, A., & Gravemeijer, K. P. E. (2006). An historical phenomenology of mean and median. *Educational Studies in Mathematics, 62,* 149–168.

Ballman, K. (1997). Greater emphasis on variation in an introductory statistics course. *Journal of Statistics Education, 5*(2), Retrieved July 31, 2007, from www.amstat.org/publications/jse/v5n2/ballman.html

Ballman, K. (2000). Real data in classroom examples. In T. L. Moore (Ed.), *Teaching statistics: Resources for undergraduate instructors* (pp. 11–18). Washington, DC: Mathematical Association of America.

Barbella, P., & Siegel, M. (2001). Exploring a queueing problem through human simulation. *Teaching Statistics, 23,* 4–7.

Barfield, W., & Robless, R. (1989). The effects of two- or three-dimensional graphics on the problem-solving performance of experienced and novice decision makers. *Behaviour & Information Technology, 8,* 369–385.

Barnette, J. J. (1978). Did Mark Twain ever hear of Sir Ronald Fisher? *The CEDR Quarterly, 11,* 8–10.

Baron, M. A., & Boschee, F. (1995). *Authentic assessment: The key to unlocking student success.* Lanham, MD: Scarecrow Press/Technomic Books.

Barr, R. B., & Tagg, J. (1995). From teaching to learning: A new paradigm for undergraduate education. *Change, 27*(6), 12–25.

Barrett, G. B. (2000). The coefficient of determination: Understanding $r^2$ and $R^2$. *The Mathematics Teacher, 93,* 230–234.

Bartz, A. E. (1981). The statistics course as a departmental offering and major requirement. *Teaching of Psychology, 8,* 106.

Bartz, A. E., & Sabolik, M. A. (2001). Computer and software use in teaching the beginning statistics course. *Teaching of Psychology, 28,* 147–149.

Batanero, C., Tauber, L. M., & Sánchez, V. (2004). Students' reasoning about the normal distribution. In D. Ben-Zvi & J. Garfield (Eds.), *The challenge of developing statistical literacy, reasoning, and thinking* (pp. 257–276). Dordrecht: Kluwer Academic.

Bear, G. (1995). Computationally intensive methods warrant reconsideration of pedagogy in statistics. *Behavior Research Methods, Instruments, & Computers, 27,* 144–147.

Becker, A. H., & Calhoon, S. K. (2000). What introductory psychology students attend to on a course syllabus. *Teaching of Psychology, 26,* 6–11.

Becker, B. J. (1996). A look at the literature (and other resources) on teaching statistics. *Journal of Educational and Behavioral Statistics, 21,* 71–90.

Becker, B. J. (2000). Multivariate meta-analysis. In H. E. A. Tinsley & S. D. Brown (Eds.), *Handbook of applied multivariate statistics and mathematical modeling* (pp. 499–525). San Diego, CA: Academic Press.

Begg, A. (1997). Some emerging influences underpinning assessment in statistics. In I. Gal & J. Garfield (Eds.), *The assessment challenge in statistics education* (pp. 17–25). Amsterdam: IOS Press.

Beins, B. (1985). Teaching the relevance of statistics through consumer-oriented research. *Teaching of Psychology, 12,* 168–169.

Beins, B. C. (1993). Writing assignments in statistics classes encourage students to learn interpretation. *Teaching of Psychology, 20,* 161–164.

Beins, B. C. (2004). *Research methods: A tool for life with research.* Boston: Allyn & Bacon.

Benedict, J. O., & Anderton, J. B. (2004). Applying the just-in-time teaching approach to teaching statistics. *Teaching of Psychology, 31,* 197–199.

Benjamin, L. T. (2002). Lecturing. In S. F. Davis & W. Buskist (Eds.), *The teaching of psychology: Essays in honor of Wilbert J. McKeachie and Charles L. Brewer* (pp. 57–67). Mahwah, NJ: Lawrence Erlbaum Associates.

Benjamini, Y. (1988). Opening the box of a boxplot. *The American Statistician, 42,* 257–262.

Ben-Zvi, D. (2000). Toward understanding the role of technological tools in statistical learning. *Mathematical Thinking & Learning, 2,* 127–155.

Ben-Zvi, D. (2004). Reasoning about variability in comparing distributions. *Statistics Education Research Journal, 3*(2), 42–63. Retrieved July 31, 2007, from www.stat.auckland.ac.nz/~iase/serj/SERJ3(2)_BenZvi.pdf

Ben-Zvi, D., & Friedlander, A. (1997). Statistical thinking in a technological environment. In J. B. Garfield & G. Burrill (Eds.), *Research on the role of technology in teaching and learning statistics* (pp. 45–55). Voorburg, The Netherlands: International Statistical Institute.

Ben-Zvi, D., & Garfield, J. (2004). Statistical literacy, reasoning, and thinking: Goals, definitions, and challenges. In D. Ben-Zvi & J. Garfield (Eds.), *The challenge of developing statistical literacy, reasoning, and thinking* (pp. 3–15). Dordrecht: Kluwer Academic.

Best, J. (2004). *More damned lies and statistics. How numbers confuse public issues.* Berkeley, CA: University of California Press, Berkeley.

Bloom, B. S., Englehart, M. D., Furst, E. J., Hill, W. H., & Krathwohl, D. R. (1956). *Taxonomy of educational objectives: The classification of educational goals, handbook I: Cognitive domain.* New York: Longmans, Green.

Bolstad, W. M., Hunt, L. A., & McWhirter, J. L. (2001). Sex, drugs, and Rock & Roll in a first-year service course in statistics. *The American Statistician, 55,* 145–149.

Bolt, M. (1996). *Instructor's resources to accompany Exploring Psychology by David G. Myers*. New York: Worth.

Bosack, T. N., McCarthy, M. A., Halonen, J. S., & Clay. S. P. (2004). Developing scientific inquiry skills in psychology: Using authentic assessment strategies. In D. S. Dunn, C. M. Mehrotra, & J. S. Halonen (Eds.), *Measuring up: Educational assessment challenges and practices for psychology* (pp. 141–170). Washington, DC: American Psychological Association.

Bossley, M., O'Neill, G., Parsons, C., & Lockwood, J. (1980). Teaching implications of statistical procedures used in current research. *Teaching of Psychology, 7*, 107–108.

Bowley, A. L. (1907). *Elements of statistics* (3rd ed.). London: P. S. King & Son.

Bradley, D. R. (1989). Using the microcomputer as a visual aid in the statistics classroom. *Behavior Research Methods, Instruments, & Computers, 21*, 96–98.

Bradley, D. R., Hemstreet, R. L., & Ziegenhagen, S. T. (1992). A simulation laboratory for statistics. *Behavior Research Methods, Instruments, & Computers, 24*, 190–204.

Bradstreet, T. E. (1996). Teaching introductory statistics courses so that nonstatisticians experience statistical reasoning. *The American Statistician, 50*, 69–78.

Bragger, J. D., & Freeman, M. A. (1999). Using a cost-benefit analysis to teach ethics and statistics. *Teaching of Psychology, 26*, 34–36.

Brakke, K., Wilson, J. H., & Bradley, D. V. (2007). Beyond basics: Enhancing undergraduate statistics instruction. In D. S. Dunn, R. A. Smith, & B. C. Beins (Eds.), *Best practices for teaching statistics and research methods in the behavioral sciences* (pp. 109–122). Mahwah, NJ: Erlbaum.

Brewer, C. L. (1997). Undergraduate education in psychology: Will the mermaids sing? *American Psychologist, 52*, 434–441.

Briggs, N. E., & Sheu, C. (1998). Using Java in introductory statistics. *Behavior Research Methods, Instruments & Computers, 30*, 246–249.

Brink, T. L. (2004). Online teaching: Problems and solutions. In B. Perlman, L. I. McCann, & S. H. McFadden (Eds.), *Lessons learned: Practical advice for the teaching of psychology* (Vol. 2; pp. 71–79). Washington, DC: American Psychological Society.

Brinthaupt, T. M. (2002). Teaching research ethics: Illustrating the nature of the researcher-IRB relationship. *Teaching of Psychology, 29*, 243–245.

Brislin, R. (2000). *Understanding culture's influence on behavior* (2nd ed.). New York: Wadsworth.

Britt, M. A., Sellinger, J., & Stillerman, L. M. (2002). A review of ESTAT: An innovative program for teaching statistics. *Teaching of Psychology, 29*, 73–75.

Broers, N. J., & Imbos, T. (2005). Charting and manipulating propositions as methods to promote self-explanation in the study of statistics. *Learning and Instruction, 15,* 517–538.

Broers, N. J., Mur, M. C., & Bude, L. (2004). *Directed self-explanation in the study of statistics.* Paper presented at the International Association for Statistical Education (IASE) Roundtable on Curricular Development in Statistics Education, Lund, Sweden. Retrieved July 31, 2007, from www.stat.auckland.ac.nz/~iase/publications/rt04/2.2_Broers_etal.pdf

Brooks, C. I. (1987). Superiority of women in statistics achievement. *Teaching of Psychology, 14,* 45.

Brooks, G. P., & Raffle, H. (2005). FISH: A new computer program for friendly introductory statistics help. *Teaching Statistics, 27,* 81–88.

Brosnan, C. A., Ericksen, L. R., & Lin, Y. (2002). Teaching nursing research using large data sets. *Journal of Nursing Education, 41,* 368–371.

Brown, M., Askew, M., Baker, D., Denvir, H., & Millett, A. (1998). Is the National Numeracy Strategy research-based? *British Journal of Educational Studies, 46,* 362–385.

Bryce, G. R. (2002). Undergraduate statistics education: An introduction and review of selected literature. *Journal of Statistics Education, 10*(2). Retrieved July 31, 2007, from www.amstat.org/publications/jse/v10n2/bryce.html

Bryce, G. R., Gould, R., Notz, W. I., & Peck, R. L. (2001). Curriculum guidelines for Bachelor of Science degrees in statistical science. *The American Statistician, 55,* 7–13.

Buche, D. D., & Glover, J. A. (1988). Teaching students to review research as an aid for problem solving. In M. E. Ware & C. L. Brewer (Eds.), *Handbook for teaching statistics and research methods* (pp. 126–129). Hillsdale, NJ: Lawrence Erlbaum.

Buck, J. L. (1985). A failure to find gender differences in statistics achievement. *Teaching of Psychology, 12,* 100.

Buck, J. L. (1990). On testing for variance effects. *Teaching of Psychology, 17,* 255–256.

Buckalew, L. W. (1983). Nonparametrics and psychology: A revitalized alliance. *Perceptual and Motor Skills, 57,* 447–450.

Buskist, W., & Davis, S. F. (Eds.). (2006). *Handbook of the teaching of psychology.* Malden, MA: Blackwell.

Butler, D. (1986). Integrating statistical software into laboratories and laboratory courses. *Behavior Research Methods, Instruments, & Computers, 18,* 214–244.

Butler, D. L. (1993). Graphics in psychology: Pictures, data, and especially concepts. *Behavior Research Methods, Instruments, & Computers, 25,* 81–92.

Butler, R. S. (1998). On the failure of the widespread use of statistics. *Amstat News, 251,* 84.

Byrne, B. M. (1996). The status and role of quantitative methods in psychology: Past, present, and future perspectives. *Canadian Psychology, 37,* 76–80.

Cacioppo, J. T., Petty, R. E., Feinstein, J. A., & Jarvis, W. B. G. (1996). Disposition differences in cognitive motivation: The life and times of individuals vary in need for cognition. *Psychological Bulletin, 119,* 197–253.

Cake, L. J., & Hostetter, R. C. (1986). ANOVAGEN: A data generation and analysis of variance program for use in statistics courses. *Teaching of Psychology, 19,* 185–188.

Callaert, H. (2000). Amazing graphs. *Teaching Statistics, 22,* 25–27.

Callahan, J. L., & Reio, T. G., Jr. (2006). Making subjective judgments in quantitative studies: The importance of using effect sizes and confidence intervals. *Human Resource Development Quarterly, 17,* 159–173.

Cannon, A., Hartlaub, B., Lock, R., Notz, W., & Parker, M. (2002). Guidelines for undergraduate minors and concentrations in statistical science. *Journal of Statistics Education, 10*(2). Retrieved July 31, 2007, from www.amstat.org/publications/jse/v10n2/cannon.html

Carlson, W. L. (1999). A case method for teaching statistics. *Journal of Economic Education, 30,* 52–58.

Carmer, S. G., & Cady, F. B. (1969). Computerized data generation for teaching statistics. *American Statistician, 23,* 33–35.

Carswell, C. M., & Ramzy, C. (1997). Graphing small data sets: Should we bother? *Behaviour & Information Technology, 16,* 61–71.

Carswell, C. M., Frankenberger, S., & Bernhard, D. (1991). Graphing in depth: Perspectives on the use of three-dimensional graphs to represent lower-dimension data. *Behaviour & Information Technology, 10,* 459–474.

Carter, K. R., & Cooney, J. B. (1983). The audio-tutorial applied in psychology classes to minimize individual differences and save class time. *Teaching of Psychology, 10,* 201–204.

Chambers, E. A. (2004). An introduction to meta-analysis with articles from *The Journal of Educational Research* (1992–2002). *The Journal of Educational Research, 98,* 35–44.

Chambers, J. M., Cleveland, W. S., Kleiner, B., & Tukey, P. A. (1983). *Graphical methods for data analysis.* New York: Chapman and Hall.

Chance, B., delMas, R., & Garfield, J. (2004). Reasoning about sampling distributions. In D. Ben-Zvi & J. Garfield (Eds.), *The challenge of developing statistical literacy, reasoning, and thinking* (pp. 295–323). Dordrecht: Kluwer Academic Publishers.

Chance, B. L. (1997). Experiences with authentic assessment techniques in an introductory statistics course. *Journal of Statistics Education, 5*(3). Retrieved July 31, 2007, from www.amstat.org/publications/jse/v5n3/chance.html

Chance, B. L. (2002). Components of statistical thinking and implications for instruction and assessment. *Journal of Statistics Education, 10*(3). Retrieved July 31, 2007, from www.amstat.org/publications/jse/v10n3/chance.html

Chance, B. L., & Rossman, A. J. (2001). Sequencing topics in introductory statistics: A debate on what to teach when. *The American Statistician, 55,* 140–144.

Chang, J., & Sue, S. (2005). Culturally sensitive research: Where have we gone wrong and what do we need to do now? In M. G. Constantine & D. W. Sue (Eds.), *Strategies for building multicultural competence in mental health and educational settings* (pp. 229–246). Hoboken, NJ: Wiley.

Chang, T. C., Lohr, S. L., & McLaren, C. G. (1992). Teaching survey sampling using simulation. *The American Statistician, 46,* 232–237.

Chew, S. L. (2007). Designing effective examples and problems for teaching statistics. In D. S. Dunn, R. A. Smith, & B. C. Beins (Eds.), *Best practices for teaching statistics and research methods in the behavioral sciences* (pp. 73–91). Mahwah, NJ: Erlbaum.

Cholkar, C. P., & Deshpande, M. N. (2004). Useful data for teaching statistics from Hockey World Cup matches. *Teaching Statistics, 26,* 20–21.

Christensen, A. R., & Stephens, L. J. (2003). Microsoft Excel as a supplement in a high school statistics course. *International Journal of Mathematical Education in Science and Technology, 36,* 881–885.

Christopher, A. (2006). Selecting a text and using publisher-produced courseware: Some suggestions and warnings. In W. Buskist & S. F. Davis (Eds.), *Handbook of the teaching of psychology* (pp. 36–40). Malden, MA: Blackwell.

Christopher, A. N., & Marek, P. (2002). A sweet tasting demonstration of random occurrences. *Teaching of Psychology, 29,* 122–125.

Christopher, A. N., & Walter, M. I. (2006). An assignment to help students learn to navigate primary sources of information. *Teaching of Psychology, 33,* 42–45.

Cleveland, W. S. (1984a). Graphs in scientific publications. *The American Statistician, 38,* 261–269.

Cleveland, W. S. (1984b). Graphical methods for data presentation: Full scale breaks, dot charts, and multibased logging. *The American Statistician, 38,* 270–280.

Cleveland, W. S. (1993). *Visualizing data.* Summit, NJ: Hobart Press.

Cleveland, W. S. (1994). *The elements of graphing data* (Rev. ed.). Summit, NJ: Hobart Press.

Cleveland, W. S., & McGill, R. (1984). Graphical perception: Theory, experimentation, and application to the development of graphical methods. *Journal of the American Statistical Association, 79,* 531–553.

Clough, J. (1993). Which knowledge and skills should psychology graduates have? Balancing the needs of the individual, employers, the science and the profession. *Australian Psychologist, 28*, 42–44.

Coakley, C. W. (1996). Suggestions for your nonparametric statistics course. *Journal of Statistics Education, 4*(2). Retrieved July 31, 2007, from www.amstat.org/publications/jse/v4n2/coakley.html

Cobb, G. (1992). Teaching statistics. In L. A. Steen (Ed.), *Heeding the call for change: Suggestions for curricular action* (pp. 3–34). Washington, DC: Mathematical Association of America.

Cobb, G. (1993). Reconsidering statistics education: A National Science Foundation conference. *Journal of Statistics Education, 1*(1). Retrieved July 31, 2007, from www.amstat.org/publications/jse/v1n1/cobb.html

Cobb, G. (2000). Teaching statistics: More data, less lecturing. In T. L. Moore (Ed.), *Teaching statistics: Resources for undergraduate instructors* (pp. 3–5). Washington, DC: Mathematical Association of America.

Cobb, G. W. (1984). An algorithmic approach to elementary ANOVA. *The American Statistician, 38*, 120–123.

Cobb, G. W. (1987). Introductory textbooks: A framework for evaluation. *Journal of the American Statistical Association, 82*, 321–339.

Cobb, G. W., & Moore, D. S. (2000). Statistics and mathematics: Tension and cooperation. *American Mathematical Monthly, 106*, 615–630.

Cobb, P. (1999). Individual and collective mathematical development: The case of statistical data analysis. *Mathematical Thinking and Learning, 1*, 5–43.

Cobb, P., & McClain, K. (2004). Principles of instructional design for supporting the development of students' statistical reasoning. In D. Ben-Zvi & J. Garfield (Eds.), *The challenge of developing statistical literacy, reasoning, and thinking* (pp. 375–395). Dordrecht: Kluwer Academic.

Cobb, P., McClain, K., & Gravemeijer, K. (2003). Learning about statistical covariation. *Cognition and Instruction, 21*, 1–78.

Cohen, B. H. (2002). Calculating a factorial ANOVA from means and standard deviations. *Understanding Statistics, 1*, 191–203.

Cohen, D. J., & Cohen, J. (2006). The sectioned density plot. *The American Statistician, 60*, 167–174.

Cohen, J. (1988). *Statistical power analysis for the behavioral sciences* (2nd ed.). Hillside, NJ: Lawrence Erlbaum Associates.

Cohen, J. (1992). A power primer. *Psychological Bulletin, 112*, 155–159.

Cohen, J. (1994). The earth is round ($p < .05$). *American Psychologist, 49*, 997–1003.

Cohen, J. B., & Firestone, J. M. (1939). On an experiment in the teaching of statistics. *Journal of the American Statistical Association, 34*, 714–715.

Cole, A., & Cole, C. (2005, May). *Hybrid vs. online statistics courses: Anxiety, problem solving and academic performance.* Poster presented at the annual meeting of Midwestern Psychological Association, Chicago, IL.

Collins, L. B., & Mittag, K. C. (2005). Effect of calculator technology on student achievement in an introductory statistics course. *Statistics Education Research Journal, 4,* 7–15.

Colvin, S., & Vos, K. E. (1997). Authentic assessment models for statistics education. In I. Gal & J. Garfield (Eds.), *The assessment challenge in statistics education* (pp. 27–36). Amsterdam: IOS Press.

Conners, F. A., Mccown, S. M., & Roskos-Ewoldsen, B. (1998). Unique challenges in teaching undergraduates statistics. *Teaching of Psychology, 25,* 40–42.

Connor, D., & Davies, N. (2002). An international resource for learning and teaching. *Teaching Statistics, 24,* 59–61.

Connor, J. M. (2003). Making statistics come alive: Using space and students' bodies to illustrate statistical concepts. *Teaching of Psychology, 30,* 141–143.

Cook, R. D. (1977). Detection of influential observations in linear regression. *Technometrics, 19,* 15–18.

Cook, R. D. (1979). Influential observations in linear regression. *Journal of the American Statistical Association, 74,* 169–174.

Cooper, G., & Sweller, J. (1987). The effects of schema acquisition and rule automation on mathematical problem-solving transfer. *Journal of Educational Psychology, 79,* 347–362.

Couch, J. V. (1997). Using the Internet in instruction: A homepage for statistics. *Psychological Reports, 81,* 999–1003.

Couch, J. V., & Stoloff, M. L. (1989). A national survey of microcomputer use by academic psychologists. *Teaching of Psychology, 16,* 145–147.

Council of National Psychological Associations for the Advancement of Ethnic Minority Interests. (2000). *Guidelines for research in ethnic minority communities.* Washington, DC: American Psychological Association.

Courtney, D. P., Courtney, M., & Nicholson, C. (1994). The effect of cooperative practice as an instructional practice at the college level. *College Student Journal, 28,* 471–477.

Cramer, K. M., & Jackson, D. L. (2006). Fans, football and federal elections: A real-world example of statistics. *Teaching Statistics, 28,* 56–57.

Croucher, J. S. (2004). An upper bound on the value of the standard deviation. *Teaching Statistics, 26,* 54–55.

Cumming, G. (1983). The introductory statistics course: Mixed student groups preferred to streamed. *Teaching of Psychology, 10,* 34–37.

Curcio, F. R. (2002). *A user's guide to Japanese lesson study: Ideas for improving mathematics teaching,* Reston. VA: National Council of Teachers of Mathematics.

Dambolena, I. G. (1984). Teaching the central limit theorem through computer simulation. *Mathematics and Computer Education, 18,* 128–132.

Day, H. D., Marshall, D. D., & Rubin, L. J. (1998). Statistics lessons from the study of mate selection. *Teaching of Psychology, 25*, 221–224.

delMas, B., & Liu, Y. (2005). Exploring students' conceptions of the standard deviation. *Statistics Education Research Journal, 4*(1), 55–82. Retrieved July 31, 2007, from www.stat.auckland.ac.nz/~iase/serj/SERJ4(1)_delMas_Liu.pdf

delMas, R. C. (2002). Statistical literacy, reasoning, and learning: A commentary. *Journal of Statistics Education, 10*(3). Retrieved July 31, 2007, from www.amstat.org/publications/jse/v10n3/delmas_discussion.html

delMas, R. C. (2004). A comparison of mathematical and statistical reasoning. In D. Ben-Zvi & J. Garfield (Eds.), *The challenge of developing statistical literacy, reasoning, and thinking* (pp. 79–95). Dordrecht: Kluwer Academic.

delMas, R. C., Garfield, J., & Chance, B. (1999). A model of classroom research in action: Developing simulation activities to improve students' statistical reasoning. *Journal of Statistics Education, 7*(3). Retrieved July 31, 2007, from www.amstat.org/publications/jse/secure/v7n3/delmas.cfm

Derry, S. J., Levin, J. R., Osana, H. P., Jones, M. S., & Peterson, M. (2000). Fostering students' statistical and scientific thinking: Lessons from an innovative college course. *American Educational Research Journal, 37*, 747–773.

Derry, S. J., Levin, J. R., & Schauble, L. (1995). Stimulating statistical thinking through situated simulations. *Teaching of Psychology, 22*, 51–57.

Dickson, K. L., Miller, M. D., & Devoley, M. S. (2004). Effect of textbook study guides on student performance in introductory psychology. *Teaching of Psychology, 32*, 34–39.

Dietz, E. J. (1993). A cooperative learning activity on methods of selecting a sample. *The American Statistician, 47*, 104–108.

Dillbeck, M. C. (1983). Teaching statistics in terms of the knower. *Teaching of Psychology, 10*, 18–20.

Dillon, K. M. (1982). Statisticophobia. *Teaching of Psychology, 9*, 117.

Dillon, K. M. (1999). I am 95% confident that the earth is round: An interview about statistics with Chris Spatz. *Teaching of Psychology, 26*, 232–234.

Dimitrova, G., Persell, C. H., & Maisel, R. (1993). Using and evaluating ISEE, a new computer program for teaching sampling and statistical inference. *Teaching Sociology, 21*, 341–351.

Dixon, P. N., & Judd, W. A. (1977). A comparison of computer-mannaged instruction and lecture mode for teaching basic statistics, *Journal of Computer-Based Instruction, 4*, 22–25.

Doane, D. P., & Tracy, R. L. (2000). Using bean and fulcrum displays to explore data. *The American Statistician, 54*, 289–290.

Dolinsky, B. (2001). An active learning approach to teaching statistics. *Teaching of Psychology, 28*, 55–56.

Dollinger, S. J. (2004). Predicting personality-behavior relations: A teaching activity. *Teaching of Psychology, 31*, 48–51.

du Feu, C. (2001). A new least-squares regression model. *Teaching Statistics, 23*, 17–19.

du Feu, C. (2005). Bluebells and bias, switchwort and statistics. *Teaching Statistics, 27*, 34–36.

Duell, M. N. (2006). Distance learning: Psychology online. In W. Buskist & S. F. Davis (Eds.), *Handbook of the teaching of psychology* (pp. 142–146). Malden, MA: Blackwell.

Dunlap, W. P., & Myers, L. (1997). Approximating power for significance tests with one degree of freedom. *Psychological Methods, 2*, 186–191.

Dunn, D. S. (1996). Collaborative writing in a statistics and research methods course. *Teaching of Psychology, 23*, 38–40.

Dunn, D. S. (2000). Letter exchanges on statistics and research methods: Writing, responding, and learning. *Teaching of Psychology, 27*, 128–130.

Dunn, D. S., & Chew, S. L. (Eds.). (2006). *Best practices for teaching introduction to psychology.* Mahwah, NJ: Lawrence Erlbaum Associates.

Dunn, D. S., McEntarffer, R., & Halonen, J. S. (2004). Empowering psychology students through self-assessment. In D. S. Dunn, C. M. Mehrotra, & J. S. Halonen (Eds.), *Measuring up: Educational assessment challenges and practices for psychology* (pp. 171–186). Washington, DC: American Psychological Association.

Dunn, P. (2004). Understanding statistics using computer demonstrations. *Journal of Computers in Mathematics and Science Teaching, 22*, 83–103.

Dunn, R. (1989). Building regression models: The importance of graphics. *Journal of Geography in Higher Education, 13*, 15–30.

Durlak, J. A. (1995). Understanding meta-analysis. In L. G. Grimm & P. R. Yarnold (Eds.), *Reading and understanding multivariate statistics* (pp. 319–352). Washington, DC: American Psychological Association.

Dyck, J. L., & Gee, N. R. (1998). A sweet way to teach students about the sampling distribution of the mean. *Teaching of Psychology, 25*, 192–195.

Dyck, J. L., & Mayer, R. E. (1989). Teaching for transfer of computer program comprehension skill. *Journal of Educational Psychology, 81*, 16–24.

Eaton, J. S. (2001). *Distance learning: Academic and political challenges for higher education accreditation* (CHEA Monograph Series 2001 No. 1). Washington, DC: Council for Higher Education Accreditation. Retrieved July 31, 2007, from www.chea.org/pdf/mono_1_dist_learning_2001.pdf

Edirisooriya, G. (2003). The gourmet guide to statistics: For an instructional strategy that makes teaching and learning statistics a piece of cake. *Teaching Statistics, 25*, 2–5.

Eisenhauer, J. G. (2003). Regression through the origin. *Teaching Statistics, 25*, 76–80.

Eisenhauer, J. G. (2006). How a dummy replaces a student's test and gets an *F* (Or, how regression substitutes for *t* tests and ANOVA). *Teaching Statistics, 28,* 78–80.

Elliott, T. R., & Umlauf, R. L. (1995). Measurement of personality and psychopathology following acquired physical disability. In L. A. Cushman & M. J. Scherer (Eds.), *Psychological assessment in medical rehabilitation* (pp. 301–324). Washington, DC: American Psychological Association.

Elmore, P. B., & Vasu, E. S. (1980). Relationship between selected variables and statistical achievement: Building a theoretical model. *Journal of Educational Psychology, 72,* 457–467.

Elmore, P. B., & Vasu, E. S. (1986). A model of statistics achievement using spatial ability, feminist attitudes and mathematics-related variables as predictors. *Educational and Psychological Measurement, 46,* 215–222.

Erwin, T. D., & Rieppi, R. (1999). Comparing multimedia and traditional approaches in undergraduate psychology classes. *Teaching of Psychology, 26,* 58–61.

Eskicioglu, A. M., & Kopec, D. (2003). The ideal multimedia-enabled classroom: Perspectives from psychology, education, and information science. *Journal of Educational Multimedia and Hypermedia, 12,* 199–221.

Estes, W. K. (1997). Significance testing in psychological research: Some persisting issues. *Psychological Science, 8,* 18–20.

Evans, J. St. B. (1976). Teaching statistics: Some theoretical considerations. *Bulletin of the British Psychological Society, 29,* 172–174.

Falk, R. (1986). Misconceptions of statistical significance. *Journal of Structured Learning, 9,* 83–96.

Farnsworth, D. L. (2000). The case against histograms. *Teaching Statistics, 22,* 81–85.

Fecso, R. S., Kalsbeek, W. D., Lohr, S. L., Scheaffer, R. L., Scheuren, F. J., & Stansny, E. A. (1996). Teaching survey sampling. *The American Statistician, 50,* 328–340.

Federer, W. T. (1978). Some remarks on statistical education. *The American Statistician, 32,* 117–121.

Feinberg, L. B., & Halperin, S. (1978). Affective and cognitive correlates of course performance on introductory statistics. *Journal of Experimental Education, 46,* 11–18.

Feinberg, M., & Siekpe, J. (2003). An empirical comparison of student user-satisfaction between SPSS and Minitab. *College Student Journal, 37,* 509–514.

Fernald, P. S., & Fernald, L. D. (1990). Normal probability curve. In V. P. Makosky, C. C. Sileo, L. G. Whittemore, C. P. Landry, & M. L. Skutley (Eds.), *Activities handbook for the teaching of psychology* (Vol. 3, pp. 181–182). Washington, DC: American Psychological Association.

Finley, D. L. (2006). Teaching introductory psychology online: Active learning is not an oxymoron. In D. S. Dunn & S. L. Chew (Eds.), *Best practices for teaching introduction to psychology* (pp. 129–142). Mahwah, NJ: Lawrence Erlbaum Associates.

Finn, J. P. (1983). Adding a student–student component to the PSI model. *Teaching of Psychology, 10,* 41–43.

Fiorini, G. R., Miller, J., & Acusta, A. P. (1998). Developing activities for the mathematics classroom. *Mathematics and Computer Education, 32,* 174–187.

Fischer, H. W., III (1996). Teaching statistics from a user's perspective. *Teaching Sociology, 24,* 225–230.

Fisher, R. A. (1937). Professor Karl Pearson and the method of moments. *Annals of Eugenics, 7,* 303–318.

Forster, P. A. (2006). Assessing technology-based approaches for teaching and learning mathematics. *International Journal of Mathematical Education in Science and Technology, 37,* 145–164.

Forster, P. A. (2007a). Critical evaluation of Internet resources for teaching trend and variability in bivariate data. *Australian Senior Mathematics Journal, 21,* 6–18.

Forster, P. A. (2007b). Technologies for teaching and learning trend in bivariate data. *International Journal of Mathematical Education in Science and Technology, 38,* 143–161.

Forsyth, D. R. (2003). *The professor's guide to teaching: Psychological principles and practices.* Washington, DC: American Psychological Association.

Forsyth, G. A. (1977). A task-first individual-differences approach to designing a statistics and methodology course. *Teaching of Psychology, 4,* 76–78.

Fraser, E. D. (1962). The teaching of statistics to psychology students. *Bulletin of the British Psychological Society, 46,* 11–16.

Freeman, A. R. (1977). *Clinical biostatistics.* St. Louis, MO: C. V. Mosby.

Friedman, H. (1987). Repeat examinations in introductory statistics courses. *Teaching of Psychology, 14,* 20–23.

Friedrich, J., Buday, E., & Kerr, D. (2000). Statistical training in psychology: A national survey and commentary on undergraduate programs. *Teaching of Psychology, 27,* 248–257.

Friel, S. N., Russell, S., & Mokros, J. R. (1990). *Used numbers: Statistics, middles, means, and in-betweens.* Palo Alto, CA: Dale Seymour.

Frigge, M., Hoaglin, D. C., & Iglewicz, B. (1989). Some implementations of the boxplot. *The American Statistician, 43,* 50–54.

Gaito, J., & Shermer, P. (1985). Expected mean squares in psychological statistics: A brief history. *Bulletin of the Psychonomic Society, 23,* 513–516.

Gal, I. (2004). Statistical literacy. In D. Ben-Zvi & J. Garfield (Eds.), *The challenge of developing statistical literacy, reasoning, and thinking* (pp. 47–78). Dordrecht: Kluwer Academic.

Gal, I., & Garfield, J. (1997). Curricular goals and assessment challenges in statistics education. In I. Gal & J. Garfield (Eds.), *The assessment challenge in statistics education* (pp. 1–13). Amsterdam: IOS Press.

Gal, I., Ginsburg, L., & Schau, C. (1997). Monitoring attitudes and beliefs in statistics education. In I. Gal & J. Garfield (Eds.), *The assessment challenge in statistics education* (pp. 37–51). Amsterdam: IOS Press.

Galotti, K. (1989). Approaches to studying formal and everyday reasoning. *Psychological Bulletin, 105*, 331–351.

García, C., & García, M. T. R. (2004). Cinema and multiple regression. *Teaching of Psychology, 31*, 56–58.

Gardner, P. L., & Hudson, I. (1999). University students' ability to apply statistical procedures. *Journal of Statistics Education, 7*(1). Retrieved July 31, 2007, from www.amstat.org/publications/jse/secure/v7n1/gardner.cfm

Garfield, J. (1993). Teaching statistics using small-group cooperative learning. *Journal of Statistics Education, 1*(1). Retrieved July 31, 2007, from www.amstat.org/publications/jse/v1n1/garfield.html

Garfield, J. (1994). Beyond testing and grading: Using assessment to improve student learning. *Journal of Statistics Education, 2*(1). Retrieved July 31, 2007, from www.amstat.org/publications/jse/v2n1/garfield.html

Garfield, J. (2000). *Evaluating the impact of statistics educational reform: A survey of introductory statistics courses: Final report for NSF Grant REC-9732404.* Retrieved July 31, 2007, from www.cehd.umn.edu/EdPsych/Projects/Impact.html

Garfield, J. (2002). The challenge of developing statistical reasoning. *Journal of Statistics Education, 10*(3). Retrieved July 31, 2007, from www.amstat.org/publications/jse/v10n3/garfield.html

Garfield, J. (2003). Assessing statistical reasoning. *Statistics Education Research Journal, 2*, 22–38. Retrieved July 31, 2007, from www.stat.auckland.ac.nz/~iase/serj/SERJ2(1).pdf

Garfield, J. B. (1995). How students learn statistics. *International Statistical Review, 63*, 25–34.

Garfield, J. B., Hogg, B., Schau, C., & Whittinghill, D. (2002). First courses in statistical science: The status of educational reform efforts. *Journal of Statistics Education, 10*(2). Retrieved July 31, 2007 from www.amstat.org/publications/jse/v10n2/garfield.html

Garfield, J., & Ben-Zvi, D. (2004). Research on statistical literacy, reasoning, and thinking: Issues, challenges, and implications. In D. Ben-Zvi & J. Garfield (Eds.), *The challenge of developing statistical literacy, reasoning, and thinking* (pp. 397–409). Dordrecht: Kluwer Academic.

Garfield, J., & Chance, B. (2000). Assessment in statistics education: Issues and challenges. *Mathematical Thinking and Learning, 2*, 99–125.

Garfield, J., Hogg, B., Schau, C., & Whittinghill, D. (2002). First courses in statistical science: The status of educational reform efforts. *Journal of Statistics Education, 10*(2). Retrieved July 31, 2007, from www.amstat.org/publications/jse/v10n2/garfield.html

Gatti, G. G., & Harwell, M. (1998). Advantages of computer programs over power charts for the estimation of power. *Journal of Statistics Education, 6*(3). Retrieved July 31, 2007, from www.amstat.org/publications/jse/v6n3/gatti.html

Gelman, A., & Glickman, M. E. (2000). Some class-participation demonstrations for introductory probability and statistics. *Journal of Educational and Behavioral Statistics, 25*, 84–100.

Gelman, A., & Nolan, D. (2002). *Teaching statistics: A bag of tricks.* New York: Oxford University Press.

Gibson, B. (2000). How many Rs are there in statistics? *Teaching Statistics, 22*, 22–25.

Giesbrecht, N., Sell, Y., Scialfa, C., Sandals, L., & Ehlers, P. (1997). Essential topics in introductory statistics and methodology courses. *Teaching of Psychology, 24*, 242–246.

Giraud, G. (1997). Cooperative learning and statistics instruction. *Journal of Statistics Education, 5*(3). Retrieved July 31, 2007, from www.amstat.org/publications/jse/v5n3/giraud.html

Gnanadesikan, M., Scheaffer, R. L., Watkins, A. E., & Witmer, J. A. (1997). An activity-based statistics course. *Journal of Statistics Education, 5*(2). Retrieved July 31, 2007, from www.amstat.org/publications/jse/v5n2/gnanadesikan.html

Goddard, D. (2005). *Making a difference, not faking a difference–Learning and using what's good and fair in biostatistics.* Paper presented at the 55th International Statistical Institute, Sydney, Australia. Retrieved July 31, 2007, from www.stat.auckland.ac.nz/~iase/publications/13/Goddard.pdf

Goernert, P. N. (1995). Employing hypothesis testing procedures with real-world binomial data. *Educational Research Quarterly, 18*(4), 15–18.

Goldman, R. N., & McKenzie, J. D., Jr. (2002). Classifying data displays with an assessment of displays found in popular software. *Teaching Statistics, 24*, 96–101.

Goldstein, M. D., & Strube, M. J. (1995). Understanding correlations: Two computer exercises. *Teaching of Psychology, 22*, 205–206.

Gore, P. A., Jr., & Camp, C. J. (1987). A radical poster session. *Teaching of Psychology, 14*, 243–244.

Gould, R. (2004). Variability: One statistician's view. *Statistics Education Research Journal, 3*(2), 7–16. Retrieved July 31, 2007, from www.stat.auckland.ac.nz/~iase/serj/SERJ3(2)_Gould.pdf

Gourgey, A. F. (2000). A classroom simulation based on political polling to help students understand sampling distributions. *Journal of Statistics*

*Education*, 8(3). Retrieved July 31, 2007, from www.amstat.org/publications/jse/secure/v8n3/gourgey.cfm

Grandzol, J. R. (2004). Teaching MBA statistics online: A pedagogically sound process approach. *Journal of Education for Business, 79*, 237–244.

Green, S. B., & Salkind, N. J. (2003). *Using SPSS for Windows and Macintosh: Analyzing and understanding data.* (3rd ed.). Upper Saddle River, NJ: Prentice Hall.

Griggs, R. A. (2006). Selecting an introductory textbook: They are not "all the same". In D. S. Dunn & S. L. Chew (Eds.), *Best practices for teaching introduction to psychology* (pp. 11–23). Mahwah, NJ: Lawrence Erlbaum Associates.

Grimm, L. G., & Yarnold, P. R. (Eds.). (1995). *Reading and understanding multivariate statistics.* Washington, DC: American Psychological Association.

Grimm, L. G., & Yarnold, P. R. (Eds.). (2000). *Reading and understanding more multivariate statistics.* Washington, DC: American Psychological Association.

Grocer, S., & Kohout, J. (1997). *The 1995 APA survey of 1992 psychology baccalaureate recipients.* Retrieved July 31, 2007, from http://research.apa.org/95survey/homepage.html

Groth, R. E. (2006). An exploration of students' statistical thinking. *Teaching Statistics, 28*, 17–21.

Guilford, J. P. (1959). Three faces of intellect. *American Psychologist, 14*, 469–479.

Gurung, R. A. R. (2003). Pedagogical aids and student performance. *Teaching of Psychology, 30*, 92–95.

Guttmannova, K., Shields, A. L., & Caruso, J. C. (2005). Promoting conceptual understanding of statistics: Definitional versus computational formulas. *Teaching of Psychology, 32*, 251–253.

Hall, A. G. (1995). A workshop approach using spreadsheets for the teaching of statistics and probability. *Computers & Education, 25*, 5–12.

Halley, F. S. (1991). Teaching social statistics with simulated data. *Teaching Sociology, 19*, 518–25.

Halpern, D. F. (2002). Teaching for critical thinking: A four-part model to enhance thinking skills. In S. F. Davis & W. Buskist (Eds.), *The teaching of psychology: Essays in honor of Wilbert J. McKeachie and Charles L. Brewer* (pp. 91–105). Mahwah, NJ: Lawrence Erlbaum Associates.

Halpern, D. F. (2004). Creating cooperative learning environments. In B. Perlman, L. I. McCann, & S. H. McFadden (Eds.), *Lessons learned: Practical advice for the teaching of psychology* (Vol. 2), (pp. 165–173). Washington, DC: American Psychological Society.

Halvorsen, K. T. (2000). Assessing mathematical statistics textbooks. In T. L. Moore (Ed.), *Teaching statistics: Resources for undergraduate instructors* (pp. 105–115). Washington, DC: Mathematical Association of America.

Halvorsen, K. T., & Moore, T. L. (2000). Motivating, monitoring, and evaluating students projects. In T. L. Moore (Ed.), *Teaching statistics: Resources for undergraduate instructors* (pp. 27–32). Washington, DC: Mathematical Association of America.

Hames, R., & Draper, P. (2004). Women's work, child care, and helpers-at-the-nest in a hunter-gatherer society. *Human Nature, 15*, 319–341.

Hamm, S. (2006, July 3). More to life than the office. *Business Week, 3991*, 68–69.

Hammerman, J. K., & Rubin, A. (2004). Strategies for managing statistical complexity with new software tools. *Statistics Education Research Journal, 3*(2), 17–41. Retrieved July 31, 2007, from www.stat.auckland.ac.nz/~iase/serj/SERJ3(2)_Hammerman_Rubin.pdf

Hand, D. J., Daly, F., Lunn, A. D., McConway, K. J., & Ostrowski, E. (Eds.). (1994). *A handbook of small data sets*. London: Chapman and Hall.

Hansen, R. S., McCann, J., & Myers, J. L. (1985). Rote versus conceptual emphases in teaching elementary probability. *Journal for Research in Mathematics Education, 16*, 364–374.

Harasim, L. M. (1990). Online education: An environment for collaboration and intellectual amplification. In L. M. Harasim (Ed.), *Online education: Perspectives on a new environment* (pp. 39–64). New York: Praeger.

Harlow, L., Burkholder, G., & Morrow, J. (2006). Engaging students in learning: An application with quantitative psychology. *Teaching of Psychology, 33*, 231–235.

Harraway, J. A., & Barker, R. J. (2005). Statistics in the workplace: A survey of use by recent graduates with higher degrees. *Statistics Education Research Journal, 4*(2). Retrieved July 31, 2007, from www.stat.auckland.ac.nz/~iase/serj/SERJ4(2)_harraway_barker.pdf

Harrington, D. (1999). Teaching statistics: A comparison of traditional classroom and programmed instruction/distance learning approaches. *Journal of Social Work Education, 35*, 343–352.

Harris, C. M., Mazoué, J. G., Hamdan, H., & Casiple, A. R. (2007). Designing an online introductory statistics course. In D. S. Dunn, R. A. Smith, & B. C. Beins (Eds.), *Best practices for teaching statistics and research methods in the behavioral sciences* (pp. 237–256). Mahwah, NJ: Lawrence Erlbaum Associates.

Harris, E. E. (1974). The teaching of sociological statistics revisited. *College Student Journal, 8*, 82–87.

Harwell, M. R., Herrick, M. L., Curtis, D., Mundfrom, D., & Gold, K. (1996). Evaluating statistics texts used in education. *Journal of Educational and Behavioral Statistics, 21*, 3–34.

Hassebrock, F., & Snyder, R. (1997). Applications of computer algebra system for teaching bivariate relationships in statistics courses. *Behavior Research Methods, Instruments, & Computers, 29*, 246–249.

Hastings, M. W. (1982). Statistics: Challenge for students and the professor. *Teaching of Psychology, 9*, 221–222.

Hatchette, V., Zivian, A. R., Zivian, M. T., & Okada, R. (1999). STAZ: Interactive software for undergraduate statistics. *Behavior Research Methods, Instruments, & Computers, 31*, 19–23.

Hauptman, J. (2004). Presentation of Type I and Type II error rates to non-statisticians. *Teaching Statistics, 26*, 46–48.

Hawkins, A. (1997). Myth-conceptions! In J. B. Garfield & G. Burrill (Eds.), *Research on the role of technology in teaching and learning statistics* (pp. 1–14). Voorburg, The Netherlands: International Statistical Institute.

Hayden, R. W. (2000). Advice to mathematics teachers on evaluating introductory statistics textbooks. In T. L. Moore (Ed.), *Teaching statistics: Resources for undergraduate instructors* (pp. 93–103). Washington, DC: Mathematical Association of America.

Henson, R. K., & Roberts, J. K. (2006). Use of exploratory factor analysis in published research: Common errors and some comment on improved practice. *Educational and Psychological Measurement, 66*, 393–416.

Hershberger, S. L. (2003). The growth of structural equation modeling: 1994–2001. *Structural Equation Modeling, 10*, 35–46.

Hertzberg, H. (2003, January 20). Dividends. *The New Yorker.* Retrieved July 31, 2007, from www.newyorker.com/archive/2003/01/20/030120ta_talk_hertzberg

Hettich, P. (1974). The student as data generator. *Teaching of Psychology, 1*, 35–36.

Hewett, T. T., & Porpora, D. V. (1999). A case study report on integrating statistics, problem-based learning, and computerized data analysis. *Behavior Research Methods, Instruments, & Computers, 31*, 244–251.

Higgins, J. J. (1999). Nonmathematical statistics: A new direction for the undergraduate discipline. *The American Statistician, 53*, 1–6.

Hittner, J. B., & Carpenter, K. M. (1994). Theoretical and applied sources for teachers of structural equation modeling. *Teaching of Psychology, 21*, 179–181.

Hoenig, J. M., & Heisey, D. M. (2001). The abuse of power: The pervasive fallacy of power calculations for data analysis. *The American Statistician, 55*, 19–24.

Hogg, R. (1992). Report of workshop on statistics education. In L. A. Steen (Ed.), *Heeding the call for change: Suggestions for curricular action* (pp. 34–43). Washington, DC: Mathematical Association of America.

Hogg, R. V. (1999). Let's use CQI in our statistics programs. *The American Statistician, 53*, 7–14.

Holmes, P. (1997). Assessing project work by external examiners. In I. Gal & J. Garfield (Eds.), *The assessment challenge in statistics education* (pp. 153–164). Amsterdam: IOS Press.

Holmes, P. (2002). Assessment: New ways of pupil evaluation using real data. *Teaching Statistics*, *24*, 87–89.

Hong, E., & O'Neil, H. F., Jr. (1992). Instructional strategies to help learners build relevant mental models in inferential statistics. *Journal of Educational Psychology*, *84*, 150–159.

Horgan, G. W. (1999). Use of spreadsheets for demonstrating experimental power and variability. *Journal of Statistics Education*, *7*(1). Retrieved July 31, 2007, from www.amstat.org/publications/jse/secure/v7n1/horgan.cfm

Hotelling, H. (1940). The teaching of statistics. *The Annals of Mathematical Statistics*, *11*, 457–470.

Hotelling, H., & Pabst, M. R. (1936). Rank correlation and tests of significance involving no assumption of normality. *The Annals of Mathematical Statistics*, *7*, 29–43.

Howell, D. C. (2007). *Statistical methods for psychology*. Belmont, CA: Thomson Wadsworth.

Hoyle, R. H. (Ed.). (1995). *Structural equation modeling: Concepts, issues, and applications*. Thousand Oaks, CA: Sage.

Hubbard, R. (1992). Teaching statistics with Minitab. *The Australian Mathematics Teacher*, *48*(4), 8–10.

Hubbard, R. (1997). Assessment and the process of learning statistics. *Journal of Statistics Education*, *5*(1). Retrieved July 31, 2007, from www.amstat.org/publications/jse/v5n1/hubbard.html

Huberty, C. J., & Barton, R. M. (1990). Applied multivariate statistics textbooks. *Applied Psychological Measurement*, *14*, 95–101.

Huberty, C. J., & Olejnik, S. (2006). *Applied MANOVA and discriminant analysis*. Hoboken, NJ: John Wiley & Sons.

Huck, S. W., Cross, T. L., & Clark, S. B. (1986). Overcoming misconceptions about z-scores. *Teaching Statistics*, *8*, 38–40.

Hudak, M. A., & Anderson, D. E. (1990). Formal operations and learning style predict success in statistics and computer science courses. *Teaching of Psychology*, *17*, 231–234.

Huelsman, T. J. (2006). Lessons learned using PowerPoint in the classroom. In W. Buskist & S. F. Davis (Eds.), *Handbook of the teaching of psychology* (pp. 94–98). Malden, MA: Blackwell.

Huff, D. (1954). *How to lie with statistics*. New York: Norton.

Hunt, N. (2005). Using Microsoft Office to generate individualized tasks for students. *Teaching Statistics*, *27*, 45–48.

Hunter, J. E., & Schmidt, F. L. (2004). *Methods of meta-analysis: Correcting error and bias in research findings*. Thousand Oaks, CA: Sage.

Hunter, W. G. (1977). Some ideas about teaching design of experiments, with 25 examples of experiments conducted by students. *The American Statistician*, *31*, 12–17.

Hurlburt, R. T. (1993). Developing estimation skills to increase students' comprehension of the mean and the standard deviation. *Teaching Sociology*, *21*, 177–181.

Hurlburt, R. T. (2001). "Lectlets" deliver content at a distance: Introductory statistics as a case study. *Teaching of Psychology*, *28*, 15–20.

Institute for Higher Education Policy. (1999, February). *Distance learning in higher education* (CHEA Update Number 1). Washington, DC: Council for Higher Education Accreditation. Retrieved July 31, 2007, from www.chea.org/pdf/dist_learn_99.pdf

International Statistical Institute. (1985). *Declaration of professional ethics*. Retrieved July 31, 2007, from http://isi.cbs.nl/ethics.htm

Jacobs, K. W. (1980). Instructional techniques in the introductory statistics course: The first class meeting. *Teaching of Psychology*, *7*, 241–242.

Jannarone, R. J. (1986). Preparing incoming graduate students for statistics. *Teaching of Psychology*, *13*, 156–157.

Joarder, A. H., & Latif, R. M. (2006). Standard deviation for small samples. *Teaching Statistics*, *28*, 40–43.

Johnson, A. C., & Drougas, A. M. (2004). Illustrating type I and type II errors via spreadsheet simulation in the business statistics course. *Decision Sciences Journal of Innovative Education*, *2*, 89–95.

Johnson, D. E. (1986). Demonstrating the central limit theorem. *Teaching of Psychology*, *13*, 155–156.

Johnson, D. E. (1989). An intuitive approach to teaching analysis of variance. *Teaching of Psychology*, *16*, 67–68.

Johnson, H. D., & Dasgupta, N. (2005). Traditional versus non-traditional teaching: Perspective of students in introductory statistics classes. *Journal of Statistics Education*, *13*(2). Retrieved July 31, 2007, from www.amstat.org/publications/jse/v13n2/johnson.html

Johnson, R. (1997). Earth's surface water percentage? *Teaching Statistics*, *19*, 66–68.

Jolliffe, F. (1997). Issues in constructing assessment instruments for the classroom. In I. Gal & J. Garfield (Eds.), *The assessment challenge in statistics education* (pp. 191–204). Amsterdam: IOS Press.

Jones, G. A., Langrall, C. W., Mooney, E. S., & Thornton, C. A. (2004). Models of development in statistical reasoning. In D. Ben-Zvi & J. Garfield (Eds.), *The challenge of developing statistical literacy, reasoning, and thinking* (pp. 97–117). Dordrecht: Kluwer Academic.

Jones, G. A., Langrall, C. W., Thornton, C. A., Mooney, E. S., Wares, A., Jones, M. R., et al. (2001). Using students' statistical thinking to inform instruction. *Journal of Mathematical Behavior*, *20*, 109–144.

Jones, G. A., Thornton, C. A., Langrall, C. W., Mooney, E. S., Perry, B., & Putt, I. J. (2000). A framework for characterizing children's statistical thinking. *Mathematical Thinking and Learning*, *2*, 269–307.

Jones, G. T., Hagtvedt, R., & Jones, K. (2004). A VBA-based simulation for teaching simple linear regression. *Teaching Statistics, 26,* 36–41.

Jones, J. H. (1993). *Badblood: The Tuskegee syphilis experiment.* New York: Free Press.

Jowett, G. H., & Davies, H. M. (1960). Practical experimentation as a teaching method in statistics. *Journal of the Royal Statistical Society, Series A, 123,* 11–35.

Kahn, A. S., & Brookshire, R. G. (1991). Using a computer bulletin board in a social psychology class. *Teaching of Psychology, 18,* 245–249.

Kardas, E. P., & Spatz, C. (2007). Teaching ethics in research methods courses. In D. S. Dunn, R. A. Smith, & B. C. Beins (Eds.), *Best practices for teaching statistics and research methods in the behavioral sciences* (pp. 150–171). Mahwah, NJ: Lawrence Erlbaum Associates.

Karp, D. R. (1995). Using SPSS for Windows to enhance, not overwhelm, course content. *Teaching Sociology, 23,* 234–240.

Katz, B. M., & Tomazic, T. J. (1990). Applied sources for teachers of multivariate statistics. *Teaching of Psychology, 17,* 256–258.

Keeler, C. M., & Steinhorst, R. K. (1995). Using small groups to promote active learning in the introductory statistics course: A report from the field. *Journal of Statistics Education, 3*(2). Retrieved July 31, 2007, from www.amstat.org/publications/jse/v3n2/keeler.html

Keith, T. Z. (2006). *Multiple regression and beyond.* Boston: Allyn and Bacon.

Keller, F. S. (1968). Goodbye teacher. *Journal of Applied Behavior Analysis, 1,* 79–89.

Kelly, A. E., Sloane, F., & Whittaker, A. (1997). Simple approaches to assessing underlying understanding of statistical concepts. In I. Gal & J. Garfield (Eds.), *The assessment challenge in statistics education* (pp. 85–90). Amsterdam: IOS Press.

Kemmerly, P. R. (1990). Nonparametric methods instruction in quantitative geology. *Journal of Geological Education, 38,* 238–242.

Kester, L., Kirschner, P. A., & van Merriënboer, J. J. G. (2004). Timing of information presentation in learning statistics. *Instructional Science, 32,* 233–252.

Key Curriculum Press. (2007a). *Fathom dynamic data software.* Retrieved July 31, 2007, from /www.keypress.com/x5656.xml

Key Curriculum Press. (2007b). *TinkerPlots dynamic data exploration.* Retrieved July 31, 2007, from www.keypress.com/x5715.xml

Kirk, R. E. (2002, August). *Teaching introductory statistics: Some things I have learned.* Paper presented at the 110th Annual Conference of the American Psychological Association, Chicago, Illinois.

Kirk, R. E. (2005). Effect size measures. In B. Everitt & D. Howell (Eds.), *Encyclopedia of statistics in behavioral science* (Vol. 2, pp. 532–542). New York: Wiley.

Kirk, R. E. (2007). Changing topics and trends in introductory statistics. In D. S. Dunn, R. A. Smith, & B. C. Beins (Eds.), *Best practices for teaching statistics and research methods in the behavioral sciences* (pp. 25–44). Mahwah, NJ: Lawrence Erlbaum Associates.

Kirkpatrick, L. A., & Feeney, B. C. (2003). *A simple guide to SPSS for Windows for versions 8.0, 9.0, 10.0, & 11.0.* (Rev. ed.). Belmont, CA: Wadsworth/Thomson Learning.

Kirsch, I. S., Jungeblut, A., & Mosenthal, P. B. (1998). The measurement of adult literacy. In S. T. Murray, I. S. Kirsch, & L. B. Jenkins (Eds.), *Adult literacy in OECD countries: Technical report on the first International Adult Literacy Survey* (pp. 105–134). Washington, DC: National Center for Education Statistics, U.S. Department of Education.

Klem, L. (1995). Path analysis. In L. G. Grimm & P. R. Yarnold (Eds.), *Reading and understanding multivariate statistics* (pp. 65–97). Washington, DC: American Psychological Association.

Klem, L. (2000). Structural equation modeling. In L. G. Grimm & P. R. Yarnold (Eds.), *Reading and understanding more multivariate statistics* (pp. 227–260). Washington, DC: American Psychological Association.

Kline, R. B. (2005). *Principles and practice of structural equation modeling* (2nd ed.). New York: Guilford Press.

Kneidel, K. (1996). How the chi-square test works: A lesson. *The American Biology Teacher, 58,* 420–423.

Koch, C., & Gobell, J. (1999). A hypertext-based tutorial with links to the Web for teaching statistics and research methods. *Behavior Research Methods, Instruments, & Computers, 31,* 7–13.

Koenig, C. S. (2006). *A compendium of introductory psychology texts.* Retrieved July 31, 2007, from the Office of Teaching Resources in Psychology Online Web site: www.teachpsych.org/otrp/resources/koenig06pdf.zip

Konold, C., & Pollatsek, A. (2002). Data analysis as the search for signals in noisy processes. *Journal for Research in Mathematics Education, 33,* 259–289.

Kosonen, P., & Winne, P. H. (1995). Effects of teaching statistical laws on reasoning about everyday problems. *Journal of Educational Psychology, 87,* 33–46.

Kosslyn, S. M. (1994). *Elements of graph design.* New York: W. H. Freeman.

Kowalski, R. M. (1995). Teaching moderated multiple regression for the analysis of mixed factorial designs. *Teaching of Psychology, 22,* 197–198.

Kraemer, H. C. (1985). A strategy to teach the concept and application of power of statistical tests. *Journal of Educational Statistics, 10,* 173–195.

Kreiner, D. S. (2006). A mastery-based approach to teaching statistics online. *International Journal of Instructional Media, 33,* 73–80.

Kvam, P. H. (2000). The effect of active learning methods on student retention in engineering students. *The American Statistician, 54,* 136–140.

Lajoie, S. P. (1997). The use of technology for modeling performance stand-
ards in statistics. In J. B. Garfield & G. Burrill (Eds.), *Research on the
Role of Technology in Teaching and Learning Statistics* (pp. 57–70).
Voorburg, The Netherlands: International Statistical Institute.

Lalonde, R. N. & Gardner, R. C. (1993). Statistics as a second language?
A model for predicting performance in psychology students. *Canadian
Journal of Behavioural Science, 25,* 108–125.

Lambiotte, J. G., Skaggs, L. P., Dansereau, D. F. (1993). Learning from
lectures: Effects of knowledge maps and cooperative review sessions.
*Applied Cognitive Psychology, 7,* 483–497.

Lan, W. Y. (1996). The effects of self-monitoring on students' course performance, use of learning strategies, attitude, self-judgment ability, and knowledge representation. *Journal of Experimental Education, 64,* 101–115.

Landrum, R. E. (2005). Core terms in undergraduate statistics. *Teaching of
Psychology, 32,* 249–251.

Lane, A., Hall, R., & Lane, J. (2002). Development of a measure of self-
efficacy specific to statistics courses in sport. *Journal of Hospitality,
Leisure, Sport and Tourism Education, 1*(2), 43–52. Retrieved April 18,
2008, from http://www.heacademy.ac.uk/assets/hlst/documents/johlste/
0017_lane_vol1no2.pdf

Lane, A. M., Hall, R., & Lane, J. (2004). Self-efficacy and statistics performance among Sport Studies students. *Teaching in Higher Education,
9,* 435–448.

Lappan, G., & Zawojewski, J. S. (1988). Teaching statistics: Mean, median,
and mode. *Arithmetic Teacher, 88,* 25–26.

Larsen, M. D. (2006). Advice for new and student lecturers on probability
and statistics. *Journal of Statistics Education, 14*(1). Retrieved July 31,
2007, from www.amstat.org/publications/jse/v14n1/larsen.html

Latour, B. (1990). Drawing things together. In M. Lynch & S. Woolgar
(Eds.), *Representation in scientific practice* (pp. 19–68). Cambridge, MA:
MIT Press.

Lauer, J. B., Rajecki, D. W., & Minke, K. A. (2006). Statistics and methodology courses: Interdepartmental variability in undergraduate majors'
first enrollments. *Teaching of Psychology, 33,* 24–30.

Laviolette, M. (1994). Linear regression: The computer as a teaching tool.
*Journal of Statistics Education, 2*(2), Retrieved July 31, 2007, from
www.amstat.org/publications/jse/v2n2/laviolette.html

Lawson, T. J., Schwiers, M., Doellman, M., Grady, G., & Kelnhofer, R.
(2003). Enhancing students' ability to use statistical reasoning with everyday problems. *Teaching of Psychology, 30,* 107–110.

Layne, B. H., & Huck, S. W. (1981). The usefulness of computational
examples in statistics courses. *The Journal of General Psychology, 104,*
283–285.

Lee, C. (1999). A computer-assisted approach for teaching statistical concepts. *Journal of Computers at Schools, 16*, 193–208.

Lee, M. P., & Soper, J. B. (1986). Using spreadsheets to teach statistics in psychology. *Bulletin of the British Psychological Society, 39*, 365–367.

Lehman, R. S. (1987). A microcomputer-dependent statistics and design course. *Behavior Research Methods, Instruments, & Computers, 19*, 128–130.

Lesh, R., Amit, M., & Schorr, R. Y. (1997). Using "real-life" problems to prompt students to construct conceptual models for statistical reasoning. In I. Gal & J. Garfield (Eds.), *The assessment challenge in statistics education* (pp. 91–104). Amsterdam: IOS Press.

Lesser, L. M. (2007). Critical values and transforming data: Teaching statistics with social justice. *Journal of Statistics Education, 15*(1). Retrieved July 31, 2007, from www.amstat.org/publications/jse/v15n1/lesser.html

Lesser, L. M., & Nordenhaug, E. (2004). Ethical statistics and statistical ethics: Making an interdisciplinary module. *Journal of Statistics Education, 12*(3). Retrieved July 31, 2007, from www.amstat.org/publications/jse/v12n3/lesser.html

Lillestøl, J. (2000). Data have no meaning when separated from their context. *Teaching Statistics, 22*, 27–29.

Lindquist, P. S., & Hammel, D. J. (1998). Applying descriptive statistics to teaching the regional classification of climate. *Journal of Geography, 97*, 72–82.

Lipsey, M. W., & Wilson, D. B. (2001). *Practical meta-analysis.* Thousand Oaks, CA: Sage.

Lloyd, M. A. (1999). As time goes by: Maintaining vitality in the classroom. In B. Perlman, L. I. McCann, & S. H. McFadden (Eds.), *Lessons learned: Practical advice for the teaching of psychology* (pp. 7–10). Washington, DC: American Psychological Society.

Lock, R. H. (1993). A comparison of five student versions of statistics packages. *The American Statistician, 47*, 136–145.

Loehlin, J. C. (2004). *Latent variable models: An introduction to factor, path, and structural equation analysis* (4th ed.). Mahwah, NJ: Lawrence Erlbaum Associates.

Loftsgaarden, D. O., & Watkins, A. E. (1998). Statistics teaching in colleges and universities: Courses, instructors, and degrees in fall 1995. *The American Statistician, 52*, 308–314.

Loftus, G. R. (1993). A picture is worth a thousand *p* values: On the irrelevance of hypothesis testing in the microcomputer age. *Behavior Research Methods, Instruments, & Computers, 25*, 250–256.

Lomax, R. G., & Moosavi, S. A. (2002). Using humor to teach statistics: Must they be orthogonal? *Understanding Statistics, 1*, 113–130.

Looney, M. A. (2002). Instructional analogies for two hypothesis-testing concepts. *Measurement in Physical Education and Exercise Science, 6*, 61–64.

Loosen, F. (1997). A concrete strategy for teaching hypothesis testing. *The American Statistician, 51,* 158–163.

Lorenz, F. O. (1987). Teaching about influence in simple regression. *Teaching Sociology, 15,* 173–177.

Lottes, I. L., Adler, M. A., & DeMaris, A. (1996). Using and interpreting logistic regression: A guide for teachers and students. *Teaching Sociology, 24,* 284–298.

Low, J. M. (1995). Teaching basic statistical concepts through continuous data collection and feedback. *Teaching of Psychology, 22,* 196–197.

Lucas, S. G., & Bernstein, D. A. (2005). *Teaching psychology: A step by step guide.* Mahwah, NJ: Lawrence Erlbaum Associates.

Ludwig, T. E., & Perdue, C. W. (2005). Multimedia and computer-based learning in introductory psychology. In D. S. Dunn & S. L. Chew (Eds.), *Best practices for teaching introduction to psychology* (pp. 143–158). Mahwah, NJ: Lawrence Erlbaum Associates.

Lutsky, N. (1986). Undergraduate research experience through the analysis of data sets in psychology courses. *Teaching of Psychology, 13,* 119–122.

MacCallum, R. C., & Austin, J. T. (2000). Applications of structural equation modeling in psychological research. *Annual Review of Psychology, 51,* 201–226.

Mackisack, M. (1994). What is the use of experiments conducted by statistics students? *Journal of Statistics Education, 2*(1). Retrieved July 31, 2007, from www.amstat.org/publications/jse/v2n1/mackisack.html

Macromedia. (2007). *Shockwave player adoption statistics.* Retrieved July 31, 2007, from www.adobe.com/products/player_census/shockwaveplayer/

Magel, R. C. (1998). Testing for differences between two brands of cookies. *Teaching Statistics, 20,* 81–83.

Mallows, C. (1998). The zeroth problem. *The American Statistician, 52,* 1–9.

Malloy, T. E., & Jensen, G. C. (2001). Utah Virtual Lab: JAVA interactivity for teaching science and statistics on line. *Behavior Research Methods, Instruments, & Computers, 33,* 282–286.

Marasinghe, M., Duckworth, W. M., & Shin, T. (2004). Tools for teaching regression concepts using dynamic graphics. *Journal of Statistics Education, 12*(2), Retrieved July 31, 2007, from www.amstat.org/publications/jse/v12n2/marasinghe.html

Marcoulides, G. A. (1990). Improving learner performance with computer based programs. *Journal of Educational Computing Research, 6,* 147–155.

Marek, P., Christopher, A. N., & Walker, B. J. (2004). Learning by doing: Research methods with a theme. *Teaching of Psychology, 31,* 128–131.

Maret, T. J., & Ziemba, R. E. (1997). Statistics and hypothesis testing in biology: Teaching students the relationship between statistical tests and scientific hypotheses. *Journal of College Science Teaching, 26,* 283–285.

Markel, M. (1999). Distance education and the myth of the new pedagogy. *Journal of Business and Technical Communication, 13*, 208–223.

Marshall, L., & Swan, P. (2006). Using M & Ms to develop statistical literacy. *Australian Primary Mathematics Classroom, 11*(1), 15–24.

Martens, A., Johns, M., Greenberg, J., & Schimel, J. (2006). Combating stereotype threat: The effect of self-affirmation on women's intellectual performance. *Journal of Experimental Social Psychology, 42*, 236–243.

Martinez-Dawson, R. (2003). Incorporating laboratory experiments in an introductory statistics course. *Journal of Statistics Education, 11*(1). Retrieved July 31, 2007, from www.amstat.org/publications/jse/v11n1/martinez-dawson.html

Marx, D. M., & Roman, J. S. (2002). Female role models: Protecting women's math test performance. *Personality & Social Psychology Bulletin, 28*, 1183–1193.

Matthews, R. (2000). Storks deliver babies (p = 0.008). *Teaching Statistics, 22*, 36–38.

Mayer, R. E. (2001). *Multimedia learning.* New York: Cambridge University Press.

Mayer, R. E. (2005). Introduction to multimedia learning. In R. E. Mayer (Ed.), *The Cambridge handbook of multimedia learning* (pp. 1–18). New York: Cambridge University Press.

McCullough, B. D., & Wilson, B. (1999). On the accuracy of statistical procedures in Microsoft Excel 97. *Computational Statistics & Data Analysis, 31*, 27–37.

McCullough, B. D., & Wilson, B. (2002). On the accuracy of statistical procedures in Microsoft Excel 2000 and XP. *Computational Statistics & Data Analysis, 40*, 713–721.

McCullough, B. D., & Wilson, B. (2005). On the accuracy of statistical procedures in Microsoft Excel 2003. *Computational Statistics & Data Analysis, 49*, 1244–1252.

McDougall, D., & Granby, C. (1996). How expectation of questioning method affects undergraduates' preparation for class. *Journal of Experimental Education, 65*, 43–54.

McGovern, T. V. (2002). Process/pedagogy. In S. F. Davis & W. Buskist (Eds.), *The teaching of psychology: Essays in honor of Wilbert J. McKeachie and Charles L. Brewer* (pp. 81–89). Mahwah, NJ: Lawrence Erlbaum Associates.

McGrath, R. E., & Meyer, G. J. (2006). When effect sizes disagree: The case of r and d. *Psychological Methods, 11*, 386–401.

McIntyre, R. B., Paulson, R. M., & Lord, C. G. (2003). Alleviating women's mathematics stereotype threat through salience of group achievements. *Journal of Experimental Social Psychology, 39*, 83–90.

McKeachie, W. J. (2002). Countdown for course preparation. In W. J. McKeachie (Ed.), *McKeachie's teaching tips: Strategies, research, and theory for college and university teachers* (11th ed., pp. 9–20). Boston: Houghton Mifflin.

McNamara, J. F., Morales, P., Kim, Y., & McNamara, M. (1998). Conducting your first meta-analysis: An illustrated guide. *International Journal of Educational Reform, 7*, 380–397.

Meehan, A. M., & Warner, C. B. (2000). *Elementary data analysis using Microsoft Excel.* Boston: McGraw-Hill.

Meletiou-Mavrotheris, M. (2003). Technological tools in the introductory statistics classroom: Effects on student understanding of inferential statistics. *International Journal of Computers for Mathematical Learning, 8,* 265–297.

Meletiou-Mavrotheris, M., Lee, C., & Fouladi, R. T. (2007). Introductory statistics, college student attitudes and knowledge—a qualitative analysis of the impact of technology-based instruction. *International Journal of Mathematical Education in Science and Technology, 38,* 65–83.

Melton, K. I. (2004). Statistical thinking activities: Some simple exercises with powerful lessons. *Journal of Statistics Education, 5*(3). Retrieved July 31, 2007, from www.amstat.org/publications/jse/v12n2/melton.html

Melvin, K. B., & Huff, K. R. (1992). Standard errors of statistics students. *Teaching of Psychology, 19,* 177–178.

Meyer, J., & Shinar, D. (1992). Estimating correlations from scatterplots. *Human Factors, 34,* 335–349.

Milgram, S. (1963). Behavioral study of obedience. *Journal of Abnormal and Social Psychology, 67,* 371–378.

Mill, D., Gray, T., & Mandel, D. R. (1994). Influence of research methods and statistics courses on everyday reasoning, critical abilities, and belief in unsubstantiated phenomena. *Canadian Journal of Behavioral Science, 26,* 246–258.

Miller, J. (1999). AnoGen: A Program for generating ANOVA data sets. *Teaching of Psychology, 26,* 230–231.

Miller, J. (2007). From research to practice. *Journal of Statistics Education, 15*(1). Retrieved July 31, 2007, from www.amstat.org/publications/jse/v15n1/miller.html

Miller, J. D., Kimmel, L., Hoffer, T. B., & Nelson, C. (2000). *Longitudinal study of American youth: User's manual.* Chicago: International Center for the Advancement of Scientific Literacy.

Mills, J. D. (2002). Using computer simulation methods to teach statistics: A review of the literature. *Journal of Statistics Education, 10*(1). Retrieved July 31, 2007, from www.amstat.org/publications/jse/v10n1/mills.html

Mills, J. D. (2003a). A theoretical framework for teaching statistics. *Teaching Statistics, 25,* 56–58.

Mills, J. D. (2003b). SPSS textbooks: A review for teachers. *Statistics Education Research Journal*, 2(2), 59–70. Retrieved July 31, 2007 from www.stat.auckland.ac.nz/~iase/serj/SERJ2(2).pdf

Mills, J. D. (2004a). Students' attitudes toward statistics: Implications for the future. *College Student Journal*, 38, 349–361.

Mills, J. D. (2004b). Learning abstract statistics concepts using simulation. *Educational Research Quarterly*, 28(4), 18–33.

Mills, J. D., & Johnson, E. L. (2004). An evaluation of ActivStats for SPSS for teaching and learning. *The American Statistician*, 58, 254–258.

Milne, A. A. (1928). *The house at Pooh Corner*. New York: Dutton Children's Books.

Mio, J. S., Barker-Hackett, L., & Tumambing, J. (2006). *Multicultural psychology: Understanding our diverse communities*. New York: McGraw-Hill.

Miserandino, M. (1999). Those who can do: Implementing active learning. In B. Perlman, L. I. McCann, & S. H. McFadden (Eds.), *Lessons learned: Practical advice for the teaching of psychology* (pp. 109–114). Washington, DC: American Psychological Society.

Mitchell, M. (1997). The use of spreadsheets for constructing statistical understanding. *Journal of Computers in Mathematics and Science Teaching*, 16, 201–222.

Mitchell, M. (2002). Constructing analysis of variance (ANOVA). *Journal of Computers in Mathematics and Science Teaching*, 21, 381–410.

Mitchell, M. L., & Jolley, J. M. (1999). The Correlator: A self-guided tutorial. *Teaching of Psychology*, 26, 298–299.

Mooney, E. S. (2002). A framework for characterizing middle school students' statistical thinking. *Mathematical Thinking and Learning*, 4, 23–64.

Moore, D. S. (1997). New pedagogy and new content: The case of statistics. *International Statistical Review*, 65, 123–165.

Moore, D. S. (1998). Statistics among the liberal arts. *Journal of the American Statistical Association*, 93, 1253–1259.

Moore, D. S. (2001a). Undergraduate programs and the future of academic statistics. *The American Statistician*, 55, 1–6.

Moore, T. J. (Ed.). (2001b). *Teaching statistics: Resources for undergraduate instructors*. Washington, DC: Mathematical Association of America.

Morgan, B. L. (2001). Statistically lively uses for obituaries. *Teaching of Psychology*, 28, 56–58.

Morrell, C. H., & Auer, R. E. (2007). Trashball: A logistic regression classroom activity. *Journal of Statistics Education*, 15(1). Retrieved July 31, 2007, from www.amstat.org/publications/jse/v15n1/lesser.pdf

Morris, E. (2001). The design and evaluation of Link: A computer-based learning system for correlation. *British Journal of Educational Technology*, 32, 39–52.

Morris, E., Joiner, R., & Scanlon, E. (2002). The contribution of computer-based activities to understanding statistics. *Journal of Computer Assisted Learning, 18*, 114–124.

Mulhern, G., & Wylie, J. (2004). Changing levels of numeracy and other core mathematical skills among psychology undergraduates between 1992 and 2002. *British Journal of Psychology, 95*, 355–370.

Mullis, I. V. S., Martin, M. O., Beaton, A. E., Gonzalez, E. J., Kelly, D. L., & Smith, T. A. (1998). *Mathematics and science achievement in the final year of secondary school: IEA's Third International Mathematics and Science Study (TIMSS).* Chestnut Hill, MA: Boston College.

Munley, P. H. (2002). Integrating multivariate statistics in a graduate research seminar in counseling psychology. *Teaching of Psychology, 29*, 63–66.

Muthén, B. (1989). The future of methodological training in educational psychology: The problem of teaching students to use new sophisticated techniques. In M. Whittrock & F. Farley (Eds.), *The future of educational psychology* (pp. 181–189). Hillsdale, NJ: Lawrence Erlbaum Associates.

Mvududu, N. (2003). A cross-cultural study of the connection between students' attitudes toward statistics and the use of constructivist strategies in the course. *Journal of Statistics Education, 11*(3). Retrieved July 31, 2007, from www.amstat.org/publications/jse/v11n3/mvududu.html

Myers, J. L., Hansen, R. S., Robson, R. C., & McCann, J. (1983). The role of explanation in learning elementary probability. *Journal of Educational Psychology, 75*, 374–381.

Nash, J. C., & Quon, T. K. (1996). Issues in teaching statistical thinking with spreadsheets. *Journal of Statistics Education, 4*(1). Retrieved July 31, 2007, from www.amstat.org/publications/jse/v4n1/nash.html

National Center of Education Statistics. (2003). *2003 National assessment of adult literacy.* Retrieved July 31, 2007, from www.nces.ed.gov/naal/

National Council of Teachers of Mathematics. (1989). *Curriculum and evaluation standards for school mathematics.* Reston, VA: National Council of Teachers of Mathematics.

National Council of Teachers of Mathematics. (2000). *Principles and standards for school mathematics.* Retrieved July 31, 2007, from http://standardstrial.nctm.org/document/index.htm

NBC. (2007). *NBC advertising standards, procedures and policies.* Retrieved July 31, 2007, from www.nbcumarketplace.com/marketplace2/_broadcast/NBC_Entertainment/downloads/advertising_guidelines.pdf

Newlin, M. H., & Wang, A. Y. (2002). Integrating technology and pedagogy: Web instruction and seven principles of undergraduate education. *Teaching of Psychology, 29*, 325–330.

Nguyen, P. (2005). Public opinion polls, chicken soup and sample size. *Teaching Statistics, 27*, 89–92.

Nicholson, J. R., Ridgway, J., & McCusker, S. (2006). Reasoning with data—time for a rethink? *Teaching Statistics, 28,* 2–9.

Nickerson, R. S. (2000). Null hypothesis significance testing: A review of an old and continuing controversy. *Psychological Methods, 5,* 241–301.

Nicol, A. A. M., & Pexman, P. M. (1999). *Presenting your findings: A practical guide for creating tables.* Washington, DC: American Psychological Association.

Nicol, A. A. M., & Pexman, P. M. (2003). *Displaying your findings: A practical guide for creating figures, posters, and presentations.* Washington, DC: America Psychological Association.

Nisbett, R. E., Krantz, D. H., & Jepson, C. (1983). The use of statistical heuristics in everyday inductive reasoning. *Psychological Review, 90,* 339–363.

Nodine, B. F. (1999). Why not make writing assignments? In B. Perlman, L. I. McCann, & S. H. McFadden (Eds.), *Lessons learned: Practical advice for the teaching of psychology* (pp. 167–172). Washington, DC: American Psychological Society.

Nodine, B. F. (2002). Writing: Models, examples teaching advice, and a heartfelt plea. In S. F. Davis & W. Buskist (Eds.), *The teaching of psychology: Essays in honor of Wilbert J. McKeachie and Charles L. Brewer* (pp. 57–67). Mahwah, NJ: Lawrence Erlbaum Associates.

Noether, G. E. (1984). Nonparametrics: The early years—impressions and recollections. *The American Statistician, 38,* 173–178.

Nolan, D., & Speed, T. P. (1999). Teaching statistics theory through applications. *The American Statistician, 53,* 370–375.

Nordmoe, E. D. (2004). Of Poohsticks and $p$-values: Hypothesis testing in the hundred acre wood. *Teaching Statistics, 26,* 56–58.

Norusis, M. J. (2002). *SPSS 11.0 guide to data analysis.* Upper Saddle River, NJ: Prentice Hall.

O'Brien, L. T., & Crandall, C. S. (2003). Stereotype threat and arousal: Effects on women's math performance. *Personality and Social Psychology Bulletin, 29,* 782–789.

Oldenburg, C. M. (2005). Use of primary source readings in psychology courses at liberal arts colleges. *Teaching of Psychology, 32,* 25–29.

Olds, E. G. (1954). The experimental approach in the teaching of statistics. *Journal of the American Statistical Association, 49,* 890–896.

Onwuegbuzie, A. J. (2000). Attitudes towards statistics assessments. *Assessment & Evaluation in Higher Education, 25,* 321–339.

Onwuegbuzie, A. J. (2004). Academic procrastination and statistics anxiety. *Assessment & Evaluation in Higher Education, 20,* 3–19.

Onwuegbuzie, A. J., & Leech, N. L. (2003). Assessment in statistics courses: More than a tool for evaluation. *Assessment & Evaluation in Higher Education, 28,* 115–127.

Onwuegbuzie, A. J., & Seaman, M. A. (1995). The effect of time constraints and statistics test anxiety on test performance in a statistics course. *Journal of Experimental Education, 61,* 115–124.

Onwuegbuzie, A. J., & Wilson, V. A. (2003). Statistics anxiety: Nature, etiology, antecedents, effects, and treatments—a comprehensive review of the literature. *Teaching in Higher Education, 8,* 195–209.

Osborne, R. E., & Wagor, W. F. (2004). Course assessment: Developing and assessing assessable objectives by using and integrative assessment model. In D. S. Dunn, C. M. Mehrotra, & J. S. Halonen (Eds.), *Measuring up: Educational assessment challenges and practices for psychology* (pp. 125–140). Washington, DC: American Psychological Association.

Ostrowski, J. W. (1988). Teaching statistics by spreadsheet: A developmental approach. *Social Science Computer Review, 6,* 210–223.

Oswald, P. A. (1996). Classroom use of the personal computer to teach statistics. *Teaching of Psychology, 23,* 124–126.

Paas, F. G. W. C. (1992). Training strategies for attaining transfer of problem-solving skill in statistics: A cognitive load approach. *Journal of Educational Psychology, 84,* 429–434

Paas, F. G. W. C., & van Merriënboer, J. J. G. (1994). Variability of worked examples and transfer of geometrical problem-solving skills: A cognitive-load approach. *Journal of Educational Psychology, 86,* 122–133.

Pachnowski, L. M., Newman, I., & Jurczyk, J. P. (1997, February). *Immediate data: The World Wide Web as a resource for teaching research methods.* Paper presented at the National Conference of the Eastern Educators Research Association, Hilton Head, SC.

Palincsar, S. S., & Brown, A. L. (1984). Reciprocal teaching of comprehension-fostering and monitoring activities. *Cognition and Instruction, 1,* 117–175.

Pan, W., & Tang, M. (2005). Students' perceptions on factors of statistics anxiety and instructional strategies. *Journal of Instructional Psychology, 32,* 205–214.

Parkes, J., & Harris, M. B. (2002). The purposes of a syllabus. *College Teaching, 50,* 55–61.

Peden, B. F. (2001). Correlational analysis and interpretation: Graphs prevent gaffes. *Teaching of Psychology, 28,* 129–131.

Peden, B. F., & Hausmann, S. E. (2000). Data graphs in introductory and upper level psychology textbooks: A content analysis. *Teaching of Psychology, 27,* 93–97.

Pena-Shaff, J., Altman, W., & Stephenson, H. (2005). Asynchronous online discussions as a tool for learning: Students' attitudes, expectations, and perceptions. *Journal of Interactive Learning Research, 16,* 409–430.

Perkins, D. V., & Saris, R. N. (2001). A "jigsaw classroom" technique for undergraduate statistics courses. *Teaching of Psychology, 28,* 111–113.

Perks, P., & Prestage, S. (2000). Bar and pie charts: Ideas for the classroom. *Teaching Statistics, 22, 52–55.*

Perlman, B., & McCann, L. I. (1999). The structure of the psychology undergraduate curriculum. *Teaching of Psychology, 26, 171–176.*

Perry, B., Jones, G. A., Thornton, C. A., Langrall, C. W., Putt, I. J., & Kraft, C. (1999). Exploring visual displays involving Beanie Baby data. *Teaching Statistics, 21, 11–13.*

Petocz, P. (2005). An upper bound on standard deviation as a function of range. *Teaching Statistics, 24, 42–44.*

Petocz, P., Gordon, S., & Reid, A. (2006). Recognizing and developing good statistics teachers. Paper presented at the International Conference on the Teaching of Statistics, Salvador, Bahia, Brazil. Retrieved July 31, 2007, from www.stat.auckland.ac.nz/~iase/publications/17/5B2_PETO.pdf

Pfannkuch, M., & Wild, C. (2004). Towards an understanding of statistical thinking. In D. Ben-Zvi & J. Garfield (Eds.), *The challenge of developing statistical literacy, reasoning, and thinking* (pp. 17–46). Dordrecht: Kluwer Academic.

Phoenix, D. A. (1999). Numeracy and the life scientist. *Journal of Biological Education, 34, 3–4.*

Pierce, M. A. (1983). Teaching the central limit theorem. *Mathematics and Computer Education, 17, 46–50.*

Pintrich, P. R., Smith, D. A., Garcia, T., & McKeachie, W. J. (1991). *A manual for the use of the Motivated Strategies for Learning Questionnaire.* Ann Arbor, MI: National Center for Research to Improve Postsecondary Teaching and Learning.

Pittenger, D. J. (1995). Teaching students about graphs. *Teaching of Psychology, 22, 125–128.*

Pittenger, D. J. (2001). Power calculator: A collection of interactive programs. *Educational and Psychological Measurement, 61, 889–894.*

Portier, S. J., Hermans, H. J. H., Valcke, M. M. A., & van den Bosch, H. M. J. (1997). An electronic workbook to study statistics: Design and evaluation. *Distance Education, 18, 59–75.*

Potter, A. M. (1995). Statistics for sociologists: Teaching techniques that work. *Teaching Sociology, 23, 259–263.*

Potthast, M. J. (1999). Outcomes of using small-group cooperative learning experiences in introductory statistics courses. *College Student Journal, 33, 34–42.*

Presley, R. J., & Huberty, C. (1988). Predicting statistics achievement: A prototypical regression analysis. *Multiple Linear Regression Viewpoints, 16, 36–77.*

Primavera, L. H., & Gorman, B. S. (1994). Issues in teaching about computing the standard deviation. *International Journal of Mathematical Education in Science and Technology, 25, 635–642.*

Proctor, J. L. (2002). SPSS vs. Excel: Computing software, criminal justice students, and statistics. *Journal of Criminal Justice Education, 13*, 433–442.

Prvan, T., Reid, A., & Petocz, P. (2002). Statistical laboratories using Minitab, SPSS and Excel: A practical comparison. *Teaching Statistics, 24*, 68–75.

Pullin, D. (2002). Testing individuals with disabilities: Reconciling social science and social policy. In R. B. Ekstrom & D. K. Smith (Eds.), *Assessing individuals with disabilities in educational, employment, and counseling settings* (pp. 11–31). Washington, DC: American Psychological Association.

Quilici, J. L., & Mayer, R. E. (2002). Teaching students to recognize structural similarities between statistics word problems. *Applied Cognitive Psychology, 16*, 325–342.

Quina, K., & Kulberg, J. M. (2003). The experimental psychology course. In P. Bronstein & K. Quina (Eds.), *Teaching gender and multicultural awareness: Resources for the psychology classroom* (pp. 87–98). Washington, DC: American Psychological Association.

Quinn, R. J. (1996). Modeling statistics lessons with preservice and inservice teachers. *Clearing House, 69*, 246–248.

Quinn, R. J. (2006). Exploring correlation coefficients with golf statistics. *Teaching Statistics, 28*, 10–13.

Quintana, S. M., & Minami, T. (2006). Guidelines for meta-analyses of counseling psychology research. *The Counseling Psychologist, 34*, 839–877.

Rajecki, D. W. (2002). Personal ad content analysis teaches statistical applications. *Teaching of Psychology, 29*, 119–122.

Rajecki, D. W., Appleby, D., Williams, C. C., Johnson, K., & Jeschke, M. P. (2005). Statistics can wait: Career plans activity and course preferences of American psychology undergraduates. *Psychology Learning & Teaching, 4*, 83–89.

Rasmussen, J. L., Rajecki, D. W., Ebert, A. A., Lagler, K., Brewer, C., & Cochran, E. (1998). Age preferences in personal advertisements: Two life history strategies or one matching tactic? *Journal of Social and Personal Relationships, 15*, 77–89.

Reading, C., & Reid, J. (2005). Consideration of variation: A model for curriculum development. In G. Burrill & M. Camden (Eds.), *Curricular development in statistics education: International association for statistical education 2004 roundtable.* Voorburg, The Netherlands: International Statistical Institute.

Reading, C., & Shaughnessy, J. M. (2004). Students' reasoning about the normal distribution. In D. Ben-Zvi & J. Garfield (Eds.), *The challenge of developing statistical literacy, reasoning, and thinking* (pp. 201–226). Dordrecht: Kluwer Academic.

Refinetti, R. (1996). Demonstrating the consequences of violations of assumptions in between-subjects analysis of variance. *Teaching of Psychology*, 23, 51–54.

Revak, M. A., & Porter, D. B. (2001). The toothless bathing beauty and the *t*-test. *Teaching Statistics*, 23, 22–23.

Rheinheimer, D. C., & Penfield, D. A. (2001). The effects of Type I error rate and power of the ANCOVA F test and selective alternatives under nonnormality and variance heterogeneity. *Journal of Experimental Education*, 69, 373–391.

Richardson, M., & Gabrosek, J. (2004). A-B-C, 1-2-3. *Mathematics Teacher*, 97, 270–282.

Richardson, M., Gabrosek, J., Reischman, D., & Curtiss, P. (2004). Morse code, Scrabble, and the alphabet. *Journal of Statistics Education*, 12(3), Retrieved July 31, 2007, from www.amstat.org/publications/jse/v12n3/richardson.html

Richardson, M., & Haller, S. (2003). Confident in a kiss? *Teaching Statistics*, 25, 6–11.

Richardson, W. K., & Segal, D. M. (1998). Teaching analysis of interaction in the 2 × 2 factorial design. *Teaching of Psychology*, 25, 297–299.

Rigby, A. S. (2000). Statistical methods in epidemiology. VI. Correlation and regression: The same or different? *Disability and Rehabilitation*, 22, 813–819.

Ritter, M. A., Starbuck, R. R., & Hogg, R. V. (2001). Advice from prospective employers on training BS statisticians. *The American Statistician*, 44, 14–18.

Roback, P., Chance, B., Legler, J., & Moore, T. (2006). Applying Japanese lesson study principles to an upper-level undergraduate statistics course. *Journal of Statistics Education*, 14(2). Retrieved July 31, 2007, from www.amstat.org/publications/jse/v14n2/roback.html

Roberge, J. J., & Flexer, B. K. (1982). The Formal Operational Reasoning Test. *The Journal of General Psychology*, 106, 61–67.

Roberts, D. M., & Bilderback, E. W. (1980). Reliability and validity of a statistics attitude survey. *Educational and Psychological Measurement*, 40, 235–238.

Robey, R. R., & Dalebout, S. D. (1998). A tutorial on conducting meta-analyses of clinical outcome research. *Journal of Speech, Language, and Hearing Research*, 41, 1227–1241.

Robinson-Cox, J. F. (1999). Having a ball with confidence intervals. *Teaching Statistics*, 21, 81–83.

Roiter, K., & Petocz, P. (1996). Introductory statistics courses—A new way of thinking. *Journal of Statistics Education*, 4(2). Retrieved July 31, 2007, from www.amstat.org/publications/jse/v4n2/roiter.html

Romero, V. L., Berger, D. E., Healy, M. R., & Aberson, C. (2000). Using cognitive learning theory to design effective on-line statistics tutorials. *Behavior Research Methods, Instruments, & Computers*, 21, 246–249.

Rosen, E. F., Feeney, B. C., & Petty, L. C. (1994). An introductory statistics class and examination using SPSS/PC. *Behavior Research Methods, Instruments, & Computers, 26*, 242–244.

Rosenberg, K. M. (2007). *The Excel statistics companion: CD-ROM and manual* (Version 2.0). Belmont, CA: Thomson Wadsworth.

Rossi, J. S. (1987). How often are our statistics wrong? A statistics class exercise. *Teaching of Psychology, 14*, 98–101.

Rossman, A. J., & Chance, B. L. (1999). Teaching the reasoning of statistical inference: A "top ten" list. *The College Mathematics Journal, 30*, 297–305.

Rumsey, D. J. (2002). Statistical literacy as a goal for introductory statistics courses. *Journal of Statistics Education, 10*(3). Retrieved July 31, 2007, from www.amstat.org/publications/jse/v10n3/rumsey2.html

Ryan, R. S. (2006). A hands-on exercise improves understanding of the standard error of the mean. *Teaching of Psychology, 33*, 180–183.

Sachau, D. A. (2000). Floating data and the problem with illustrating multiple regression. *Teaching of Psychology, 27*, 53–54.

Sain, R., & Brigham, T. A. (2003). The effect of a threaded discussion component on student satisfaction and performance. *Journal of Educational Computing Research, 29*, 419–430.

Samaniego, F. J., & Watnik, M. R. (1997). The separation principle in linear regression. *Journal of Statistics Education, 5*(3), Retrieved July 31, 2007, from www.amstat.org/publications/jse/v5n3/samaniego.html

Sanford, F. H., & Fleishman, E. A. (1950). A survey of undergraduate psychology courses in American colleges and universities. *American Psychologist, 5*, 33–37.

Saucier, C. (2000). *Web animation and interactivity: The ultimate guide to Web design.* Houston, TX: Jamsa Press.

Saville, D. J., & Wood, G. R. (1986). A method for teaching statistics using N-dimensional geometry. *The American Statistician, 40*, 205–214.

Scepansky, J., & Carkenord, D. M. (2004). Senior year retention of methods and statistics concepts. *Teaching of Psychology, 31*, 9–12.

Schacht, S. P., & Stewart, B. J. (1992). Interactive/user-friendly gimmicks for teaching statistics. *Teaching Sociology, 20*, 329–332.

Schau, C., & Mattern, N. (1997). Assessing students' connected understanding of statistical relationships. In I. Gal & J. Garfield (Eds.), *The assessment challenge in statistics education* (pp. 91–104). Amsterdam: IOS Press.

Schau, C., Stevens, J., Dauphinee, T. L., & Del Vecchio, A. (1995). The development and validation of the Survey of Attitudes Toward Statistics. *Educational and Psychological Measurement, 55*, 868–875.

Scheaffer, R. L., Gnanadesikan, M., Watkins, A., & Witmer, J. (1996). *Activity-based statistics.* New York: Springer-Verlag.

Scheffé, H. (1943). Statistical inference in the non-parametic case. *The Annals of Mathematical Statistics, 14*, 305–332.

Schield, M. (2005a). Statistical literacy: An evangelical calling for statistical educators. *Statistical Literacy Project*. Paper presented at the 55th International Statistical Institute, Sydney, Australia. Retrieved July 31, 2007, from www.statlit.org/PDF/2005SchieldISI.pdf

Schield, M. (2005b). *Statistical prevarication: Telling half truths using statistics*. Paper presented at the IASE Satellite Conferences: Statistics Education and the Communication of Statistics, Sydney, Australia. Retrieved July 31, 2007, from www.stat.auckland.ac.nz/~iase/publications/14/schield.pdf

Schmidt, F. L. (1996). Statistical significance testing and cumulative knowledge in psychology: Implications for training of researchers. *Psychological Methods, 1*, 115–129.

Schram, C. M. (1996). A meta-analysis of gender differences in applied statistics achievement. *Journal of Educational and Behavioral Statistics, 21*, 55–70.

Schulze, R. (2004). *Meta-analysis: A comparison of approaches*. Cambridge, MA: Hogrefe & Huber.

Schumacker, R. E., & Lomax, R. G. (2004). *A beginner's guide to structural equation modeling* (2nd ed.). Mahwah, NJ: Lawrence Erlbaum Associates.

Schumm, W. R., Webb, F. J., Castelo, C. S., Akagi, C. G., Jensen, E. J., Ditto, R. M. et al. (2002). Enhancing learning in statistics classes through the use of concrete historical examples: The space shuttle Challenger, Pearl Harbor, and the RMS Titanic. *Teaching Sociology, 30*, 361–375.

Schutz, P. A., Drogosz, L. M., White, V. E., & DiStefano, C. (1998). Prior knowledge, attitude, and strategy use in an introduction to statistics course. *Learning and Individual Differences, 10*, 291–308.

Schwartz, D. L., & Goldman, S. R. (1996). Why people are not like marbles in an urn: An effect of context on statistical reasoning. *Applied Cognitive Psychology, 10*, S99–S112.

Schwartz, D. L., & Martin, T. (2004). Inventing to prepare for future learning: The hidden efficiency of encouraging original student production in statistics instruction. *Cognition & Instruction, 22*, 129–184.

Sciutto, M. J. (2002). The methods and statistics portfolio: A resource for the introductory course and beyond. *Teaching of Psychology, 29*, 213–215.

Sedlmeier, P. (2000). How to improve statistical thinking: Choose the task representation wisely and learn by doing. *Instructional Science, 28*, 227–262.

Seier, E., & Robe, C. (2002). Ducks and green – An introduction to the ideas of hypothesis testing. *Teaching Statistics, 24*, 82–86.

Seltzer, W. (2005). *Official statistics and statistical ethics: Selected issues*. Paper presented at the 55th International Statistical Institute, Sydney,

Australia. Retrieved July 31, 2007, from http://unstats.un.org/unsd/WS%20%202005%20ISI%20paper.pdf

Seltzer, W., & Anderson, M. (2001). The dark side of numbers: The role of population data systems in human rights abuses. *Social Research, 68,* 481–513.

Serlin, R. C., & Levin, J. R. (1985). Teaching how to derive directly interpretable coding schemes for multiple regression analysis. *Journal of Educational Statistics, 10,* 223–238.

Sgoutas-Emch, S. A., & Johnson, C. J. (1998). Is journal writing an effective method of reducing anxiety towards statistics? *Journal of Instructional Psychology, 25.*

Shadish, W. R., Cook, T. D., & Campbell, D. T. (2001). *Experimental and quasi-experimental designs for generalized causal inference.* Boston, MA: Houghton Mifflin.

Shah, P., & Carpenter, P. A. (1995). Conceptual limitations in comprehending line graphs. *Journal of Experimental Psychology: General, 124,* 43–61.

Sharpe, N. R. (2000). Curriculum in context: Teaching with case studies in statistics courses. In T. L. Moore (Ed.), *Teaching statistics: Resources for undergraduate instructors* (pp. 35–40). Washington, DC: Mathematical Association of America.

Shatz, M. A. (1985). The Greyhound strike: Using a labor dispute to teach descriptive statistics. *Teaching of Psychology, 12,* 85–86.

Shaughnessy, J. M. (1977). Misconceptions of probability: An experiment with a small-group activity-based model building approach to introductory probability at the college level. *Educational Studies in Mathematics, 8,* 285–316.

Sherman, R. C., Buddie, A. M., Dragan, K. L., End, C. M., & Finney, L. J. (1999). Twenty years of PSPB: Trends in content, design, and analysis. *Personality and Social Psychology Bulletin, 25,* 177–187.

Shultz, K. S., & Koshino, H. (1998). Evidence of reliability and validity for Wise's Attitude Toward Statistics Scale. *Psychological Reports, 82,* 27–31.

Sieber, J. E., & Trumbo, B. E. (1991). Use of shared data sets in teaching statistics and methodology. In J. E. Sieber (Ed.), *Sharing social science data: Advantages and challenges* (pp. 128–138). Newbury Park, CA: Sage Publications.

Siegel, S., & Castellan, N. J., Jr. (1988). *Nonparametric statistics for the behavioral sciences* (2nd ed.). New York: McGraw-Hill.

Simonite, V. (2000). Two-way interactions – They're top of the pops. *Teaching Statistics, 22,* 58–60.

Simonoff, J. S. (1997). The "unusual episode" and a second statistics course. *Journal of Statistics Education, 5*(1). Retrieved July 31, 2007, from www.amstat.org/publications/jse/v5n1/simonoff.html

Simonoff, J. S. (1998). Move over, Roger Maris: Breaking baseball's most famous record. *Journal of Statistics Education, 6*(3). Retrieved July 31, 2007, from www.amstat.org/publications/jse/v6n3/datasets.simonoff.html

Singer, J. D., & Willett, J. B. (1990). Improving the teaching of applied statistics: Putting the data back into data analysis. *The American Statistician, 44,* 223–230.

Singleton, R., Jr. (1989). On teaching sampling: A classroom demonstration of concepts, principles, and techniques. *Teaching Sociology, 17,* 351–355.

Smith, B. (2003). Using and evaluating resampling simulations in SPSS and Excel. *Teaching Sociology, 31,* 276–287.

Smith, G. (1998). Learning statistics by doing statistics. *Journal of Statistics Education, 5*(3). Retrieved July 31, 2007 from www.amstat.org/publications/jse/v6n3/smith.html

Smith, L. D., Best, L. A., & Stubbs, D. A. (2003). Bolstering science and practice through graphism. *American Psychologist, 58,* 818–819.

Smith, L. D., Best, L. A., Stubbs, D. A., Archibald, A. B., & Roberson-Nay, R. (2002). Constructing knowledge: The role of graphs and tables in hard and soft psychology. *American Psychologist, 57,* 749–761.

Smith, L. D., Best, L. A., Stubbs, D. A., Johnson, J., & Archibald, A. B. (2000). Scientific graphs and the hierarchy of the sciences: A Latourian survey of the inscription practices. *Social Studies of Science, 30,* 73–94.

Snee, R. D. (1993). What's missing in statistical education? *The American Statistician, 47,* 149–154.

Souhrada, T. (2006). *NUMB3RS activity: Logging witnesses.* Retrieved July 31, 2007, from www.education.ti.com/educationportal/activityexchange/download_file.jsp?cid=US&fileurl=Math%2FProbabilityStatistics%2F6745%2F6745_Act2_LoggingWitnesses_AllsFair_final.pdf

Sowey, E. R. (2001). Striking demonstrations in teaching statistics. *Journal of Statistics Education, 9*(1). Retrieved July 31, 2007, from www.amstat.org/publications/jse/v9n1/sowey.html

Spatz, C. (2008). *Basic statistics: Tales of distributions.* Belmont, CA: Thomson Wadsworth.

Spencer, S. J., Steele, C. M., & Quinn, D. M. (1999). Stereotype threat and women's math performance. *Journal of Experimental Social Psychology, 35,* 4–28.

Spinelli, M. A. (2001, September/October). The use of technology in teaching business statistics. *Journal of Education for Business,* 41–44.

Stallings, W. M. (1993). Return to our roots: Raising radishes to teach experimental design. *Teaching of Psychology, 20,* 165–167.

Stanton, J. M. (2001). Galton, Pearson, and the peas: A brief history of linear regression for statistics instructors. *Journal of Statistics Education, 9*(3), Retrieved July 31, 2007, from www.amstat.org/publications/jse/v9n3/stanton.html

Stapleton, L. M., & Leite, W. L. (2005). A review of syllabi for a sample of structural equation modeling courses. *Structural Equation Modeling, 12,* 642–664.

Starke, M. C. (1985). A research practicum: Undergraduates as assistants in psychological research. *Teaching of Psychology, 12,* 158–160.

Starkings, S. (1997). Assessing student projects. In I. Gal & J. Garfield (Eds.), *The assessment challenge in statistics education* (pp. 139–151). Amsterdam: IOS Press.

Stedman, M. E. (1993). Statistical pedagogy: Employing student-generated data sets in introductory statistics. *Psychological Reports, 72,* 1036–1038.

Stephenson, W. R. (2001). Statistics at a distance. *Journal of Statistics Education, 9*(3). Retrieved July 31, 2007, from www.amstat.org/publications/jse/v9n3/stephenson.html

Stern, S. E. (1999). The effect of gender on the number of shoes owned: Gathering data for statistical and methodological demonstrations. In L. T. Benjamin, B. F. Nodine, R. M. Ernst, & C. B. Broeker (Eds.), *Activities handbook for the teaching of psychology* (Vol. 4, pp. 74–76). Washington, DC: American Psychological Association.

Stigler, J., & Hiebert, J. (1999). *The teaching gap.* New York: Free Press.

Stinnett, R. B. (2000). *Day of deceit: The truth about FDR and Pearl Harbor.* New York: The Free Press.

Stockburger, D. W. (1982). Evaluation of three simulation exercises in an introductory statistics course. *Contemporary Educational Psychology, 7,* 365–370.

Stoloff, M. L., & Couch, J. V. (1987). A survey of computer use by undergraduate psychology departments in Virginia. *Teaching of Psychology, 14,* 92–94.

Strube, M. J., & Goldstein, M. D. (1995). A computer program that demonstrates the difference between main effects and interactions. *Teaching of Psychology, 22,* 207–208.

Sturm-Beiss, R. (2005). A visualization tool for one- and two-way analysis of variance. *Journal of Statistics Education, 13*(1). Retrieved July 31, 2007, from www.amstat.org/publications/jse/v13n1/sturm-beiss.html

Suich, R. C., & Turek, R. J. (1989). Prediction versus independence in contingency tables. *Teaching Statistics, 11,* 42–43.

Suich, R. C., & Turek, R. J. (2003). Intuition in using nominal variables for prediction. *Teaching Statistics, 25,* 86–89.

Sullivan, M. M. (1993, November). *Students learn when they assume a statisticians role.* Paper presented at the nineteenth Annual Conference of the American Mathematical Association of Two-Year Colleges, Boston, MA.

Summers, J. J., Waigandt, A., & Whittaker, T. A. (2005). A comparison of student achievement and satisfaction in an online versus a traditional face-to-face statistics class. *Innovative Higher Education, 29,* 233–250.

Summers, L. H. (2005, January 14). Remarks at NBER Conference on Diversifying the Science & Engineering Workforce. Retrieved July 31, 2007, from Harvard University, Office of the President Web site: www.president.harvard.edu/speeches/2005/nber.html

Sweller, J. (1988). Cognitive load during problem solving: Effects on learning. *Cognitive Science, 12*, 257–285.

Sweller, J., Chandler, P., Tierney, P., & Cooper, M. (1990). Cognitive load and selective attention as factors in the structuring of technical material. *Journal of Experimental Psychology: General, 119*, 176–192.

Sweller, J., & Cooper, G. A. (1985). The use of worked examples as a substitute for problem solving in learning algebra. *Cognition and Instruction, 2*, 59–89.

Sweller, J., van Merriënboer, J. J. G., & Paas, F. G. W. C. (1998). Cognitive architecture and instructional design. *Educational Psychology Review, 10*, 251–296.

Symanzik, J., & Vukasinovic, N. (2003). Comparative review of ActivStats, CyberStats, and MM*Stat. MSOR Connections, 3(1). Retrieved July 31, 2007, from http://ltsn.mathstore.ac.uk/newsletter/feb2003/pdf/activstatscyberstatsmmstat.pdf

Symanzik, J., & Vukasinovic, N. (2006). Teaching an introductory statistics course with CyberStats, an electronic textbook. *Journal of Statistics Education, 14*(1). Retrieved July 31, 2007, from www.amstat.org/publications/jse/v14n1/symanzik.html

Tabachnick, B. G., & Fidell, L. S. (1991). Software for advanced ANOVA courses: A survey. *Behavior Research Methods, Instruments, & Computers, 23*, 208–211.

Tabachnick, B. G., & Fidell, L. S. (2007). *Using multivariate statistics* (5th ed.). Boston: Pearson Education.

Tanner, M. A. (1985). The use of investigations in the introductory statistics course. *The American Statistician, 39*, 306–310.

Tariq, V. N. (2002). A decline in numeracy skills among bioscience undergraduates. *Journal of Biological Education, 36*, 76–83.

Tarpey, T., Acuna, C., Cobb, G., & De Veaux, R. (2002). Curriculum guidelines for Bachelor of Arts degrees in statistical science. *Journal of Statistics Education, 10*(2). Retrieved July 31, 2007, from www.amstat.org/publications/jse/v10n2/tarpey.html

Taub, G. E. (2003). A review of ActivStats For SPSS: Integrating SPSS instruction and multimedia in an introductory statistics course. *Journal of Educational and Behavioral Statistics, 28*, 291–293.

Taylor, S., & Muncer, S. (2000). Redressing the power and effect of significance. A new approach to an old problem: Teaching statistics to nursing students. *Nurse Education Today, 20*, 358–364.

Tempelaar, D. T., Gijselaers, W. H., & Schim van der Loeff, S. (2006). Puzzles in statistical reasoning. *Journal of Statistics Education, 14*(1).

Retrieved July 31, 2007, from www.amstat.org/publications/jse/v14n1/tempelaar.html

The School Spirit Study Group. (2004). Measuring school spirit: A national teaching exercise. *Teaching of Psychology, 31*, 18–21.

Thisted, R. A. (1979). Teaching statistical computing using computer packages. *The American Statistician, 33*, 27–30.

Thompson, B. (2002a). "Statistical," "practical," and "clinical": How many kinds of significance do counselors need to consider? *Journal of Counseling and Development, 80*, 64–71.

Thompson, B. (2002b). What future quantitative social science research could look like: Confidence intervals for effect sizes. *Educational Researcher, 31*(3), 25–32.

Thompson, B. (2000c). Ten commandments of structural equation modeling. In L. G. Grimm & P. R. Yarnold (Eds.), *Reading and understanding more multivariate statistics* (pp. 261–283). Washington, DC: American Psychological Association.

Thompson, B. (2000d). Canonical correlation analysis. In L. G. Grimm & P. R. Yarnold (Eds.), *Reading and understanding more multivariate statistics* (pp. 285–316). Washington, DC: American Psychological Association.

Thompson, B. (2004). *Exploratory and confirmatory factor analysis: Understanding concepts and applications.* Washington, DC: American Psychological Association.

Thompson, W. B. (1994). Making data analysis realistic: Incorporating research into statistics courses. *Teaching of Psychology, 21*, 41–43.

Timmerman, T. A. (2000). Survey design and multiple regression: Frequently encountered, but infrequently covered. *Teaching of Psychology, 27*, 201–203.

Townsend, M. A. R., Moore, D. W., Tuck, B. F., & Wilton, K. M. (1998). Self-concept and anxiety in university students studying social science statistics within a co-operative learning structure. *Educational Psychology, 18*. Retrieved January 17, 2006, from Academic Search Elite database.

Tremblay, P. F., & Gardner, R. C. (1996). On the growth of structural equation modeling in psychological journals. *Structural Equation Modeling, 3*, 93–104.

Tremblay, P. F., Gardner, R. C., & Heipel, G. (2000). A model of the relationships among measures of affect, aptitude, and performance in introductory statistics. *Canadian Journal of Behavioural Science, 32*, 40–48.

Tromater, L. J. (1985). Teaching a course in computer-assisted statistical analysis. *Teaching of Psychology, 12*, 225–226.

Truran, H., & Arnold, A. (2002). Using consultation for teaching elementary statistics. *Teaching Statistics, 24*, 46–50.

Tudor, G. E. (2006). Teaching introductory statistics online – Satisfying the students. *Journal of Statistics Education, 14*(3). Retrieved July 31, 2007, from www.amstat.org/publications/jse/v14n3/tudor.html

Tufte, E. R. (2001). *The visual display of quantitative information* (2nd ed.). Cheshire, CT: Graphics Press.

Turek, R. J., & Suich, R. C. (1999). An asymptotic test on the Goodman-Kruskal λ. *Journal of Nonparametric Statistics, 11,* 377–392.

Tyrrell, S. (2003). By comparison: A procession of incomes. What do you really mean? *Teaching Statistics, 25,* 59–61.

UNESCO. (2000). *World education report: The right to education—Towards education for all throughout life.* Paris: UNESCO.

United Nations Statistical Commission. (1994). Fundamental principles of official statistics. Retrieved July 31, 2007, from http://unstats.un.org/unsd/methods/statorg/FP-English.htm

U.S. Government Accountability Office. (2005). *College textbooks: Enhanced offerings appear to drive recent price increases* (GOA Publication No. GAO-05-806). Washington, DC: Author.

Utts, J. M. (2003). What educated citizens should know about statistics and probability. *The American Statistician, 57,* 74–79.

Utts, J. M., Sommer, B., Acredolo, C., Maher, M. W., & Matthews, H. R. (2003). A study comparing traditional and hybrid Internet-based instruction in introductory statistics classes. *Journal of Statistics Education, 11*(3). Retrieved July 31, 2007, from www.amstat.org/publications/jse/v11n3/utts.html

van Merriënboer, J. J. G., & Sweller, J. (2005). Cognitive load theory and complex learning: Recent developments and future directions. *Educational Psychology Review, 17,* 147–177.

Vanhoof, S., Sotos, A. E. C., Onghena, P., Verschaffel, L., Van Dooren, W., & Van den Noortgate, W. (2006). Attitudes toward statistics and their relationship with short- and long-term exam results. *Journal of Statistics Education, 14*(3). Retrieved July 31, 2007, from www.amstat.org/publications/jse/v14n3/vanhoof.html

Vardeman, S. B., & Morris, M. D. (2003). Statistics and ethics: Some advice for young statisticians. *The American Statistician, 57,* 21–26.

Vaughan, T. S. (2003). Teaching statistical concepts with student-specific datasets. *Journal of Statistics Education, 4*(1). Retrieved July 31, 2007, from www.amstat.org/publications/jse/v11n1/vaughan.html

Vaughan, T. S., & Berry, K. E. (2005). Using Monte Carlo techniques to demonstrate the meaning and implications of multicollinearity. *Journal of Statistics Education, 13*(1). Retrieved July 31, 2007, from www.amstat.org/publications/jse/v13n1/vaughan.html

Velleman, P. F., & Moore, D. S. (1996). Multimedia for teaching statistics: Promises and pitfalls. *The American Statistician, 50,* 217–225.

von Hippel, P. T. (2005). Mean, median, and skew: Correcting a textbook rule. *Journal of Statistics Education, 13*(2), Retrieved July 31, 2007, from www.amstat.org/publications/jse/v13n2/vonhippel.html

Walker, H. M. (1936). Needed improvements in the teaching of statistics. *Teachers College Record, 37,* 607–617.

Walker, H. M. (1951). Statistical literacy in the social sciences. *The American Statistician, 5*, 6–12.

Wallman, K. K. (1993). Enhancing statistical literacy: Enriching our society. *Journal of the American Statistical Association, 88*(421), 1–8.

Walsh, A. (1987). Teaching understanding and interpretation of logit regression. *Teaching Sociology, 15*, 178–183.

Walsh, J. F. (1991). Using summary statistics as data in ANOVA: A SYSTAT macro. *Teaching of Psychology, 18*, 249–251.

Walsh, J. F. (1992). A simple procedure for generating nonnormal data sets: A FORTRAN program. *Teaching of Psychology, 19*, 243–244.

Walsh, J. F. (1993). Crafting questionnaire-style data: An SAS implementation. *Teaching of Psychology, 20*, 188–190.

Walters, A. K. (2006, July 7). New laws on the books. *The Chronicle of Higher Education, 52*(44), A35.

Wang, A. Y., Newlin, M. H., & Tucker, T. L. (2001). A discourse analysis of online classroom chats: Predictors of cyber-student performance. *Teaching of Psychology, 28*, 222–226.

Ward, B. (2004). The best of both worlds: A hybrid statistics course. *Journal of Statistics Education, 12*(3). Retrieved July 31, 2007, from www.amstat.org/publications/jse/v12n3/ward.html

Ward, E. F. (1984). Statistics mastery: A novel approach. *Teaching of Psychology, 11*, 223–225.

Ware, M. E., Badura, A. S., & Davis, S. F. (2002). Using student scholarship to develop student research and writing skills. *Teaching of Psychology, 29*, 151–154.

Ware, M. E., & Brewer, C. L. (Eds.). (1999). *Handbook for teaching statistics and research methods* (2nd ed.). Mahwah, NJ: Lawrence Erlbaum Associates.

Ware, M. E., & Chastain, J. D. (1989). Computer-assisted statistical analysis: A teaching innovation? *Teaching of Psychology, 16*, 222–227.

Ware, M. E., & Chastain, J. D. (1991). Developing selection skills in introductory statistics. *Teaching of Psychology, 18*, 219–222.

Ware, M. E., & Johnson, D. E. (Eds.). (2000). *Handbook of demonstrations and activities in the teaching of psychology: Introductory, statistics, research methods, and history* (Vol. I, 2nd ed.). Mahwah, NJ: Lawrence Erlbaum Associates.

Warner, C. B., & Meehan, A. M. (2001). Microsoft Excel as a tool for teaching basic statistics. *Teaching of Psychology, 28*, 295–298.

Watson, J. M. (1997). Assessing statistical thinking using the media. In I. Gal & J. Garfield (Eds.), *The assessment challenge in statistics education* (pp. 107–121). Amsterdam: IOS Press.

Watson, J. M. (2004). Developing reasoning about samples. In D. Ben-Zvi & J. Garfield (Eds.), *The challenge of developing statistical literacy, reasoning, and thinking* (pp. 277–294). Dordrecht: Kluwer Academic Publishers.

Watson, J. M., & Kelly, B. A. (2002). *Can grade 3 students learn about variation?* Paper presented at the Sixth International Conference on the Teaching of Statistics, South Africa.

Weaver, F. S. (1989). Introductory statistics: Questions, content, and approach. In F. S. Weaver (Ed.), *New directions for teaching and learning: No. 38. Promoting inquiry in undergraduate learning* (pp. 79–84). San Francisco: Jossey-Bass.

Weaver, K. A. (1999). The statistically marvelous medical growth chart: A tool for teaching variability. *Teaching of Psychology, 26*, 284–286.

Webster, E. (1992). Evaluation of computer software for teaching statistics. *Journal of Computers in Mathematics and Science Teaching, 11*, 377–391.

Weinfurt, K. P. (1995). Multivariate analysis of variance. In L. G. Grimm & P. R. Yarnold (Eds.), *Reading and understanding multivariate statistics* (pp. 245–276). Washington, DC: American Psychological Association.

Weldon, K. L. (2000). A simplified introduction to correlation and regression. *Journal of Statistics Education, 8*(3), Retrieved July 31, 2007, from www.amstat.org/publications/jse/secure/v8n3/weldon.cfm

Wender, K. F., & Muehlboeck, J. (2003). Animated diagrams in teaching statistics. *Behavior Research Methods, Instruments, & Computers, 35*, 255–258.

West, R. W., & Ogden, R. T. (1998). Interactive demonstrations for statistics education on the World Wide Web. *Journal of Statistics Education, 6*(3), Retrieved July 31, 2007, from www.amstat.org/publications/jse/v6n3/west.html

Whigham, D. (1998). How to Excel with normal distributions. *Teaching Statistics, 20*, 84–85.

White, W. (2001). Connecting independence and the chi-square statistic. *Mathematics Teacher, 94*, 134–136.

Wild, C. J. (1994). Embracing the "wider view" of statistics. *The American Statistician, 48*, 163–171.

Wild, C. J., & Pfannkuch, M. (1999). Statistical thinking in empirical enquiry. *International Statistical Review, 67*, 223–265.

Wilensky, U. (1997). What is normal anyway? Therapy for epistemological anxiety. *Educational Studies in Mathematics, 33*, 171–202.

Wilkins, J. L. M., & Ma, X. (2002). Predicting student growth in mathematical content knowledge. *Journal of Educational Research, 95*, 288–298.

Wilkinson, L. (1994). Less is more: Two- and three-dimensional graphics for data display. *Behavior Research Methods, Instruments, & Computers, 26*, 172–176.

Wilkinson, L. (1999). Graphs for research in counseling psychology. *The Counseling Psychologist, 27*, 384–407.

Wilkinson, L., & the Task Force on Statistical Inference. (1999). Statistical methods in psychology journals: Guidelines and explanations. *American Psychologist, 54*, 594–604.

Wirth, S. (2003). King Kong, storks, and birth rates. *Teaching Statistics, 25,* 29–32.

Wise, S. L. (1985). The development and validation of a scale measuring attitudes toward statistics. *Educational and Psychological Measurement, 45,* 401–405.

Wiseman, F. (2004). A useful example when teaching hypothesis testing. *Teaching Statistics, 26,* 59–61.

Wiseman, F., & Chatterjee, S. (1997). Major League Baseball player salaries: Bringing realism into introductory statistics courses. *The American Statistician, 51,* 350–352.

Wishart, J. (1939). Some aspects of the teaching of statistics. *Journal of the Royal Statistical Society, Part IV,* 532–551.

Woehlke, P. L., & Leitner, D. W. (1980). Gender differences in performance on variables related to achievement in graduate-level educational statistics. *Psychological Reports, 47,* 1119–1125.

Wolfle, L. M. (2003). The introduction of path analysis to the social sciences, and some emergent themes: An annotated bibliography. *Structural Equation Modeling, 10,* 1–34.

Wolfowitz, J. (1942). Additive partition functions and a class of statistical hypotheses. *The Annals of Mathematical Statistics, 13,* 247–279.

Wood, W. C., & O'Hare, S. L. (1992). A spreadsheet model for teaching regression analysis. *Journal of Education for Business, 67,* 233–237.

Woolf, L. M. (2001). *Teaching research ethics within the context of human rights and history.* Poster presented at the Twenty-Third Annual National Institute of the Teaching of Psychology, St. Petersburg Beach, Florida. Retrieved July 31, 2007, from www.webster.edu/~woolflm/handout/handout.html

Woolf, L. M., & Hulsizer, M. R. (2007). Understanding the mosaic of humanity through research methodology: Infusing diversity into research methods courses. In D. S. Dunn, R. A. Smith, & B. C. Beins (Eds.), *Best practices for teaching statistics and research methods in the behavioral sciences* (pp. 237–256). Mahwah, NJ: Lawrence Erlbaum Associates.

Woolf, L. M., Hulsizer, M. R., & McCarthy, T. (2002a). *International psychology: A compendium of textbooks for selected courses evaluated for international content.* Retrieved July 31, 2007, from the Office of Teaching Resources in Psychology Online Web site: www.teachpsych.org/otrp/resources/woolf02intcomp.pdf

Woolf, L. M., Hulsizer, M. R., & McCarthy, T. (2002b). *International psychology: Annotated bibliography, relevant organizations, and course suggestions.* Retrieved July 31, 2007, from the Office of Teaching Resources in Psychology Online Web site: www.teachpsych.org/otrp/resources/woolf02intbib.pdf

Wulff, S. S., & Wulff, D. H. (2004). "Of course I'm communicating; I lecture every day": Enhancing teaching and learning in introductory statistics. *Communication Education, 53,* 92–103.

Wybraniec, J., & Wilmoth, J. (1999). Teaching students inferential statistics: A "tail" of three distributions. *Teaching Sociology, 27,* 74–80.

Yu, P. L. H., Chan, J. S. K., & Fung, W. K. (2006). Statistical exploration from SARS. *The American Statistician, 60,* 81–91.

Zacharopoulou, H. (2006). Two learning activities for a large introductory statistics class. *Journal of Statistics Education, 14*(1). Retrieved July 31, 2007, from www.amstat.org/publications/jse/v14n1/zacharopoulou.html

Zanakis, S. H., & Valenza, E. R. (1997). Student anxiety and attitudes in business statistics. *Journal of Education for Business, 72*(5), 10–16.

Zeidner, M. (1991). Statistics and mathematics anxiety in social science students—some interesting parallels. *British Journal of Educational Psychology, 61,* 319–328.

Zerbolio, D. J. (1989). A "bag of tricks" for teaching about sampling distributions. *Teaching of Psychology, 16,* 207–209.

Zhu, E., & Kaplan, M. (2002). Technology and teaching. In W. J. McKeachie (Ed.), *McKeachie's teaching tips: Strategies, research, and theory for college and university teachers* (11th ed., pp. 204–223). Boston: Houghton Mifflin.

# Index